COMMERCIAL BANKING IN THE UNITED STATES:
A History

BENJAMIN J. KLEBANER
The City College of the City University of New York

The Dryden Press
Hinsdale, Illinois

To Ruth, My Helpmeet

Copyright © 1974 by The Dryden Press
A division of Holt, Rinehart and Winston, Inc.
All rights reserved
Library of Congress Catalog Card Number: 74-45
ISBN: 0-03-084701-X
Printed in the United States of America
456 090 987654321

PREFACE

This volume offers the reader without any special background in economics or finance a concise picture of the evolution of American commercial banking practice, structure, and regulation from the beginnings in the late eighteenth century down to the present day. The greater part of the text is devoted to the eventful period since 1913. Stress is placed on the role of commercial banks as providing the bulk of the means of payment in the United States and on their role as a source of funds. Thereby it is hoped that the reader will gain a better understanding of current developments and tendencies.

The subject matter of the comprehensive treatise by John J. Knox and his collaborators (1900) was arranged by state and region. A number of monographs in banking history treat the subject by state.* A great many volumes cover the history of a particular bank, generally superficially, detailing personalities rather than activities. The present study summarizes essential aspects of the evolution of the American banking picture as a whole over the span of almost two centuries.

Horace White's highly successful textbook *Money and Banking* was "illustrated by American history" as the subtitle stated. For decades his imitators gave a great deal of space to American banking history. Post-1945, and espec-

---

*A fairly extensive listing of state banking histories is included in the bibliography of J. Van Fenstermaker, *The Development of American Commercial Banking: 1782-1837* (Ohio: Bureau of Economic and Business Research, Kent State University, 1965), pp. 103-105.

ially more recent texts, however, generally devote no more than a few pages to the subject. By placing banking in historical perspective, this volume should enable the reader to understand better the contemporary American commercial banking scene.

The author is indebted to William Beranek of the University of Pittsburgh and to J. Van Fenstermaker of the University of Mississippi for their critical comments on earlier data of the manuscript. These readers are in no way responsible for whatever flaws remain.

Benjamin J. Klebaner

New York, N.Y.
December, 1973

CONTENTS

Chapter 1   **The Spread of Commercial Banking**   1
Chapter 2   **Bank Notes and Deposits Before 1863**   17
Chapter 3   **Bank Loans Before 1863**   29
Chapter 4   **Government and the Banks Before 1863**   39
Chapter 5   **Antebellum Banking in the Balance**   47
Chapter 6   **Heyday of the Unit Bank**   53
Chapter 7   **Banks and the Means of Payment, 1863-1913**   63
Chapter 8   **Loans and Investments, Investment Banking, and Trust Companies, 1863-1913**   75
Chapter 9   **Failure and Panic**   87
Chapter 10   **Banking, the Government, and the Economy, 1863-1913**   95
Chapter 11   **The Formative Years of the Federal Reserve System, 1914-1920**   103
Chapter 12   **Banking in the 1920's**   111
Chapter 13   **The Banking Collapse, 1930-33**   131
Chapter 14   **Banking Operations in the Aftermath of the Collapse, 1933-1945**   145
Chapter 15   **A Dynamic Industry Since 1945**   167
Chapter 16   **Some Perspectives on American Banking**   187
   Selected References   193
   Index   197

CHAPTER I

SPREAD OF COMMERCIAL BANKING

Colonial Period

The American colonies had no banks for clearing business transactions, and the underdeveloped state of short-term credit arrangements hampered commerce. As much of the *specie* (silver and gold) from trade with the Spanish and Portuguese empires was used as payment for imports from England, small denomination coins were in short supply. Instead beaver skins and tobacco were widely used for money in the seventeenth century.

The first issue of bills of credit anywhere was by Massachusetts in 1690 to finance a military expedition against the French in Canada. By 1712 the rest of New England, New York, New Jersey, and South Carolina had issued paper money; the remaining colonies (except for North Carolina) followed suit by 1760. Another source of paper money were the public land banks sponsored by each of the colonial governments except Virginia's. Starting with South Carolina's in 1712, they issued bills of credit to borrowers who offered real estate as collateral.[1] There were also some privately owned note-issue schemes, such as the Massachusetts Land Bank Company, but London ordered them to cease in 1741. Further issues of legal tender bills of credit were forbidden to the New England colonies a decade later and to the other American colonies in 1764. In 1773 the English Parliament explained that the prohibition extended only to legal tender laws applicable to private indebtedness; the colonies could issue notes for taxes and other public dues.

Colonial Americans thought of a bank as "a batch of paper money." Whatever banking functions, in the modern sense, the colonists required were performed by merchants with access to British capital through their London and Glasgow connections. Into the early nineteenth century tradesmen extended long credits on their books, transferred debits and credits between customers, and made loans of their own and their neighbors' capital, even in so economically advanced a state as Massachusetts. Before the coming of bank notes in Georgia, merchants' promises-to-pay circulated in their immediate vicinity. And "crackerbarrel bankers"[2] served many communities before incorporated banks made their appearance.

The Earliest Banks

In 1781 there were no examples in America (and few elsewhere) to cite when Alexander Hamilton argued that banks "have proved to be the happiest engines that were invented for advancing trade." On the continent of Europe the main function of banks continued to be money changing, as in the Middle Ages. Business manuals of the seventeenth and eighteenth centuries defined a banker as one who dealt in bills of exchange, operated with foreign correspondents, and speculated on the rate of exchange between currencies. London goldsmiths, however, early in the 1600's were discounting inland bills and placing their own notes into circulation.

One week after a Continental Congress ordinance incorporated in perpetuity the Bank of North America, on January 7, 1782, the first commercial bank to be chartered on the continent opened in Philadelphia. Intended by Robert Morris as "a principal pillar of American credit," he predicted, in a circular letter to the governors of the thirteen states, that the bank would "facilitate the management of the finances of the United States." The hard-pressed Confederation received over $1.25 million in loans from the bank in its first three years. Even more significant were its wartime operations as a commercial bank and as a vehicle for the revival of credit and confidence. The bills of the Bank of North America were the first paper issued in the country that were convertible into specie.

The Philadelphia bank's success inspired imitators. A proposal for a Bank of Maryland in 1784 pointed out that the state needed "an institution which naturally increases the medium of trade, promotes punctuality in the performance of contracts, facilitates the payment of public dues, furnishes a safe deposit for cash, aids the anticipation of funds on paying common interest, advances the value of country produce, and facilitates the negotiations of the foreigner, while it provides an advantage to the stockholder." But the Baltimore bank had to wait until 1790 to receive a charter. The legislature of the Bay State, however, needed little prompting to grant the February 1784 petition of Boston merchants for the Massachusetts Bank. The Bank of New York opened as an unincorporated institution in 1784 because political opposition delayed the grant of a charter until 1791. Thus three commercial banks were active when the Constitutional Convention assembled in 1787. The oldest was located a short distance from the meeting place. Although a majority of delegates were friendly to banks, the Constitution nowhere specifically referred to them. Apparently its authors sought to avoid unnecessary controversy, as the public was not so well disposed. By the time Hamilton persuaded President Washington of the constitutionality of the federally chartered Bank of the United States in 1791, Baltimore and Providence had been added to the list of commercial centers that boasted an incorporated bank. In 1794, a century after the founding of the Bank of England, the British Isles had five chartered banks. In the same year, only thirteen years after the chartering of the Bank of North America, there were eighteen banks in the United States.

Among American business corporations of the eighteenth century, banks were pre-eminent. Twenty-nine were in operation in 1800, including the federally chartered First Bank of the United States, which had five branches. Five of the first eight banks to be chartered by the various states are still in business; twelve of the twenty-eight listed for the year 1800 have been in continuous operation for some 175 years. (See Table 1). In New England, every town with a population of at least 5,000 at the time of the 1800 census had a bank, except for Marblehead and Bridgewater in Massachusetts and Norwalk, Connecticut; six communities with fewer than 5,000 nevertheless boasted a bank, making sixteen in all. The rest of the nation had altogether thirteen banks, two in areas with populations under 5,000. Four localities outside of New England with populations over 5,000 did not have a bank in 1800: Schenectady, New York; the Virginia ports of Norfolk (which did have a branch of the Bank of the United States) and Richmond, and Savannah, Georgia. The four states with no bank in 1800 had at least one within the decade: North Carolina and New Jersey in 1804, Vermont in 1806, and Georgia in 1810.

The earliest banks aspired to a position of exclusivity in the state or at least the locality. The Bank of North America squelched an effort to establish a second bank in 1784 by making available additional stock at a price below the original subscription. Pennsylvania did not charter a second bank until 1793. Eight years after the Bank of Massachusetts opened in the expectation of being the sole one in the commonwealth, a second Boston bank was chartered. "Old Massachusetts" apparently gave rivals "a doubtful welcome and

TABLE 1　*Incorporated Banks in Operation by 1800*

Location	Date Opened	Date Chartered (where different)	Original Name	Subsequent Development or Present Name
Philadelphia	1782	1781	Bank of America	First Pennsylvania Bank
	1791		Bank of the United States[a] (branch locations shown separately)	Closed 1811
	1793		Bank of Pennsylvania	Failed in 1857
New York City	1784	1791	Bank of New York	Bank of New York
	1792		New York Branch, Bank of the U.S.	Closed 1811
	1799		Manhattan Company Bank	Chase, Manhattan Bank, N.A.
Boston	1784		Massachusetts Bank	First National Bank of Boston
	1792		Boston Branch, Bank of the U.S.	Closed 1811
	1792		Union Bank	Absorbed by State Street Trust Co. in 1925
Baltimore	1790-1	1790	Bank of Maryland	Failed in 1834
	1792		Baltimore Branch, Bank of the U.S.	Closed 1811
Charleston	1792	1801	Bank of South Carolina	Closed 1865
	1792		Charleston Branch, Bank of the U.S.	Closed 1811

TABLE 1   *(continued)*

Location	Date Opened	Date Chartered (where different)	Original Name	Subsequent Development or Present Name
	1795-6	1795	Bank of Baltimore	Union Trust Company of Maryland
Maine (then part of Mass.)	1799		Portland Bank	Suspended operations 1815
New Hampshire	1792		New Hampshire Bank, Portsmouth	?
Massachusetts (outside Boston)	1792	1799	Essex Bank, Salem	expired 1819; closed affairs 1822
	1795		Bank of Nantucket	suspended 1812; liquidated by 1816
	1795		Merrimack Bank, Newburyport	Merchant's National Bank of Newburyport
	1800		Gloucester Bank	Gloucester National Bank of Gloucester
Rhode Island	1791		Providence Bank	Industrial National Bank of Rhode Island
	1795		Bank of Rhode Island, Newport	voluntarily liquidated 1900
	1800		Bank of Bristol	?
	1800		Washington Bank, Westerly	Washington Trust Co.
Connecticut[b]	1792		Union Bank, New London	Branch of Connecticut Bank & Trust Co., Hartford since 1963

TABLE 1   *(continued)*

Location	Date Opened	Date Chartered (where different)	Original Name	Subsequent Development or Present Name
	1792		Hartford Bank	Hartford National Bank & Trust Co.
	1792		New Haven Bank	First New Haven National Bank
	1796		Bank of Norwich	Voluntarily liquidated 1889
New York (outside N.Y. city)	1792		Bank of Albany	Suspended 1861
	1792		Bank of Columbia, Hudson	Suspended 1829
Delaware	1795	1796	Bank of Delaware, Wilmington	Consolidated with Security Trust Co. 1929
District of Columbia	1793		Bank of Columbia, Georgetown	Failed by 1826
Virginia	1793	1792	Bank of Alexandria	Failed in 1834
	1800		Norfolk Branch, Bank of the U.S.	Closed 1811

[a]Branches of the Bank of the United States opened by 1800 are shown separately. This bank also opened branches in Savannah, Washington, D.C., and New Orleans after 1800. Many of these branches were acquired by newly-organized state banks when the federal bank's charter expired in 1811.

[b]The Middletown Bank was incorporated in October, 1795 but did not open until May, 1801. In 1955 it merged into the Hartford National Bank.

hard terms."[3] In Connecticut, the Hartford Bank was able to retain its position of local exclusivity for 22 years.

Established banks feared that newcomers would deplete specie reserves and reduce their profits. Nevertheless, competition could not be staved off indefinitely. Pressures for additional facilities came from customers dissatisfied with existing banks. While the older Philadelphia institutions catered mainly to merchants engaged in foreign trade, the Bank of Pennsylvania, established in 1793, chiefly served retailers. Yet a newer group of merchants who considered themselves unfairly treated by existing institutions launched the Philadelphia Bank in 1803. A powerful argument for a third bank in Baltimore in 1804 was that existing local banks limited their loans to a small circle and were suspected of favoritism.

Hamilton foresaw nothing but pernicious consequences from a new bank in New York. With three banks doing business in the city, he wrote in 1791, there would be "such a mass of artificial credit as must endanger every one of them, and do harm in every view." Nevertheless by 1805 New York, Philadelphia, Boston, and Baltimore each had three banks. Those four trade centers had an additional twenty banks by 1818. Yet, as late as 1837 the historian Richard Hildreth could make reference to "the rabid and desparate fury with which all old banks have ever opposed and calumniated all new ones."

Between 1791, when the First Bank of the United States was chartered, and 1816, when the Second Bank was incorporated, the total number grew from 6 to 246. In commercial centers, banks were founded with a specie capital base and made short-term loans to merchants. In agricultural localities, the main or sole capital was the state's credit (for example, the Bank of the State of South Carolina). A third type combined banking with an unrelated activity. Aaron Burr's Bank of the Manhattan Company (1799) was the offspring of a corporation to provide New York City with wholesome water. The Miami Exporting Company of Cincinnati, chartered in 1803 to ship farm produce to New Orleans, went into banking at once. Concealment of purpose was used in the early days to overcome the aversion of legislatures to granting banking privileges to persons in political opposition; Burr, a Democrat, faced a legislature dominated by Federalists.

Mushrooming of Banks

By 1811 Secretary of the Treasury Gallatin could inform the Senate that "the banking system is now firmly established; and in its ramifications, extends to every part of the United States." Banks multiplied twelve-fold during the first two decades of the nineteenth century. Authorized capital stock of state-chartered banks rose from $3 million to $168 million between 1790 and 1830. By 1840 there were three times as many banks as in 1820, and the more than 1500 banks of 1860 were twice the 1840 total. The increase in banks after 1820 was not much more rapid than the growth of national income or population. Even for the pre-1820 period banking growth has been found not to have been "inordinately rapid in comparison with other aspects of economic development."[4] That is not to argue that there were no excesses in specific places and at certain times. In 1815 it was alleged that "villages without trade or importance of any kind must have their two or three banks."[5] And according to a clergyman in Jefferson County, Ohio, where seven banks were established in 1814, "a money mania like an epidemic seized the people." In 1814 Georgia's output of goods and services were at least equal to North Carolina's or Louisiana's, but Georgia had only one third their banking capital and less than one-sixth of South Carolina's. Meanwhile 165 banks closed between 1811 and 1830. Among the reasons given was "too great a multiplication of banks, in places not adapted to the proper and regular banking business."[6]

In anticipation of the expiration of the federal charter of the Second Bank of the United States in 1836, the number of banks doubled between 1832 and 1837. Many hoped to attract deposits of the federal government which, as a Treasury department circular of 26 September 1833 explained, would enable the banks "to afford increased facilities to commerce and to extend your accommodations to individuals." The Virginia economist George Tucker observed in 1839 that rashness resulting from characteristically American "ardor of enterprise had manifested itself most markedly in banking."[7] Although the ardor cooled for some years following the panic of 1837, by 1851 banks were being added at the rate of one a month in New York City, followed by another fifteen in the succeeding 2 years. One contemporary banker in the nation's financial hub estimated that "not a few" of his colleagues lacked business education and could not even "conduct the simplest commercial correspondence."[8]

Bank buildings outside the larger centers were likely to be inexpensive, one-story frame structures with one or two rooms, a far cry from the classic Greek temple built for the headquarters for the Second Bank of the United States. A simple wooden counter, which might also serve as a seat, separated the customer from the banker. The sheet iron safe was locked by a large key. Individual cages were not required, as commonly one man had all the responsibilities, from president to janitor. With the spread of banking facilities, however modest in appearance, barter transactions declined.[9] But villages in western New York state resorted to barter because as late as 1836 it was difficult for them to obtain "current money." And although Chicago had over 4,000 inhabitants in 1840 and opened its canals and first railroad connection in 1846, over half of the city's transactions in the early 1840's with surrounding territories were without the intermediation of money. Nevertheless, the proliferation of banks brought more and more Americans into the orbit of the money economy.

Free Banking

For many decades the privilege of incorporation was available only by special act of the legislature. Bank chartering in New York "became so shameless and corrupt that it could be endured no longer," Millard Fillmore recalled in 1848. The remedy was a law considered by a contemporary "as equal to a second declaration of independence." Under the Free Banking Act of April 1838, any who wished could associate themselves for banking purposes by meeting the specifications of a general law. Bank notes had to be secured by bonds of New York and the United States or by mortgages on New York real estate.

Thirteen months before New York passed that historic measure, while the bill was still before the assembly, Michigan, which was largely settled by emigrants from New York, enacted the earliest free banking act. Hailed by the governor as "destroying . . . the odious features of a bank monopoly and giving equal rights to all classes of the community," the Michigan law of March 1837 led to the establishment of over forty banks within a year. All were in receivership before another year had elapsed. "An Act to more effectively protect the public against various frauds" repealed free banking in April 1839. After Georgia's enactment of December 1838, the free banking movement stalled for over a decade. New Jersey and Alabama had a free banking act in 1850. In 1851, Massachusetts, Ohio, and Illinois authorized free banking; Connecticut, Vermont, Wisconsin, Indiana, and Tennessee did so in 1852; Louisiana in 1853; Michigan and Iowa in 1857; Minnesota in 1858; Kansas in 1859; and Pennsylvania in 1860.

New York's law of 1838 was described by Bray Hammond, the leading student of antebellum banking, as "the most important event in American banking history [,establishing] a distinctively American system of banking."[10] New York's 1846 constitution precluded special charters for banks, but most other free banking states continued this practice. Thus Vermont, Connecticut, and Massachusetts did not charter a single free bank in the 1850's. Few free banks were organized where more profitable arrangements could be made by special enactments embodying less restrictive conditions than those in the state's free banking law.

Some free banking states omitted the prudential provisions of the New York law, thereby making it possible for nonresidents to found banks that did little, if any, business at the place of issue. The organizers transmuted their depreciated state bonds into bank notes while enjoying the interest on the securities. If any significant amount of bank notes were presented for redemption, the state authority would divide the insufficient proceeds from the sale of the bonds. Indiana's governor described the weaknesses of that state's law in 1853:

> The speculator comes to Indianapolis with a bundle of bank notes in one hand and the stock in the other; in twenty-four hours he is on the way to some distant point of the Union to circulate what he denominates a legal currency authorized by the Legislature of Indiana. He has nominally located his bank in some remote part of the State, difficult of access, where he knows no banking facilities are required, and intends that his notes shall go into the hands of persons who will have no means of demanding their redemption.

The Boston entrepreneur Nathaniel Appleton pleaded in 1831 that banking "should be open to as free a competition as any other branch of commercial business." Roger Taney, Andrew Jackson's secretary of the treasury, argued in 1834 for opening the "certain and liberal [profits of banking] to the most free competition [so that] its advantages [could be] shared by all classes of society." In the quarter of a century after Jackson left the White House most northern states put an end to exclusive banking privilege. Fourteen of the twenty-three Union states had such a policy when free banking was made part of the National Bank Act of 1863.

Bank Capital

At least before free banking opened the gates wide, bank stock appeared to promise great profits. Though highly regarded as an investment, bank stock did not generally yield exceptional earnings. Pennsylvania banks averaged dividends of 7 percent in 1835 and 1859. Nevertheless, eagerness to subscribe to stock of new banks was not limited to the early days of the Republic when they were a novelty. Scandal and riot accompanied the awarding of stock for the Girard Bank in 1832, although the legislature had set a maximum to be allocated each day in an effort to avoid trouble in the City of Brotherly Love. Indeed, the opening of the stock subscription books was the occasion for "the most disgraceful riots that occur in Philadelphia." [11]

Enthusiasm for bank stock was not necessarily accompanied by an inclination or capacity on the owner's part to subscribe in specie or equivalents. By 1830 the New England states began to insist that capital be paid in cash when the bank was being organized. Wildcat banking was characterized by inadequate actual paid-in capitalization.

Often all or most stockholders were required to be residents of the state. Less developed areas in the South and West attracted outside capital. In 1838, thirty-three banks in Ohio, Kentucky, Tennessee, and Mississippi were owned mainly by capitalists in New York, Philadelphia, or Boston. Residents of eastern cities, mainly Philadelphians, owned Tennessee bank stock throughout the period 1815-1840.

After the panic of 1837 the principle of making the bank shareholder liable as an individual, beyond the amount he had already invested, came to be considered as a remedial measure. Effective in 1850, New York bank shareholders were made responsible for an amount equal to what they had paid in. This "double liability" provision had become common in most states by 1860; more significant, it was made part of the National Bank Act of 1863.

Private Banks

Commercial banks used the corporate form extensively from an early date, but unincorporated individuals and partnerships ("private banks") were also important. Massachusetts and New Hampshire enacted the earliest ban on unincorporated banking associations in 1799, followed by New York in 1804. Pressured by incorporated banks and desirous of regulating firms issuing what circulated as money, at least six other states joined in prohibiting private banks by 1827. New York's 1804 law affected the activities of unincorporated companies; in 1818 individuals and associations were also barred from carrying on operations that the law authorized incorporated banks to conduct. This proscription was liberalized in 1837 to allow individuals to receive deposits and make discounts, but private bank-note issues continued to be illegal. Elsewhere, banks without charters generally avoided issuing bank notes. The outstanding antebellum private bank belonged to Stephen Girard. He bought the Philadelphia headquarters of the First Bank of the United States on its closing, and he succeeded to most of its business in 1812. Soon after his death at the end of 1831, Girard's bank was wound up.

Alexander Brown and Sons started as a linen import business in Baltimore in 1800. The firm came to be even more involved in foreign exchange dealings and in extension of credit to importers. Branches were opened in Philadelphia, New York, and Boston, as well as in Liverpool and London. The American branches went their separate ways in 1839. The New York partnership is still in business as Brown Brothers Harriman & Company, whose banking activities date from 1818, while Baltimore is the headquarters of the investment bank Alex. Brown & Sons.

George Smith, unable to secure a bank charter in Wisconsin or Illinois, did succeed in obtaining the reenactment of the charter for The Wisconsin Marine and Fire Insurance Company in 1839. It had the power to receive deposits though not to issue bank notes. Smith's certificates of deposit, redeemable at par in a number of midwestern commercial centers, took the place of bank notes. Almost $1.5 million of those were in circulation in 1852, when a new general banking law in Wisconsin forced the redemption of Smith's certificates and his incorporation as a bank.

In the West, private banks may have been more numerous than authorized ones during 1830-1844. By 1860 deposits in the 437 private banks of Ohio, Indiana, Illinois, Michigan, and Wisconsin were more than the combined deposit and note liabilities of the chartered banks in those states. The growth of private banking was stimulated by the collapse of numerous incorporated banks after 1837. One estimate puts their total at 398 in 1853 and 1108 in 1860, a more rapid relative increase than the number of incorporated banks.[12] Reputable private banks had concentrated "mercantile banking [in their hands] because of the superior facility they afford over associations of irresponsible men doing business in palaces at enormous expense," *Hunts' Merchants Magazine* explained in 1843.

In accordance with the hard money sentiments of their inhabitants, five states refused to incorporate note-issuing banks: Texas (1845-1869; 1876-1904), Iowa (1846-1857) Arkansas (1846-1864), California (1849-1879), and Oregon (1857-1880). In 1844, Congress refused to renew the charters of the six banks then operating in the District of Columbia. A committee explained that "Congress owes it to the people of this country . . . to try the experiment in this District of doing without banks and paper money. . . ." Actually, four of the six continued to operate and to issue bank notes in denominations over $5. In 1852, in addition to those states, there were no active incorporated banks in Florida, Illinois, Wisconsin, or Minnesota. The absence of chartered banks in nine of the thirty-three states and organized territories reflected agrarian hostility to the instability banks were thought to create, as reflected in post-1837 experience.

Indiana and Missouri restricted banking to a state-regulated institution, as did Iowa after 1857. Iowa borrowers requiring long-term credit had to resort to private banks as the State Bank (1858-1865) was limited to maturities of up to four months. The monopoly in these three states was confined to the bank-note issue privilege. On the eve of the Civil War there were twenty-eight private banks in Missouri outside St. Louis; Boonville and Hannibal each had three. Many Missouri towns continued to depend on them long after the war. States without any incorporated banks were not devoid of banking facilities. In Iowa, between 1846-1857, land agents bought federal lands which were sold to the settlers on credit. Land agents also received deposits, sold drafts on domestic and foreign commercial centers, and exchanged bank notes. Shortly after the Fort Dodge land office opened in 1855, seven private banks were in operation, one in a tent. A banker wishing to issue bank notes, which was illegal in Iowa, would acquire an out-of-state bank (Nebraska was a favored state) and proceed to circulate those notes in the Iowa office. This was the flaw in the argument of those who believed like William Gouge in 1835, that by getting rid of paper money and money corporations "we shall get rid of very efficient instruments of evil."

Branch Banking

The Second Bank of the United States reached a maximum of twenty-five branches in 1830 including the eight cities where the First Bank had located branches. Branching was not confined to the two federally sponsored banks however, nor did it disappear with the termination of their charter. Incomplete information submitted to the secretary of the treasury reported 100 branches in 1834 and 174 in 1861. While few northern banks had any, branches were significant in the South and West, especially in Virginia, Louisiana, Kentucky, Missouri, Ohio, Indiana, and Iowa. Branches proved convenient for Virginia river towns with insufficient capital for independent banking facilities.

The State Bank of Indiana was described by its former head Hugh McCulloch as "a bank of branches." Each of the ten branches had assets that belonged exclusively to their shareholders. But each branch was liable for all the debts of every other branch. The parent bank in Indianapolis served as supervisor. The successor Bank of the State of Indiana with twenty branches continued the arrangement of mutual control and inspection. The State Bank of Ohio had thirty-six branches by 1860. Each had to contribute an amount equal to 10 percent of its note circulation to a safety fund. The State Bank of Iowa (1858-1865) had a 12.5 percent safety fund levy for bank notes and, like Indiana and Ohio, supervised its fifteen branches through a central board of directors. In Louisiana, the fifteen banks chartered between 1818 and 1836 were headquartered in New Orleans. They were also authorized to open a total of forty-six branches in twenty-six different towns, of which thirty six were actually opened although the number dropped sharply after 1837. Greater safety was achieved by these institutions as they pooled the illiquid rural loans with the more diversified commercial loans of the great international seaport.

Whether a single office or part of a branch system, whether chartered or unincorporated, banks came to be increasingly used by the business community. Originally confined to the major seaports on the Atlantic coast, commercial banking spread rapidly to all settled parts of the young nation. The United States did not lag behind Europe in the spread of the specialized financial institution.

Notes

1. For details, see Theodore Thayer, "The Land-Bank System in the American Colonies," *Journal of Economic History* 13 (1953), p. 148.

2. H. F. Williamson, ed. *Growth of the American Economy* (New York: Prentice-Hall, 1951), p. 232.

3. Norman S. B. Gras, *Massachusetts First National Bank of Boston* (Cambridge: Harvard University Press, 1937), p. 37.

4. John Gurley and Edward Shaw, "Money," in *American Economic History*, ed. Seymour E. Harris (New York: McGraw Hill, 1961), p. 109.

5. Quoted in Earl Sylvester Sparks, *History and Theory of Agricultural Credit in the United States* (New York: T. Y. Crowell, 1932), p. 228.

6. Timothy Pitkin, *Statistical View of the Commerce of the United States of America*, 2d ed. (New Haven: Durrie & Peck, 1835), p. 433.

7. George Tucker, *Theory of Money and Banks Investigated* (Boston: Little, Brown, 1839), p. 259.

8. Quoted in Henry W. Lanier, *Century of Banking in New York* (New York: Gillis Press, 1922), p. 213.

9. One storekeeper in Worcester, Massachusetts (population 2000 around 1803) sold spices, salt and molasses for "country pay" consisting of vegetables and woolens. Mildred McClary Tymeson, *Worcester Bank Book from Country Barter to County Bank* (Worcester, 1966), p. 9.

10. Bray Hammond, "Free Banks and Corporations: The New York Free Banking Act of 1838," *Journal of Political Economy*, 44 (1936), p. 184.

11. William M. Gouge, *Short History of Paper-Money and Banking in the United States* (New York: B. & S. Collins, 1835), p. 75.

12. Richard Sylla, "American Capital Market 1846-1914" (Ph.D. diss., Harvard University, 1969), pp. 26, 37.

CHAPTER II

BANK NOTES AND DEPOSITS BEFORE 1863

Bank Note Usage

Commercial banks issued the only paper money circulating in the United States before 1862. Very soon after the first banks opened, their notes came to exceed coins. Specie averaged perhaps $3.00 or $4.00 per capita in the earliest years of the Republic, while bank notes in circulation amounted to some $3.50 per capita in 1800. By 1819 the United States had carried "the system of a paper currency . . . to a greater extent than anywhere else in the world," Alexander Baring, the leading British banker in the American trade, told a Parliamentary committee.[1] In addition to bank notes payable on demand a number of other types of bank liabilities circulated between 1812-1840. "Post notes," payable at some future date, were originally for the purpose of transmitting funds safely to distant places. They were illegal in New York as of 1828, but as late as 1837 Safety Fund banks petitioned unsuccessfully for authority to issue them. In 1840 New York made the issuance of post notes a misdemeanor. On the way out by 1840, they were later forbidden by the National Bank Act. Nevertheless currency transactions remained complicated. Notes of solvent banks fetched varying amounts, depending on distance from the place where they were redeemable.

A large variety of counterfeits plagued business. In addition to the spurious notes of nonexistent banks, there were genuine notes with forged signatures or with raised denominations. Sometimes notes of failed banks were altered with the name of a solvent one. Some were simply notes of old, closed banks. Amidst this confusion a worn, dirty note was considered more likely to be genuine than a clean one. Pinholes (made by banks as they filed the note) further attested to their authenticity.

Businessmen receiving sizeable amounts of diverse paper would have to pay attention to these banknotes. The counterfeit detector required diligent study six days a week. When John Thompson, author of the most famous counterfeit detector announced his new "bank note reporter" in 1841 he pointed to "frequent complaints of want of confidence in the existing publications" and promised to alert the public to unsound issues "regardless alike of the favor or ill-will of the great financiers." In 1859 one bogus Ohio bank bribed a publisher $1900 to "quote the money right." Thompson was sued for denouncing fraudulent issues but won each time. *Bicknall's Counterfeit Detector and Bank-Note List* started the year 1839 with 1,395 descriptions of counterfeit or altered notes in denominations from $1.00 to $500.00. By 1859 the *Nicholas Bank-Note Reporter* had 5,400 separate descriptions of spurious notes. There were 30 different counterfeits of the Bank of Delaware alone, including a dozen $5.00 notes, seven $10.00 notes, and one $100.00 note. *Monroe's Descriptive List of Genuine Bank Notes* (1859) itemized 1,323.

The United States Mint did not coin anything in the range between $1.00 and $2.50, and only a few $5.00 coins. Foreign coins could be used as legal tender by weight; the Spanish dollar was the largest coin in general circulation. The First Bank of the United States issued no notes under $10.00 while the Second was forbidden notes under $5.00. State bank notes filled the resulting vacuum. Notes under $5.00 came under prohibition by Massachusetts and Virginia in 1792. New York closed the door on notes under $10.00, in stages, by September 1836. The 1835 law, like others of its class, aimed to provide a better currency composed partly of coin, and to avoid further victimization of workingmen by counterfeits. Elimination of small bills would prevent the mass of the population being directly injured by banks. In 1852, there were some who agreed with New Jersey's governor that "the State which soonest adopts the use of coin, by the expulsion of paper in the smaller business transactions, will outstrip all others in the permanent prosperity of every branch of useful industry." On the eve of the Civil War, notes under $5.00 were illegal in Maine, Pennsylvania, Maryland, Virginia, Alabama, and Louisiana. However such bans were not always enforced or enforceable.

Albert Gallatin (Jefferson's Secretary of the Treasury) decried notes under $10.00 as a "public nuisance" in 1831, but prohibitory legislation, however well-intended, flew in the face of a public demand for small notes. In Missouri where the minimum denomination issued by the State Bank was $20.00, the illegal issues of private banks circulated widely. Small notes continued to be issued in New York despite the ban; in 1855 the law was repealed because of its nonenforcement. The state was flooded with $1.00, $2.00, $3.00, and $4.00 bank notes from interior states and New England.

As early as 1805 Massachusetts banks were issuing twenty-five cent notes. During the post-1815 depression, fractional notes were widespread in such sums as 5 cents, 6¼ cents, 10 cents, 12½ cents, 20 cents, and 25 cents. Although many states had restricted denominations to a round minimum of $1.00, $2.00 or $5.00 by 1830, laws against fractional notes were rarely enforced. And where enforced, it was not usual to find fractional parts of $1.00 notes in circulation. With improved coinage, fractional notes were almost entirely driven out after 1840, only to reappear a decade later as the silver in quarter dollars came to be worth more than their face value. From 1850 to 1853 New England banks desisted from issuing fractional notes, resorting instead to an old device of issuing bank notes in such odd sums at $1.25 or $1.75. Finally in 1853 Congress reduced the silver content of fractional coins. During the Civil War, as the value of the metal rose above the amount stamped on the coin, bank notes were cut up, and odd-sum and fractional bank notes were issued. So rapidly did these notes wear out, most banks found that the cost of reissue exceeded the interest income to the bank. Finally in July 1862 the issuance of bank notes in denominations of less than $1.00 was made a federal offense.

Earlier interest on the national level in sound bank notes took the form of the chartering of the First and Second Bank of the United States. During their 40 years as federal instrumentalities (1791-1811 and 1816-1836 respectively) the tendency of state banks to overissue notes was somewhat held in check. The resumption of specie payments, a prime objective in chartering the Second Bank, by restoring confidence diminished the discount on State bank note issues in the 1820's. Bank notes came increasingly to be held in lieu of specie and were returned less frequently to the issuing bank. The Second Bank's regulatory role thus served to enhance the acceptability of notes of State banks while at the same time antagonizing many of them.

Monopoly was among the misleading accusations against the Second Bank. Actually in 1830 it had only about one-fifth of the total note circulation and the same proportion of bank loans, while its share of specie and bank deposits was about one third. The Second Bank's notes did carry the special privilege of being receivable for public dues, a reflection of the bank's unique relationship to the federal government. Notes of the Bank of the

United States were held in excellent repute, the $19 million outstanding in 1831 circulating as far away as Montreal and Mexico City. Indeed, the Senate Finance Committee found in 1830 "a state of currency approaching as near to perfection as could be desired." Five years after the Second Bank's federal charter expired, however, the currency situation was "worse than that of any other country," according to Gallatin, then a leading New York banker.

Individual states, acting alone, could accomplish little, as Pennsylvania's governor pointed out in 1858. Cooperation, especially with adjoining states, was needed but not forthcoming. The free banks of Illinois, Indiana, and Wisconsin flooded Iowa, without any chartered banks of its own in the mid-1850's, with "some of the worst money in the Union."[2] Notes of over 300 banks circulated in Iowa City in 1856, mostly below par. General Sherman's brother recalled how his bank would sort them. Those from Eastern Pennsylvania, New York, and New England, "choice par funds, rating next to gold," would be shipped to New York in return for domestic exchange; from Ohio, Indiana, Missouri, Virginia, Maryland, and Kentucky came some of the best bank notes, "bankable funds." The Illinois and Wisconsin compartment in the currency tray was reserved for banks mainly in Chicago and Milwaukee, among the few legitimate ones in the state. Most troublesome were the "Western mixed" bank notes: stump-tail [from Illinois and Wisconsin], red-horse, wild-cat, brindle-pup, and red-dog [from Indiana and Nebraska].[3]

On 8 August 1861 the Chicago *Tribune* announced that "all banks of issues are a curse to the community." On 13 December 1861 that leading Republican organ made reference to "the ragged and doubtful issues of 1,600 [banking] corporations." Political opponents of the State Bank of Illinois described its notes as "bank rags" and "printed lies." The West's disgust with all bank notes and the region's near-unanimous desire for a uniform national currency was reported in 1863 by a "western banker" in a leading business magazine. About 7,000 different kinds of bank notes plus more than 5,500 varieties of fraudulent notes circulated in the loyal states by 1862. Senator John Sherman of Ohio remarked in 1863 that there were only 253 banks whose notes had not been altered or imitated. In another speech on the floor of the Senate he quoted the *London Times*: "Through the evils of the war the people will at least gain that deliverance from the previous confusion of their currency which to Europeans appears a barbarism." Greenbacks and national bank notes provided the remedy.

Redemption of Bank Notes

States bestowed on incorporated, but not on private, banks the note issue privilege. With this usually went the legal obligation to redeem notes on demand in specie or its equivalent. As fulfillment was often difficult, banks developed a variety of evasive strategems. Loans were made with the understanding that the borrower would see to it that the bank notes provided would not be returned for redemption before a minimum interval had elapsed. In Portsmouth, New Hampshire, a borrower from the Union Bank agreed on 1 August 1825 to keep $12,000 of its marked bills in circulation for one year, by redeeming them "weekly or as often as may be requested, in such manner as shall be satisfactory to the Bank." The borrower would then put these notes into circulation again. A Wilmington customer borrowed $20,000 from the Farmers Bank of Delaware with the understanding that he would redeem $10,000 of the bank's notes as soon as the cashier received them. Connecticut legislated against the practice in 1837, only to find some banks making loans to out-of-state borrowers willing to offer this guarantee. This "protected circulation," specially marked for the purpose, amounted to over $1.3 million in 1853; in 1854 Connecticut again prohibited the practice. Borrowers who were slow to redeem the notes given them were naturally preferred. Those who had directly or indirectly taken specie from the bank in connection with a previous loan were ineligible to borrow from the Cheshire Bank in Keene, New Hampshire, according to its 1804 rules.

Notes payable at some place other than the bank's own location became customary in the old Southwest. Tennessee's Union Bank had over $1.5 million payable in New Orleans in 1837 and another, larger amount payable in Philadelphia. Two Wall Street banks made Toms River the official place of issue. In 1851 that village consisted of four stores and a public house. The latter's owner doubled as president of one of the two banks. When redemption was requested, a Toms River bank could send to New York for specie and meet the deadline under a New Jersey law giving a bank three days grace.

Notes were very commonly put into circulation in a place distant from the bank of issue, sometimes by a mutual exchange between two banks. In 1846 the governor of Virginia complained that Richmond banks paid out the notes of their distant branches rather than their own. The Bank of Southern Illinois, established to circulate notes in more populous places, counted on the fact that few would ever take the trouble to present them for redemption in Bolton, a locale with one family in a remote part of Williamson County. In 1857 Illinois instituted a requirement that at least 200 people had to reside in an area where the bank was located. The Bolton type banks were the exception, however. Most Western banks were in recognized places "as accessible as travel conditions of the day permitted."[4]

Another tactic that the Illinois legislature attempted to eliminate in 1857 was the requirement that notes had to be presented one at a time and payment in small change. In 1837 all Charleston, South Carolina, bankers were said to delay payment of even small sums for hours. The teller would take out one small coin at a time, "toss it up, ring it, turn it over in his hand, engage in conversation, and then walk back to the counter." In 1840 the Philadelphia free trade journalist Condy Raguet could declaim against "those miserable and discreditable expedients so frequently resorted to by banks on the eve of insolvency. . . ."

The hospitality for which southerners and westerners were famous did not extend to strangers coming to redeem local bank notes. In 1818 Georgia authorized the Bank of Darien to require a written oath that the redeemed notes did not belong to any other bank or corporation. Between 1855 and 1859 persons who presented notes for redemption in Ohio, Indiana, and Missouri were threatened with lynching or being tarred and feathered. Early in 1855 residents of Versailles, Kentucky, passed a formal resolution denouncing an agent from Lexington, Kentucky, who had been appearing to redeem notes of the local bank. He was hanged in effigy and promised an early demise if he ever again molested their bank's specie.

The long forebearance of Americans who did not exercise their right to claim specie from banks astonished David Ricardo, who was an outstanding London banker as well as a major economist. In 1821 his correspondent Raguet explained that a person seeking to redeem bank notes "would have been persecuted as an enemy to society;" not a single case had been brought before a Philadelphia justice of the peace when the banks suspended specie payments during the War of 1812. An Englishman who had resided in Cincinnati in the 1830's was amused by the care taken by American merchants to prevent bank runs and to keep specie out of use. Specie withdrawal would diminish the bank's lending capacity and lead to a multiple contraction of the money supply. In the judgment of the astute French economist Michel Chevalier, Americans "firm faith in paper [was] founded in reason." But such confidence was not always warranted. When Michigan's Bank Commissioners inspected the Jackson County Bank in 1838 the $8,000 in "specie" was in chests filled mostly with nails and broken window glass. Just a few days previously the bank had certified to the state that it possessed $20,000 in specie.

Early in Indiana's free banking era it was possible to establish a new bank without a building or any of the usual accoutrements. An engraving plate to print $50,000 in bills cost about $1,500. Bonds of a state (often Southern) selling below face value would be shipped to the care of the state auditor. When the official countersigned the bills, the "banker" could pay for the

bonds and have surplus notes left over. The Adams Express Company provided some restraint with a special squad in the early 1850's to redeem
Indiana issues for their own account as well as on behalf of clients.

During periods of general suspension of specie payments, though banks
remained open, most ceased to redeem their obligations. Such episodes occurred in 1814 (outside New England), 1818, 1837, 1839-1841, and 1857.
The Civil War suspension began in 1861 and lasted 18 years. In addition to
those widespread general suspensions, there were numerous partial ones associated with bank failures in various localities. The typical customer's dilemma
was depicted by General Sherman, who was connected with one of San
Francisco's private banks during a run in 1855.

> At our counter happened the identical case, narrated of others, of the
> Frenchman, who was nearly squeezed to death in getting to the counter,
> and when he received his money, did not know what to do with it. "If
> you got the money, I no want him; if you no got him, I want it like the devil!

Protection of Noteholders

Every bank chartered under New York's Safety Fund Law of 1829 paid an
amount equal to 0.5 percent of its capital yearly for 6 years. Obligations of
failed banks were paid out of the fund, which had a $10,000 balance on its
termination in 1866. However, a considerable portion of the claims had been
lost or forgotten owing to the lapse of time in some bank failures. The Safety
Fund idea spread to Vermont (1831), Indiana (1834), Michigan (1836), Ohio
(1845), and Iowa (1858). In New York, Vermont, and Michigan all banks
chartered after the passage of the Safety Fund Act were compelled to join the
system. Michigan, the only one of the six requiring its free banks to join,
exhausted its Safety Fund by around 1842, effectively terminating the system there. The scheme ended in the five remaining states when the 1866
federal tax eliminated state bank notes.

Beginning with Connecticut in 1831, a number of states gave noteholders
of failed banks the status of preferred creditors. They "were mostly of that
class which is least able to bear losses," Hugh McCulloch of Indiana remarked
in connection with the 1857 collapse. When a northern Pennsylvania bank's
Philadelphia agent ceased to redeem its notes the result was

> Hundreds of poor laborers were to be seen running in every direction
> with their hands full of the trash and not able to induce a broker to give
> a sixpence in the dollar for them. We passed in the market a woman who

makes her living by selling butter, eggs, and vegetables, who had almost all she was worth, about $17, in Towanda Bank notes. When apprized that it was worthless, she sank down in agony upon her stool and wept like a child. This is but one of a hundred similar cases.[5]

Par Redemption

With the introduction of the Suffolk system, notes of New England banks circulated at par throughout that region. Boston merchants, unlike businessmen of other major commercial centers, did not have to contend with discounts on the notes of banks in their immediate trade area. Part of the success derived from the greater conservatism of Boston's entrepreneurs; the Lowells, Lawrences, and Appletons were among the Suffolk Bank's directors. What had originated as a measure to restrain the flood of country bank notes (thought to deprive Boston banks of an opportunity for issuing additional notes themselves), developed into the first successful regional clearing system in the United States.

In 1825 the associated banks of Boston agreed that the Suffolk Bank should receive country notes at par from them. In turn, a New England bank was expected to keep a non-interest-bearing permanent clearing balance. Suffolk also accepted at par bills of sound New England banks even if their balances were kept with another Boston bank. At least in New England the view was that a bank had no right to complain if it was called on to redeem its notes. Daily redemption averaged $400,000 in 1834 and $750,000 by 1850. In 1857, $400 million—10 times the average circulation of New England's banks—was sorted and counted annually. The country banks, which felt themselves unduly restrained and chafed under Suffolk's autocratic attitude, organized the Bank of Mutual Redemption in 1858. Even so, Suffolk retained the loyalty of about half of all the country banks.

The Second Bank of the United States began to buy and sell domestic bills of exchange on all the cities where it had branches in 1817 and came to dominate the market for domestic exchange. When its federal charter expired in 1836 the state banks succeeded to this business. Complaints of excessive charges became commonplace.

As with international currency movements, costs of shipping precious metals set limits to the domestic exchange rates. The 1834-1837 increase in the Treasury price of gold served to reduce the rate. Between New York and Boston, for example, gold would be transported before the rate could climb to a 0.25 percent premium; in the pre-1834 silver era, the differential might be 1 percent as the specie shipment for any given dollar amount was much bulkier.

While notes of the First Bank of the United States were acceptable all over the American continent, it was remarked in 1809 that one could not be sure that any other paper money would be accepted in payment for dinner even fifty miles from the issuing bank's locality. Visitors to the United States were cautioned about the fact that a given bank note would be worth progressively less as one proceeded further from the place of issue.

A number of states tried to limit or eliminate the discount on their bank's notes. In 1851 New York, in a measure, which the superintendent of banks claimed "literally closed the door to illegitimate banking," required its banks to provide for the redemption of their notes at New York City, Albany, or Troy at a 0.25 percent discount instead of the 0.5 percent permitted since 1840. Pennsylvania's attempt to require par redemption at Philadelphia or Pittsburgh in 1850 was unsuccessful. Outside New England, par bank notes were issued only in Illinois and Indiana (with their state banks) and in Louisiana (where branches of New Orleans banks served lesser communities). The "uniform bank currency" for which presidential candidate Henry Clay campaigned in 1844 came at last in 1863. The national bank note, redeemable at par throughout the United States, was not subject to exchange charges. The average cost of exchange between the East and the South and West had declined between 80 and 90 percent from the antebellum level, according to the 1876 estimate of the Comptroller of the Currency.

Deposits as Money

Counterparts of the various types of deposits in use today can be found in the first American banks, albeit in a primitive form. At first, checks were used in local payments and as a way of withdrawing cash from one's demand deposit account. In the first decade of the nineteenth century, checks came to be a medium of more than local settlements, and in the next decade, of more than local exchange. The modern usage of checks to pay debts or obtain currency was explained in a popular businessman's manual of 1838. According to Raguet, except for small retail transactions, almost all payments were made by checks in cities all over the United States in 1840. In the 1850's the number of bank accounts multiplied twenty-fold.[6] By 1860 most Massachusetts shopkeepers and substantial mechanics and professionals had joined the large merchants in keeping bank accounts.

Hamilton was already aware in 1790 that borrowers often transferred the proceeds of a loan through the vehicle of a check, which was in turn passed on by the recipient. In 1809 Gallatin put deposits on a par with bank notes as constituting "the circulating medium substituted by the banking operations to money; for payments from one individual to another are equally made by drafts on the bank, or by the delivery of bank notes." As Raguet told the Pennsylvania Senate in 1821, bank deposits were a part of the currency. In 1860 Samuel Hooper, who played an important role in Congress in the passage of the national banking legislation, wrote that "the great mass of deposits in the banks of the large commercial cities originate in discounts made by banks, and is therefore the creation of the banks." Although most writers in the antebellum period came to recognize the monetary nature of demand deposits, the general public held to the literal, erroneous view that these deposits represented mainly money brought to the bank for safekeeping.

This failure to comprehend that bank lending involved deposit creation explains the virtually universal distinction between banks of deposit and discount and banks of note issue. As late as 1838 a University of Pennsylvania economist, Henry Vethake, held that "the furnishing of a paper circulation was the essential feature of the banking system." Daniel Webster affirmed a year later that without note issue an institution was not a bank. At the end of 1841 Gallatin stated that in the United States paper money issue was implied by banking. Yet, Bray Hammond conjectured that as early as 1811 deposits were at least as large as note issues. This was the case from the start of the incomplete statistical series in 1834 published by the Secretary of the Treasury. Deposits excluding balances owed to other banks, however, did not consistently exceed bank notes until 1856. Available data do not distinguish between demand and time deposits. Fritz Redlich, an eminent twentieth-century historian, surmised that in 1820 three fourths were time, but during the period 1815-1840 the trend was increasingly toward demand deposits.

As early as 1791 the Bank of New York had almost 50 percent more deposits than bank notes. In 1829 the percentage ratio of notes to deposits for country banks stood at 177; for banks in seven leading cities, 74; and for New York City, 51. By 1849 it was 27 percent for New York City, while for country banks in the Empire state the ratio was 223 percent; a decade later the ratios had fallen to 9 and 78 percent respectively. Banks in the North rarely issued the legally authorized maximum amount of notes. In New England the ratio in 1850 was 42 percent of the maximum and by 1860 only 36 percent.

The rising volume of checks led to the opening of the New York Clearing House in October 1853 (80 years after London; 19 years before Paris and Vienna) for the daily settlement of net balances arising among the city's fifty-two banks. Boston opened the next clearinghouse about two and a half years later. Philadelphia's, conceived before the 1857 crisis, came into existence only afterward in 1858. Also in 1858, as an outgrowth of the crisis, Baltimore's banks selected the Union Bank of Maryland as their clearing agent. Boston and Philadelphia followed the New York example and established a distinct instrument for the purpose. Cleveland in 1858 and Worcester in 1861 were the only other localities with a clearinghouse arrangement before the establishment of the national banking system. Interbank deposits reflected bank relationships beyond the local level. Banks were placing deposits with each other in the 1790's. By 1812 Massachusetts country banks kept deposits in Boston, while banks in the Hub kept deposits with one another. In 1813 the Massachusetts Bank had deposits in the Bank of New York and the Bank of North America. The rival Union Bank of Boston kept accounts with the Mechanics Bank and the Bank of the Manhattan Company in New York and with the Farmers and Mechanics Bank in Philadelphia. Important interbank balances were also kept in Troy, Baltimore, and New Orleans in the 1830's. Such deposits were useful for note redemption and check collection. Large banks paid interest on interbank deposits. In New York City this competitive device was more often used by private bankers and trust companies than by the incorporated banks. By 1850, almost 600 of the 700 chartered banks in the nation kept $17 million in New York, in amounts from $15,000 to $100,000. A decade later, 1600 incorporated banks and 900 private banks held $25 million of bankers' balances in the money metropolis, mostly in a few Wall Street banks.

The compensating balance required of would-be borrowers developed well before 1861. Men secured the favor of banks "by leaving a considerable amount *constantly on deposit*," the economist Amasa Walker noted in 1857. He went on to note that the practice had become a "sort of [general rule] to which men are expected to conform themselves, if they wish liberal assistance from the banks."

As the American economy developed, becoming increasingly market-oriented in the process, the public came to rely on banks for most of the means of payment. Depending on the state and the period in question, bank notes and deposit accounts ranged in quality from excellent to scandalous, with a tendency for improvement in former frontier communities. Uniformly high standards awaited the coming of the national banking system in 1863. Meanwhile the influx of California gold after 1848 led to some substitution of specie for bank money, especially bank notes. [7]

Notes

1. Quoted in Bray Hammond, *Banks and Politics in America from the Revolution to the Civil War* (Princeton: Princeton University Press, 1957), p. 189.

2. Fred Merritt, *Early History of Banking in Iowa* (Iowa City: University of Iowa Press, 1900), p. 137.

3. Quoted in Howard H. Preston, *History of Banking in Iowa* (Iowa City: State Historical Society of Iowa, 1922), pp. 59-60. On the eve of the Civil War, bonds of Southern states were the backing for two thirds of the notes of Illinois banks, and an even greater proportion of Wisconsin's free banks. Missouri state bonds were selling at 80 percent of par in July, 1860; by December they were at 61 percent. All but 17 of Illinois' 104 banks were insolvent by the summer of 1861. See William Gerald Shade, *Banks or No Banks. The Money Issue in Western Politics 1832-1865* (Detroit: Wayne State University Press, 1972), pp. 205-206.

4. Carter H. Golembe, *"State Banks and the Economic Development of the West 1830-1844"* (Ph.D. diss., Columbia University, 1952), pp. 63-64.

5. (Gouge's) *Journal of Banking*, 24 Nov. 1841, p. 168, quoting the Philadelphia *Public Ledger*.

6. John A. Ferris, *Financial Economy of the United States* (San Francisco: A. Roman, 1867), p. 231. The 1859 *Annual Report* of the New York Superintendent of Banks made the same twenty-fold estimate.

7. Edward J. Stevens, "Composition of the Money Stock Prior to the Civil War," *Journal of Money, Credit and Banking*, 3 (1971), p. 100.

CHAPTER III

BANK LOANS BEFORE 1863

Types of Borrowers

Lenders of the colonial period might be neighbors or friends. By the second half of the eighteenth century, newspapers were the main vehicle for bringing borrower and lender together in the more populous communities. In time, banks came to assume a critical role as sources of financing. "Every business man is at the present time compelled to borrow of banks," the Connecticut Bank Commissioners stated with some exaggeration in 1853.

The earliest banks in Philadelphia, New York, Boston, and Baltimore specialized in commercial credit at short term. Banks had "a close connection with the whole mercantile interest," the Philadelphia merchant Pelatiah Webster explained in 1791. Half a century later Gallatin recalled that when banks were instituted their original purpose was to accommodate commercial interests. Agrarian hostility derived from the feeling that banks would not be of direct assistance to farmers and would act only to channel loanable funds away from agriculture. A supporter of that view was James Sullivan, the Massachusetts attorney general. "Banks can never supply the farmer with loans, and if all the spare money is vested in bank stocks, there never can be sufficient quantity in the hands of private persons to supply those who wish to take on land security," he wrote in *The Path of Riches* (1792).

After striving in vain to block the chartering of banks to serve merchants, agricultural interests turned to the establishment of their own institutions. Most petitions for banks in Virginia came from small towns and rural areas as early as 1816. In July 1817 Marylanders were called upon to establish a bank that would afford landholders "the same facilities of obtaining money for the cultivation and improvement of their estates, which persons engaged in commerce obtain from the commercial banks . . . for the carrying on of trade."

The policy of compelling some lending to agriculture began when Massachusetts required the Union Bank of Boston to make one-fifth of its loans to agricultural parties outside Boston in amounts ranging from $100 to $1000 for at least one year on the security of real estate. All but one of the fourteen Massachusetts banks chartered during 1802 and 1803 had to make one-eighth of their loans to agriculture on the same terms. Starting with the 1811 charter of the Merchants Bank and the State Bank, one-tenth of the funds had to go to agricultural as well as manufacturing interests. The same was the case with thirty of the thirty-four Massachusetts banks chartered between 1812 and 1815, but with only six of the twenty-eight chartered between 1815 and 1826. Each of the forty-one banks chartered by Pennsylvania in 1814 had to make available up to one-fifth of its capital to farmers, merchants, and manufacturers of their respective districts in 1-year loans, a provision continued in the general banking law of 1824.

The Bank of Indiana adopted the policy in 1843 of financing not only the flow of farm products to market but also the increase of cattle and hogs by "judicious loan to farmers." Hugh McCulloch, then manager of the Fort Wayne branch, reported this "greatly stimulated and increased production." Southern banks lent to merchants on the security of the great staples; in turn these made credit available to planters.

Loans on real estate were made throughout the nation, but some banks in the North came to dislike the long term and the difficulty in receiving prompt payment at maturity. Yet in Charleston, South Carolina, five of the six banks that did not lend on real estate and bonds suspended in 1839, at the same time that the Bank of South Carolina, with extensive real estate loans, paid its notes in specie. Cincinnati banks preferred real estate loans to trade bills in the 1830's. On two occasions when the speculators could not meet their obligations, almost the entire city was sold by the Second Bank of the United States. Finding loans for the purchase or improvement of land to be "sluggish and unreliable," the Bank of the State of Indiana turned away from them after 1843.

During the colonial era, provincial and private loan offices made a limited number of loans on mortgage security for a limited period. Further, all the original colonies except Virginia established a public land bank. The earliest,

Charleston's Land and Loan Bank of the Carolinas (1712), had £52,000 to lend. While agriculture was obviously favored, any landowner was eligible to borrow; merchants and other nonagriculturalists also took advantage of these land banks. Those colonial enterprises were probably the inspiration for the real estate banks found in the antebellum South (and for the twentieth-century federal land banks for farmers). Property banks aimed at attracting foreign capital by the sale of bonds secured by real estate mortgages.

Louisiana incorporated the first one, the Consolidated Association of Planters, in 1827 and later chartered two others. Louisiana's property banks also made loans on urban real estate. These property banks in addition had the note issue privilege and performed commercial banking functions. Arkansas' Real Estate Bank was founded in 1836 in conformity with the constitutional provision for a "banking institution calculated to aid and promote the agricultural interests." That state's first commercial banks were chartered in 1838 in the hope of increasing land values by "coining the wild lands of Arkansas into money." There were other Southern banks founded for the express purpose of lending on real estate. The Union Bank of Louisiana (1812), a prototype of several later ones, was empowered to lend on real estate and slaves. The Planters Bank of Mississippi (1830) could lend on mortgage security up to one third the value of the property.

Manufacturing activities also received some financing from bank loans. On Hamilton's suggestion, the Bank of New York advanced $45,000 to the Society for Establishing Useful Manufactures in 1792 to permit completion of its factories in Paterson, New Jersey. Baltimore's Mechanics Bank was chartered in 1806 "to give aid especially to practical mechanics and manufacturers." Up to $80,000 (equal to one-eighth of the bank's paid-in capital) could be loaned to those categories, secured by property, with no borrower receiving more than $3,000. Bankers before 1860 were generally dubious about the prospects of manufacturing and insisted on collateral security.

Internal improvements projects received significant bank funds. Banks provided over one-fifth of some $40 million spent in Ohio, Wisconsin, Illinois, and Indiana, partly in short-term loans in anticipation of proceeds from long-term flotations. Girard's Bank made a $266,000 loan to the Schuylkill Navigation Company in 1827; the Mt. Carbon Railroad received $30,000 in 1830 and the Danville & Pottsville Railroad, $20,000 in 1831. New Orleans banks were called upon to assist two large railroad undertakings in the 1850's. The Philadelphia Bank, with only $46,000 in railway and canal securities in 1861, had increased its investment to $600,000 by 1863, mostly in the Pennsylvania, Reading, and Lehigh Railroads.

Some states granted transportation companies banking privileges in the hope of accelerating construction. The Georgia Railroad and Banking Company (whose bank has been in business since 1833) constructed a line from Augusta to Athens, while the Central Railroad and Banking Company connected Savannah with Macon. Between 1835 and 1837 South Carolina, Georgia, Mississippi, and Louisiana chartered sixteen combined banking and railroad companies, authorizing them to issue $33 million in bank stock. Half of the capital of those corporations could be used for banking, and they could issue notes up to three times their banking capital.

Instead of financial subsidy, New Jersey attached a banking privilege to the charter of the Morris Canal and Banking Company "for the encouragement of so great an undertaking as the erection of said canal, and in some measure to induce capitalists and others to subscribe." The right to engage in banking for 35 years was made contingent on completion of the canal, which connected Newark with Phillipsburg in 1831. Within a decade, the corporation was in receivership. On reorganizing in 1844, it became exclusively a canal company. Louisiana's first improvement bank, the Canal Bank, had to devote $1 million of its $4 million capital for a canal from Lake Pontchartrain to New Orleans (1831). In Michigan, note issues of its banking subsidiary made possible the early completion of the Erie and Kalamazoo Railroad.

While New Jersey, Louisiana, and Michigan got what they bargained for, the outcome was not everywhere so successful. From 1831 to the crash in 1837 Mississippi "was gridironed with imaginary railroads and beridden with railroad banks. There was more watered stock sold than there were cross-ties laid."[1] South Carolina's eminent Senator Robert Hayne headed a project to link Charleston with the Ohio River. The South Western Railroad opened a bank in 1839 which lasted until 1868 when its charter expired. The railroad, projected to reach Louisville and Cincinnati, got only as far as Columbia.

Commercial banks that created purchasing power in the form of bank notes to finance jointly owned nonbank enterprises were by no means confined to canals and railroads. A bank belonging to the Dry Dock Company[2] opened in New York City in 1825, a year after the Chemical Manufacturing Company had its charter amended to include banking. In 1844 that corporation ceased to be involved in manufacturing. Chemical Bank, long known as "Old Bullion" because it alone among New York City banks did not suspend specie payments in 1857, has been among the ten largest in the nation in recent years. Kentucky had the Sanders Manufacturing Company in 1818. New Jersey granted the Salem Banking and Steam Mill Company a charter in 1822. In 1826 it disposed of the flour mill used by local farmers, remaining a bank until 1967 when it merged with the First National Bank of South Jersey. The New Orleans Gas Light and Banking Company (1829) financed the completion of what was reputed to be the best street lighting system in any American city, while the Commercial Bank (1833-1843) operated the city's waterworks. The Exchange Bank constructed the St. Charles Hotel in the American quarter of New Orleans to meet terms of its 1835 charter. Most banks established to provide capital funds for nonbanking enterprises collapsed in 1837.

On more than one occasion, state governments turned for loans to the banks they had chartered. Massachusetts, Pennsylvania, Maryland, Virginia, and South Carolina had to borrow over $5 million to cover defense outlays during the War of 1812. Pennsylvania called on its banks to lend it up to 5 percent of their capital in 1840. Louisiana owed its banks $1.1 million by the end of 1841.

Bank underwriting of and trading in investment securities provided industry and government with capital funds. In the period following the War of 1812 banks bought stocks and resold them in small lots or acted as agents selling on commission. From the 1820's to the early 1840's, investment banking activities of commercial banks were especially notable in New York City, Philadelphia, and Albany. By the 1850's, however, most of the investment banking business, except for purely local issues, was in the hands of private bankers.

Banks also made loans with securities as collateral. And a New York legislative committee report of 1837 criticized banks for facilitating speculation. The widespread use of bank loans extended on security collateral, as the practice had evolved by the 1850's, was "a distinctly American development."[3] By 1850 interbank balances, which could be withdrawn at any time, had become an important source of call money. After 1857, as New York Stock Exchange settlements due after a specified period declined greatly and stock broker's credit extension to their customers increased, virtually all speculative trades came to depend on call loans, payable on demand. Antebellum banks kept their secondary reserves almost exclusively in the form of call loans, as there did not exist an open market in commercial paper (promises to pay after several months, usually 90 days, issued by leading businesses). Agitation demanding the elimination of call loans as secondary reserves began in the aftermath of the Panic of 1857 and continued well into the twentieth century.

Banks in major cities often specialized in the financing of specific business activities, as reflected in their names. In 1860 there were over sixty farmers banks, fifty mechanics, forty-five merchants, thirty involving commerce (or commercial), twenty traders, and fifteen manufacturers. The four St. Louis banks established in 1857 derived their capital from distinct groups:

the Bank of St. Louis from steamboat men and manufacturers; the Merchants Bank, dry goods and grocers; the Southern Bank, boots, shoes, and the mechanical trades; and the Exchange Bank, lumber. The City Bank in New York began as a source of funds for shipping interests, later developing into a lender for merchants handling such raw materials as cotton and sugar. Antebellum bank loan portfolios were notably heterogeneous. The variety of purposes, types, and (as will be shown next) maturities, reflected the diverse needs of the developing economy.

Loan Maturities

Even the earliest banks broke their own rules and granted loans to their founders for other than short-term business purposes. In 1786 the Bank of North America was discounting commercial paper based on the sale of goods, with no more than 45 days to maturity (earlier, only 30 days), and no renewals. Twenty years later it was making longer terms available and renewing frequently. In 1803 the Philadelphia Bank made its first discounts for 60 days but by 1807 had a 4-month limit. Philadelphia banks generally confined themselves to 60-day discounts early in the nineteenth century; within 30 years, competition had raised the customary limit to from 4 to 6 months. In 1812 almost half of the notes discounted by Girard's Bank were for 60 days or less; by 1831 over half were for at least 6 months. Following the example of the First Bank of the United States, the Second Bank placed a 60-day limit on its discounts; soon after it began operations the rule was abandoned. By 1827 the limit was 6 months. By 1830, with ample funds to reinvest as a result of the repayment of the federal debt, the Second Bank bought mortgage-secured paper payable in New Orleans in 1 to 3 years.

Punctuality in commercial payments was a practice introduced by banks. Indeed, that was an important reason for their unpopularity in the early days. However, by 1816 the average American bank had over half of its loans on a basis where the bank might "but it is understood won't call in 60 days—much of it arose from the assurance of the Bank that it would not be called for many months—some part of it for several years," reported a committee of the Virginia legislature. By the 1820's and 1830's, banks were discounting at longer term than in earlier times.

Accepted theory followed Adam Smith in confining banks to the discount of short-term, strictly business paper. Actual practice, as various legislative committees discovered after the 1837 crisis, diverged sharply from the principles enunciated in the *Wealth of Nations*. In the century after 1830 maturities did not change much—1 to 6 months with renewals. Some renewals continued for years, making the 60- or 90-day limit set by a bank's by-laws much longer in practice.

The British principle of lending on "real bills of exchange," resting on goods moving from merchants and manufacturers to consumers was the exception in American banking. Here renewable accommodation paper based on secured promissory notes was popular. When accommodation paper was discounted, the borrower anticipated it would be renewed, whereas in the case of business paper, payment at maturity was expected.

The importer sold to country storekeepers on nominal 6-month credits, which actually lasted for a year or longer. The country merchant in turn sold on book credit to people who did not expect to make a settlement in less than a year. Banks in the larger cities moved away from accomodation paper, and such loans were rare by 1850. Among country banks, however, accomodation paper continued to be popular. Three month accomodation paper, with the borrower confident of renewal, financed the construction of vessels and factories. Textile manufacturers customarily received 8-, 10-, and 12-month credits from Rhode Island banks, although for a time after the panic of 1857 a 6-month term was the limit. A comprehensive study of 2,385 loans extended to eight New England textile firms from 1840 to 1860 shows commercial banks making 87 percent of those outstanding for a 1- to 6-month term and 63 percent of those for a 6- to 12-month period. Banks provided 58 percent of the local loans borrowed by those companies.

Edmond Forstall, a thoughtful New Orleans banker, convinced Louisiana in 1842 to require banks in that great trade center to hold short-term, self-liquidating assets along the lines of the British "real-bills" principle. New Orleans banks had to offset demand liabilities by one third specie and two thirds paper due in 90 days. In the earlier years of the Forstall system, any renewal of 90-day paper was regarded as equivalent to protest, and its maker was publicly dishonored.[4] When a bank's specie holdings fell below one third, it could not make any further discounts. Except for the prohibition of renewals, these principles prevailed until the late 1850's. New Orleans businessmen thought they were at a disadvantage in competition with those in New York, Philadelphia, Charleston, and other rival ports where loans could be had or renewed for 6-months or a year at 6 percent.

Although short-term lending was the law only in New Orleans, banks in other commercial centers also made it their practice. Typically, however, an antebellum bank simultaneously extended both short- and long-term credit. Agrarian and frontier pressures for long-term credit affected rural banking practices and also led to the establishment of public banks for long-term loans, as in Georgia. Indeed, part of the attractiveness of free banking was its lack of "inhibitions as to long-term credit."[5]

Biases in Lending

Particularly in the early decades, political loyalties influenced the judgment of bank directors responsible for passing on loan applications. Jeffersonian Republicans, who thought the Federalist dominated Bank of New York had acted illiberally toward them, formed the Bank of the Manhattan Company. A Republican who disagreed with his Federalist colleagues in the Bank of Albany (which he had helped to found) proceeded to organize the New York State Bank. Politics also showed up in the state owned banks. Legislators would select directors who promised to lend to their constituents. Over half of the total $15.3 million owed the Bank of the State of Alabama (founded in 1823) at the time it was placed in liquidation in 1844 was bad or doubtful. In contrast, the State Bank of Indiana in which the state had a half interest, had less than $50,000 in bad debts in its 25-year history. Even small sums were loaned only after careful investigation of the borrower's standing, habits, and character.

A unique approach to credit analysis was followed by the Bank of the City of Chicago. President Paine refused loans to those who drank, smoked, or gambled or who exacted usury. Loans were intended to facilitate "the natural exchange between the producer and consumer, whether of body, soul, or spirit, and for the time necessary to produce the exchange."[6] A spiritualist meeting place in the rooms above the bank housed a High Priestess who consulted the spirit of Alexander Hamilton before a loan was made. The counsel of the first Secretary of the Treasury must have been sound. The bank paid all its creditors in full after it was closed by the police in 1852.

Directors and their friends were commonly believed to receive specially favorable loan terms while refusing loans to others offering superior security. Yet in Vermont in 1837 the bank commissioners found that in all but two banks the proportion of loans to directors was "extremely small;" the two in question were loans of perhaps no more than the directors would have received had they not been on the board. In Virginia in the early 1840's directors had borrowed $2.4 million, an amount almost equal to one-fourth of the capital of the reporting banks. A hostile critic claimed that "most directors serve, and value their places, merely to borrow as much money as possible."[7]

Loans secured by bank stock might assist shareholders, but they sometimes were used to evade laws governing the amount of paid-in capital. Such loans might also tend to favor the bank's owners or directors. Stockholders were already principal and preferred borrowers in the first days of the Bank of North America. In 1819 Hezekiah Niles cited the case of the City Bank of Baltimore, which had loaned out over $400,000 to every official save the porter and one clerk, to denounce banking as "a cheat . . . a machine for the exclusive benefit of a few scheming men." When eleven banks in or near Boston (whose capital had never been paid in) failed in 1837-1838, a local paper denounced "the manufacture of banks by those who sought to borrow all the fictitious capital they could create." It is not surprising, however, that aspiring borrowers were often the organizers of a new bank in a capital-hungry community.

Legislation to deal with abuses from loans on bank stock set maximum limits or prohibited such loans outright. Some states tried to prevent favoritism and to diffuse the benefits of banks as widely as possible by limiting the amount that could be loaned out to any one borrower; $50,000, for example, was the limit in Pennsylvania and Maryland.

Banks were accused of channeling loans in undesirable directions by not being of help to farmers, by primarily encouraging speculation, and by discriminating in their loan decisions. Such indictments reflected borrower disappointment as much as an accurate representation of the facts. However, a recent scholarly investigation discovered antebellum Louisiana banks showing "some preferences" to large planters over small farmers, to merchants over planters, and to public works.[8] The most effective solution for these complaints was available in the free banking states, where persons who considered an existing bank unfair could readily organize a new one.

Notes

1. Quoted in Frederick A. Cleveland and Fred W. Powell, *Railroad Promotion and Capitalization* (New York: Longmans Green, 1909), p. 171.

2. In 1867 the Eleventh Ward Bank succeeded to the banking business of this firm. In 1902 it merged into the Corn Exchange Bank.

3. Joseph Hedges, *Commercial Banking and the Stock Market before 1863* (Baltimore: Johns Hopkins Press, 1938), p. 76.

4. Bray Hammond, "Long and Short Term Credit in Early American Banking," *Quarterly Journal of Economics* 49 (1934), p. 100.

5. *Ibid.*, p. 96.

6. Quoted in Cyril James, *Growth of Chicago Banks* (New York; Harper, 1938), p. 222.

7. Edmund Ruffin, *Farmer's Register* 10 (30 April 1842), p. 181. The editor's war against banking and currency extravagances lost this outstanding agricultural journal many of its subscribers, forcing it to suspend publication in its tenth year. See Avery Craven, *Edmund Ruffin, Southerner: A Study in Secession* (New York: Appleton-Century-Crofts, 1932), pp. 61ff.

8. George D. Green, "Banking in Antebellum Louisiana," *Journal of Economic History* 26 (1966), p. 581.

CHAPTER IV

GOVERNMENT AND THE BANKS BEFORE 1863

The State as Sponsor or Shareholder

Eight states organized wholly owned banks before 1838. Vermont, with a state bank from 1806 to 1812, was the first. The State Bank of Illinois (1821-1831) was the only other one in the North. The six in the South began with the successful Bank of the State of South Carolina (1812-1870) and ended with the Bank of Tennessee (1838-1866), the second effort in that state. The Bank of the State of Alabama operated from 1823 to 1845; the Central Bank in Georgia, 1828 to 1842; and the Bank of the State of Arkansas, 1837 to 1843. The Bank of the State of Tennessee (1820-1831) and the state-owned banks in Illinois and Kentucky (1820-1834) were opened to relieve the agrarian distress resulting from the 1819 depression in the aftermath of heavy borrowing in the preceding two years.

Each new slave state across the Southern tier from Florida to Arkansas established one or more banks to further the production and marketing of cotton and sugar. Beginning with Louisiana in 1824, states in the Southwest and the West had incurred indebtedness of over $65 million by 1840 to provide banking capital. In the South and West, already endowed by nature with an adequate transportation system, the state-sponsored banks "formed the counterpart of the internal improvement program of the North and East."[1] Louisiana's debt, the largest in the South and outranked only by New

York's and Pennsylvania's, was 95 percent for banking (especially property banks); the state's bonds provided almost half of Louisiana's banking capital as of 1838. The state was not ordinarily a stockholder in the real estate and property banks, but it usually received a portion of the profits in return for the guaranty its credit provided the bank.

Most states except New Jersey and several of the smaller ones in New England owned at least some bank stock by 1812. Massachusetts made its first subscription in 1793; by 1812 it owned one-eighth of the bank stock in the state, which it sold in 1821. Pennsylvania's first purchase was one-third of the stock in the Bank of Pennsylvania (1793). The state's total investment reached $2.1 million, at par, by 1815 and was sold in 1843.

The outstanding State Bank of Indiana (1832-1857) was half privately owned. Those shareholders could borrow from the state (not the bank) five-eighths of the subscription price, with the stock and real estate serving as collateral. When the bank was liquidated and its business taken over by the privately owned Bank of the State of Indiana (1855-1865), the state received a handsome profit. Most states, however, were not so fortunate in their investments.

Stock ownership by the state held out the lure of profits that would diminish or even eliminate the need for taxation. Revenue could also be obtained by exacting a bonus for a charter. Pennsylvania received $12,000 from the Bank of North America for a new charter in 1814, and the Louisiana State Bank paid $100,000 in 1818. The first state to tax bank stock was Georgia in 1805, followed by New Jersey in 1810, and Massachusetts in 1812. Bank dividends were first taxed in Pennsylvania in 1814, an example followed by Ohio in 1815 and Virginia in 1846. Taxation of dividends and capital stock became more common than bonuses after 1820. By 1864 a dozen Philadelphia banks planned to halve their tax burden by converting to national bank status.

Government Supervision

Ten states with significant shareholdings appointed directors in one or more banks, but stock ownership was not a prerequisite for state efforts at control of banking. Bank charters contained bank regulation of a sort. Early ones did not spell out the powers of banks in any detail. On incorporating the Commercial Bank of Albany in 1825, New York specified for the first time that the bank was authorized to

have and possess all incidental and necessary powers to carry on the business of banking—by discounting bills, notes, and other evidences of debt; by receiving deposits; by buying gold and selling bills of exchange, and by issuing bills, notes and other evidences of debt; but the said company shall have and possess no other powers whatever, except such as are expressly granted by this act.

That definition, carried over in New York's Free Banking Act of 1838 and in the 1863 National Currency Act, became basic in state and federal banking legislation. The final clause with its broad restriction appeared for the first time in the 1825 charter. Earlier incorporation acts had enumerated various restraints. Thus of ninety-seven New York charters still in effect in 1839, ninety-two forbade dealings in real estate (except for mortgage transactions and the banking house); eighty-eight forbade dealing in any merchandise or bonds of the states or United States, except in liquidating loan collateral.

The American discovery of "giving publicity to their actual condition" was hailed by the Virginia economist George Tucker in 1839 as the most effective check "to the imprudence of banks." States began to require regular reporting in the early 1800's. However, banks often disregarded the reporting requirement or submitted inaccurate or misleading statements. Even honest, exact reports could not reveal developments in the intervening period, as Pennsylvania's governor noted in 1846. The insistence of Massachusetts on frequent, regular reports, "perpetuated a hypothetical, not an actual control that permitted transgressors to 'cover real delinquency by a show of correctness' and to 'mislead the public' by an appearance of supervision which really did not exist."[2] In Illinois, from 1817 to 1863 private banks had a "very much more creditable [record than the] elaborately safeguarded state institutions."[3]

New York set up the earliest special bank supervisory authority under the Safety Fund Act of 1829. Three commissioners made on-the-spot investigations of each bank's affairs at least four times a year. Within a decade, goaded by the 1837 Panic, New York's example had been copied by all of New England except New Hampshire and by Mississippi and Michigan.

In 1843, the very year that New Hampshire provided for an annual, unannounced inspection, New York abolished the commissioners, the legislature reasoning that they were superfluous when bankers were honest and of no avail when bankers were dishonest. Pennsylvania's governor remarked in 1846 that inspections in states with bank commissioners "are apt to induce a dangerous reliance on the vigilance of such officers." Similarly, the eminent economist John R. McCulloch noted in London in 1845 that the various state regulations such as those requiring payment of part of the capital before a new bank could open, publication of statements of condition, or inspection by public officials, were "in fact worse than worthless. Such regulations cannot be enforced, so that their real effect is, by giving an appearance of credit and respectability to the worst description of banks, to lull suspicion, and facilitate fraud."

New York abandoned its laissez-faire attitude toward bank examinations in 1851, establishing its banking department on a permanent basis. Massachusetts followed a parallel course, by restoring in 1851 the bank commissioners office that had been in existence from 1838 to 1843. It had been abolished on the pretext of an economy drive but the actual reason was country bank hostility. The basic official check on New York banks, however, remained the quarterly report of condition. The superintendent could examine the bank only if an irregularity was suspected. And he might well hesitate because even rumors of an examination could lead to a run on the bank. So as not to further "delude the unwary public," the superintendent asked, in vain, for the elimination of his examining powers in 1858. His examination authority remained confined to cases where he suspected illegal or unsound activities until 1884. Most other states did not go even to the limited extent that New York did in the continuous regulation of banks. Pennsylvania recognized the need but merely added banking to the responsibilities of the Auditor General in 1860.

In 1841, Gallatin, then an eminent conservative New York City banker, wrote that there was universal agreement that every phase of banking save the note issue function "not only must be open to all, but requires no more restrictions than any other species of commerce." A similar distinction between deposit and discount operations "open to all" and bank note issue "confined to the few" and subject to state restraint, was drawn by Millard Fillmore as New York State comptroller in 1848. In the following year, California's first constitution allowed banks to accept deposits but made issuance of paper money a crime. Oregon in 1857 did the same. The statement "Take away from the banks of the United States the power of issuing paper money, and the whole difficulty of banking vanishes," appeared in *Hunt's Merchants Magazine* in 1858. That the real banking problem of the day involved deposit regulation even more than the protection of note issues was correctly pointed out by the Philadelphia ironmaster Stephen Colwell in *The Ways and Means of Payment* (1859), but not many of his contemporaries were convinced.

Impressed with the benefits of free competition in all economic activities, the historian Hildreth in 1840 advocated "as much liberty for capitalists to invest their money in a bank as in a cotton mill." In practice, the goal of this free banking spokesman was realized; the absence of an effective supervisory mechanism meant that statutory constraints were largely meaningless.

Legal Reserve Requirements

By 1861 a dozen states sought to prevent overissue of bank notes by requiring legal reserves. Early charters limited the bank's liabilities to some multiple of its (supposedly specie) capital, in effect specifying legal reserves. Virginia was first, in 1837, to express the requirement directly in terms of a percentage of (note) liabilities. New York followed in 1838, but in 1840 country bank opposition led to repeal of the 12.5 percent specie requirement for redemption of the notes outstanding. Meanwhile Georgia (1838), Ohio (1839), Connecticut (1848), Indiana (1853), and Missouri (1857) instituted reserve requirements.

Louisiana provided the most important precedent for the reserve provision in the 1863 federal law. An 1842 statute specified for the first time a specie reserve, of one third, for both deposits and bank notes. Edmond Forstall, president of the Citizens Bank of New Orleans, explained to his fellow legislators as early as February 1837 (three months before the Panic) that deposits were a threat no less than bank notes. The legal requirement he advocated was enacted five years after the Panic of 1837, but already in 1839 the associated banks of New Orleans had agreed among themselves to follow the practice. Louisiana's Free Banking Act of 1853 required reserves for bank deposits but not for bank notes.

Early in 1858 New York's governor pointed with envy to "the chief banks of New Orleans, [which] above all banks of the country, were enabled to resist the pressure of universal suspension elsewhere and maintain their integrity." The legislature refused to enact his proposed 25 percent reserve requirement for deposits. Nevertheless, all but four of the forty-six New York Clearing House members voluntarily agreed to keep a 20 percent cash reserve in March 1858 and increased it to 25 percent in 1860.

With the experience of the 1857 suspension of specie payments in view, President Buchanan suggested that the states legislate a one third reserve requirement for both notes and deposits. But only a few took action of any sort. After years of opposition by bankers who viewed such a measure as unnecessary meddling, Massachusetts passed a law in 1858 that established a 15 percent legal reserve for deposits and for notes. Iowa, also in 1858,

insisted on a 25 per cent cover for both deposits and notes. Maine (1858) and
Pennsylvania (1860) required a reserve only for bank notes.

The Federal Government and the Independent Treasury

Although banking was mainly a state concern before 1863, the federal
government's role was not inconsiderable. Both the First and the Second
Bank of the United States were chartered by the Congress to serve the needs
of the United States Treasury for a federal depository and fiscal agent to
transfer funds and make payments where needed. The First Bank had effectu-
ated the transmission of public funds more easily, to a greater extent, and
with greater security against possible loss than any of the existing state institutions, Secretary of the Treasury Gallatin (1801-1814) pointed out. During
the War of 1812 the federal government felt keenly the absence of those
facilities. The bank note currency of the different seaports depreciated in
varying degrees, resulting in a variable de facto tariff rate from 1812 through
1816. Congress aimed to eliminate this inequity by chartering the Second
Bank of the United States in 1816, which aided the state banks to resume
specie payment, and accepted only convertible bank notes.

Even in the heyday of the federal banks, the Treasury found it necessary
to use some state banks; fifteen were used in the early 1830's where there was
no nearby branch of the Bank of the United States. A policy of running down
holdings of United States balances was announced in the Fall of 1833 as part
of Jackson's war against Nicholas Biddle, head of the great federal bank. The
"pet banks," as the opposition newspapers labeled them, were now to receive
Treasury deposits. Purportedly safe, all but four of the eighty-eight depositories joined the general suspension of specie payments in May 1837. The
Treasury lost perhaps $500,000 in unrecovered deposits and unredeemable
bank notes. From 1789 to 1841 the federal government lost an estimated
$5 million from bad bank notes and another $900,000 in uncollectable
deposits.

Soon after the start of the Panic of 1837 Gouge urged the separation of
government from the banks to shear the institutions of half their power to do
evil. He insisted that the Treasury could easily and safely conduct its affairs[4]
without resorting to any bank or using any kind of bank paper. Separation
was the objective of the Independent Treasury that was instituted in Martin
Van Buren's administration in 1840 and repealed the following year when the
Whigs gained power. Reestablished in 1846, it did not go out of existence
officially until 1920. The United States Treasury had made use of a federally
chartered institution for almost 40 years and of state chartered banks during

the entire span from 1789 to 1846. Henceforth the government was to be its own banker. Treasury receipts and payments were to be in gold, silver, and Treasury notes. Secretary of the Treasury Robert J. Walker hoped the measure he sponsored would increase the amount of specie in circulation as well as restrain banks from issuing notes in excess.

In December 1857 President James Buchanan could boast that "thanks to the Independent Treasury, the government has not suspended [specie] payments, as it was compelled to do by the failure of the banks in 1837." However, early in 1862, a few weeks after the banks suspended, the Treasury did likewise. The use of state banks as depositories for federal bond subscriptions, the issuance of irredeemable United States Notes ("greenbacks"), and authorization of national banks as depositories represented further departures from principle. The only significant role of the Independent Treasury during the Civil War period was the collection of custom duties in specie and its disbursement for public debt interest payments.

The Independent Treasury system's impact on the economy was minimal in its earliest years when federal collections and spending averaged about $1 million a week. However, the arrangement had the potential of interfering with the nation's banking operations, disturbing and embarrassing them, as Calvin Colton correctly foresaw in 1849. The ideal of the separation of bank and state became more and more unrealistic later in the nineteenth century, as the federal budget grew and the ramifications of commercial banking reached every part of the nation and every sector of economic activity.

Notes

1. Guy S. Callender, "The Early Transportation and Banking Enterprises of the States in Relation to the Growth of Corporations," *Quarterly Journal of Economics* 17 (1902), p. 162.

2. Oscar and Mary F. Handlin, *Commonwealth: A Study of the Role of Government in the American Economy: Massachusetts 1774-1861*, rev. ed. (Cambridge: Harvard University Press 1969), p. 121.

3. George W. Dowrie, *The Development of Banking in Illinois, 1817-1863* (Urbana: University of Illinois Press 1913), p. 130.

4. William M. Gouge, *An Inquiry into the Expediency of Dispensing with Bank Agency and Bank Paper in the Fiscal Concerns of the United States* (Philadelphia: William Stavely, 1837), p. 15.

CHAPTER V

ANTEBELLUM BANKING IN THE BALANCE

Banks and Business Fluctuations

Like most of their contemporaries, Presidents Van Buren and Buchanan blamed the operations of banks for the major financial crises and ensuing depressions that occurred during their administrations, in 1837 and 1857 respectively. Buchanan denounced "our extravagant and vicious system of paper currency and bank credits," warning that crises would recur "so long as the amount of the paper currency and bank loans and discounts of the country shall be left to the discretion of 1,400 irresponsible banking institutions, which . . . will consult the interest of their stockholders rather than the public welfare." Reviewing the monetary history of the United States from 1800 to 1875, the economist-legislator Amasa Walker saw panics and suspensions as the consequence of allowing banks to manufacture the circulating medium.[1]

Fluctuations in bank-created money in that period have usually been considered as being due mainly to variations in aggregate specie, related in turn to the United States balance of international payments position. This explanation had become general among bankers and legislators by the mid-nineteenth century. Already in 1848 Pennsylvania's governor had noted the tendency of an import of specie to increase bank notes "by enlarging the means of the banks to extend their issues." However, sharp rises in the volume of bank

notes and deposits outstanding per dollar of specie reserves, antecedent to
financial collapses from 1834 to 1860, have raised doubts about the traditional explanation.[2] Perhaps the role of banking for the entire pre-1861
period can best be characterized as did Parsons for the period 1815-1840:
"While the banks did not originate business fluctuations, they transmitted
and magnified the impulses making for expansion or contraction."[3] Banks
would become more cautious about the quality and maturity of their loans
after each crisis, only to relax their standards as business recovered.

Losses from Banking

The first bank failure in the United States occurred in 1809 in Gloucester,
Rhode Island; the Farmers' Exchange Bank had assets of $8,646, but its
circulation came to $580,000.

About one-fourth of the total number of banks went out of business in the
next 6 years following the Panic of 1837. The American banking system had
not a single "redeeming quality about it," wrote Henry Vethake, a University
of Pennsylvania economist, in 1839. He viewed it from beginning to end as "a
compound of quackery and imposture." Almost 40 years later the eminent
economist Francis A. Walker commented that conditions had "almost justified" Vethake's severe language.

Of the 2,500 banks organized between 1781 and 1861, almost two fifths
had closed within 10 years of opening. The direct financial loss inflicted on
banks' creditors by these failures has not been reliably estimated. John
Sherman told his fellow senators in January 1863 that bank note holders lost
about 5 percent each year in the period to 1864. Comptroller of the Currency
John Knox made no effort to reckon the losses to depositors and shareholders; he argued that note holders were probably the principal losers and
also estimated the amount at 5 percent. Jay Cooke, the famous financial
figure of the Civil War era, put the combined cost of bank failures, fraudulent
notes, and the expense of domestic exchange in excess of $50 million a year.
The amount of broken bank notes from the beginning to 1861 was elsewhere
put at $100 million.[4] Secretary of the Treasury Levi Woodbury estimated
that the cumulative depreciation of the currency during periods of bank
suspension aggregated $95 million by 1841, $72 million of which had
occurred from 1837 to 1841 alone.

Losses were not uniformly distributed throughout the country. Ten of the
sixteen New Orleans banks in business in 1837 had gone into liquidation by
1844. From 1831 to 1844 Ohio bank note holders lost $1.4 million as forty-
seven banks failed. However, under New York's Safety Fund system note
holders lost on the average less than one-eight of 1 percent during 1829-1866;

similar slight losses were experienced under the Suffolk Bank system from 1840-1860. Virginia bank note holders and depositors lost nothing whatsoever before 1861.

In 1818 Hezekiah Niles, editor of the Baltimore *Weekly Register*, which regularly included news of bank antics, received a letter from a man who was ruined by a bank and driven to the frontier where he "blesses God that he is out of the reach of a bank." In that attitude he was in the company of some outstanding public figures. In 1811 the 76-year old John Adams mentioned his life-long abhorrence of "our whole banking system." Five years later Thomas Jefferson referred to banks of issue as "more dangerous than standing armies." From retirement Andrew Jackson wrote to Sam Houston in 1845 urging that the Texas constitution ban paper-issuing banks "to protect your morals and to cap the climax of your prosperity, and to protect the labor of your country."[5] The Lone Star State followed his advice.

Benefits of Banking

To opponents, banks represented a departure from agrarian virtue, and the triumph of commercialization.

Clearly, however, a majority of Americans wished to bring themselves nearer to banking facilities rather than the reverse. They subscribed to Noah Webster's 1802 characterization of banks as "highly useful to a commercial country." William Henry Harrison, the successful presidential candidate, told a large Ohio audience in September 1840 that he favored paper money and the credit system because "a properly devised banking system alone possesses the capability of bringing the poor to a level with the rich."[6]

The French economist Chevalier observed in his travels in the United States in the 1830's that banks had "served the Americans as a lever to transfer to their soil . . . the agriculture and manufactures of Europe, and to cover their country with roads, canals, factories . . . with everything that goes to make up civilization."[7] A German traveller in 1839 was usually given the explanation that the system of bank credit had made possible the impressive material progress achieved in a short span of years.[8] "Is there any instance in any of the United States, where any town or city has increased to any considerable extent without the aid of banking institutions," a delegate to the Pennsylvania constitutional convention of 1837 asked rhetorically.[9] New banks were sought as a means of fostering entrepreneurial zeal. Comptroller Knox considered the antebellum state banks as having been of great benefit to the commerce and industry of the United States. That banking before 1861 had "contributed to the development of capital resources," was conceded by as unsympathetic a modern historian as Fritz Redlich.[10] Banks had participated in the process of economic development by increasing the productivity of existing capital and facilitating the transfer of resources to those activities promising greater profit. In Louisiana banks aided development from subsistence farming to the commercial cultivation of cotton or sugar. In the 1830's as much as $20 million of development capital is estimated to have been attracted from outside the state (including foreign investors) by the sale of bank stocks and of Louisiana bonds to finance banking activities.[11]

Rondo Cameron has argued that "the rapidity of American economic growth and industrialization owes much to the restless spirits who did not shrink from devising radical and untried instruments to cope with what they regarded as an intolerable shortage of money."[12] When residents of Orford, New Hampshire, petitioned the legislature for a bank charter in 1807, they pointed to "the great scarcity of money" and expressed the conviction that "a competent supply of a circulating medium is highly beneficial to the commercial, agricultural and manufacturing interest of this State and of our common Country."[13] The Jacksonian leader Isaac Hill commented in 1826 as chairman of the Banking Committee of the New Hampshire legislature that "it is not surprising that the inhabitants of so many towns are anxious for a bank or banks, when are considered the facility of obtaining loans, the convenience of a place of deposit, and the patronage which is enjoyed by those who manage the funds of the institution."

The colorful tales of wildcat banking make lively reading but have distorted the perspective of antebellum banking. In the main, banks were under the control of local businessmen rather than outside adventurers. Quantitatively, the impact of the wildcat banks "was probably negligible."[15]

Gold and silver came to $20 million in 1805 and to $150 million by 1850, when they represented 3.6 percent of reproducible tangible wealth in the United States (a peak proportion for the nineteenth century). Per capita, specie amounted to $3.19 in 1805 and doubled by 1850. Bank notes and deposits made possible the economizing of a more costly form of money, specie. Indeed, to a hard money economist of a later period, Francis A. Walker, the specie basis of antebellum banking seemed "almost insanely small."[14] The social saving to the American economy from the use of bank notes was recently estimated to amount to 0.35 percent of the GNP from 1839-1848 and 0.43 percent in the following decade.[16]

On the eve of the Civil War, the greater part of the circulating medium derived from the expanding numbers of commercial banks, which were bringing former frontier areas into the money economy. Most bank notes circulated at par in the bank's home territory; at a distance, they might be negotiated at a discount that did not exceed the costs of shipment. Banks had become inextricably "interwoven with the commercial operations of society," a House of Representatives committee remarked in 1830. The multiplication of banks, as the Philadelphia ironmaster-economist Stephen Colwell observed in 1859, clearly demonstrated the public attitude that they were "an advantage if not a necessity." After almost 80 years of national experience with banks, most Americans looked upon them with favor.

Notes

1. Amasa Walker, *The National Currency and the Money Problem* (New York: Holt 1876), p. 18.

2. Thomas D. Willett, "International Specie Flows 1834-60," *Journal of Economic History* 28 (1968), p. 47. And in a review of Peter Temin's study of the Jacksonian economy, Anna J. Schwartz, contrary to Temin, points out that with an annual increase in specie of 18 percent in both subperiods, the money stock rose 3.5 percent from 1831-1834 but 23.5 percent from 1834-1836 *Journal of Economic History* 30 (1970), p. 479.

3. Burke A. Parsons, "British Trade Cycles and American Bank Credit: Some Aspects of Economic Fluctuations in the United States 1815-1840" (Ph.D. diss., University of Texas, 1958), p. 340.

4. *Hunt's Merchants Magazine*, Feb. 1862, p. 121; quoted in Davis R. Dewey, *State Banking Before the Civil War* (Washington: Government Printing Office, 1910), p. 16.

5. Quoted in Joseph M. Grant, "Analysis of Evolution of the State Banking System of Texas," (Ph.D. diss., University of Texas, 1970), p. 4.

6. Quoted in Abby L. Gilbert, "Of Banks and History," *West Virginia History* 34 (1972), p. 35.

7. Michael Chevalier, *Society, Manners and Politics in the United States* (Boston: Weeks, Jordan, 1839).

8. Franz Anton Ritter von Gerstner, *Berichte aus den Vereingten Staaten* (Leipzig: Melzer, 1839), p. 30.

9. Thomas H. Sill, *Speech . . . on Corporations, Banks, and Currency* (Philadelphia: Kay, 1838), p. 14.

10. Fritz Redlich, *Molding of American Banking* (New York: Hafner, 1947), Vol. I, p. 66.

11. George D. Green, *Finance and Economic Development in the Old South* (Stanford: Stanford University Press, 1972), p. 62.

12. Rondo Cameron, *Banking in Early Stages of Industrialization* (New York: Oxford University Press, 1967), p. 304.

13. Norman Walker Smith, "History of Commercial Banking in New Hampshire, 1792-1843," (Ph.D. diss., University of Wisconsin, 1967), p. 107.

14. Francis A. Walker, *Money in Its Relations to Trade and Industry* (New York: Holt, 1879), p. 271. Then at Yale, Walker was later made first president of M.I.T.

15. Hugh Rockoff, "Money, Prices and Banks in the Jacksonian Era," in Robert W. Fogel and Stanley Engerman, eds., *Reinterpretation of American Economic History* (New York: Harper and Row, 1971), p. 454.

16. Stanley Engerman, "A Note on the Economic Consequences of the Second Bank of the United States," *Journal of Political Economy* 78 (1970), p. 727.

CHAPTER VI

HEYDAY OF THE UNIT BANK

Early Years of the National Banking System

For over a quarter of a century the states had exercised unchallenged control of banking policy. The National Currency Act of February 1863 marked the beginning of a new era. Federal chartering and regulation of commercial banks were major positive and enduring consequences of a war that had strengthened Washington's power and influence in other areas. The 1863 legislation, amended in June 1864 in accordance with the recommendations of Comptroller Hugh McCulloch, the first administrator of the national banking system, remained unchanged in most essentials thereafter until 1913. The half century preceding the passage of the Federal Reserve Act thus constitutes a meaningful historical epoch in American banking history.

The National Currency Act, renamed the National-Bank Act in 1874, drew its inspiration from antebellum banking experience and from the statutes of several states. New York's free banking law was especially significant, contributing the idea of a government bond-backed currency. An issuing bank would receive notes of uniform design when it placed the bond collateral with the Comptroller of the Currency, the newly created official in charge of national banks. A Massachusetts law of 1858, in turn based on Louisiana's famous 1842 act, provided the concept of required reserves against both deposits and bank notes.[1]

Federal guarantee of national bank notes was the major new element in the 1863 law. When the Treasury redeemed the notes of a failed bank, the United States bonds that had served as collateral would be cancelled. Additional protection for the note holder came from his legal claim on the general assets of the national bank and from shareholder liability up to an amount equal to the par value of the stock he owned. This "double liability" carried by national bank stock until 1937 was another feature taken from the New York law (and found in some other states as well).

Opponents of a third bank of the United States could rejoice that Congress had not reincarnated such a "monster." Thirty years after Jackson had the public deposits removed from Biddle's bank, the federal government made provision for a uniform bank currency, while avoiding, as McCulloch pointed out in November 1864, "the creation of a moneyed power in a few hands over the politics and business of the country." Jay Cooke, the great Civil War bond salesman and organizer of the First National Bank in both Philadelphia and Washington, and of New York's Fourth National, viewed the national banking system as combining the finest features of American experience, "the unity of action and general control, and the uniformity of currency—which were the best features of the United States Bank—with the diffusion of issue and freedom in local management which characterize the State system."

Proponents of the new system expected that all the state banks would quickly be absorbed. However, during the life of the original act (25 February 1863-3 June 1864) only 24 of the 456 charters issued represented conversions of state banks. Charter No. 1 went to the First National Bank of Philadelphia, newly organized by Jay Cooke. The First National Bank of Chicago, one of today's giants, was No. 8. New York City's First National Bank, No. 29, was founded by John Thompson,[2] publisher of the widely used *Bank Note Reporter*, whose list of state bank notes would soon be obsolete. Cleveland's First National Bank received charter No. 7; Cincinnati's, No. 24; Washington's, No. 26; St. Louis's, No. 89; Boston's (a converted state bank), No. 200; and Baltimore's First National, No. 204. Under the provisions of the original 1863 act, seven national banks were chartered in Philadelphia, five in Chicago, and four each in St. Louis and Cincinnati.

At first the proud New York City Clearing House refused to admit national banks to membership. They were considered dangerous institutions which would repeat the dismal record of the free banks chartered by Western States in the 1850's. By way of rebuttal, McCulloch, the first Comptroller of the Currency, pointed to significant statutory safeguards. National bank capital had to be paid up in full. The bank notes were secured by United

States bonds valued at no more than 90 percent of par value. The Treasury stood ready to redeem instantly the notes of all failed national banks. Moreover, Treasury appointees would make frequent examinations of national banks. Some bankers were concerned that Congress might enact hostile legislation or meddle in banks' affairs for political reasons. McCulloch was confident, however, that "there was as little to fear from Congressional as from State legislation." He was of the opinion that, if anything, trouble could arise from "the control which the banks might have over Congress, rather than in annoying interference by Congress with their legitimate business."

Long established banks balked at Secretary of the Treasury Salomon P. Chase's insistence that time-honored names be dropped and replaced with the designation of "first, second and third, up to tenth, twentieth or fiftieth National Bank in some one of a thousand towns or cities," as Stephen Colwell remarked. An 1864 amendment giving state banks the right to retain their names removed this obstacle to conversion. The oldest, the Bank of North America, received charter No. 602 on converting in 1864. Both the Bank of Massachussetts, No. 794, and the Bank of New York, No. 1393, converted in 1865.

The process of absorbing state banks under the 1863 act proceeded so slowly that national bank notes constituted less than 15 percent of all bank-issued currency in mid-1864. At that point Senator John Sherman introduced his bill to tax state bank notes out of existence, explaining that "the national banks were intended to supersede the state banks." When the 10 percent annual levy took effect in mid-1866, only those with a national charter could be banks of issue. Numerous state banks converted as soon as the punitive tax was enacted in March 1865. Many larger ones among them (having few if any notes) were less concerned with the tax than with the threatened loss of correspondent balances, as only deposits with other national banks counted toward their legal requirement. Fewer than 300 banks chose to retain their state charters. They had either previously confined themselves to deposit banking or now retired their note issues and discovered that deposit credits were acceptable in connection with loan-making.

On 4 March 1865, the day after the prospective tax was enacted, national banks numbered 855 with a capital of $192 million. When the state bank note tax went into effect on 1 July 1866, there were over 1,634 national banks, and total capital was more than twice what it had been 16 months earlier. Nevertheless, state and private banks had 40 percent of all commercial bank deposits held by the public in 1867, and 50 percent by 1871.[3]

Free banking, the principle already in effect in a majority of Northern states, was contemplated by the authors of the National Bank Act. However, the statutory limit on the amount of national bank notes somewhat restrained the formation of national banks in the early years. The $300 million aggregate was to be allocated by state, half on the basis of population and the rest in relation to "existing banking capital, resources and business." Although an 1865 law confined a bank's noteissue to 90 percent of its paid-in capital, all of the $300 million had been apportioned by November 1866. Only thirty-nine charters were granted in 1866 and another thirty-one in the next 3 years.

Faced with the note issue ceiling, the first three Comptrollers of the Currency considered themselves as having some discretion in granting a charter. Before sending the necessary forms, McCulloch asked about the local economy, existing banks, and the background of the organizers. He commonly sought to discourage applicants; he was anxious to secure the conversion of existing state banks rather than the formation of new national banks in states with adequate banking capital.

Banks east of the Appalachians got the greater part of the note issue. Illinois, Wisconsin, and Missouri had a smaller total bank note circulation in 1870 than before the Civil War. While Indiana, Iowa, and Minnesota had more, the increase was by no means commensurate with the growth of their trade over the decade 1860-1870. Complaints from the West and South led Congress to raise the limit by $54 million in 1870. In the wake of the major depression precipitated by the Panic of 1873, the maximum was eliminated. Senator Sherman (at whose insistence the original absolute limit was included) now proclaimed, "Banking shall be free." Every application conforming to legal requirements since 14 January 1875, when the limit was removed, had been granted, Comptroller Knox reported. With the 1875 amendment, it became truly appropriate to speak of the "National Free Banking Law of the United States," as did Silas Stilwell, one of the authors of the 1863 act.

Dual Banking System Takes Root

Charters issued to national banks had a 20-year life, and the system's abandonment loomed as a distinct possibility for a long time. Starting in 1876 the Greenback Party demanded abundant paper currency, issued only by the federal government. Other enemies of national banks merely sought the repeal of the 10 percent tax (as late as 1892 this was a plank in the Democratic platform) so that state banks might flourish, especially in less developed sections of the country. An 1882 law extending the charter of existing national banks for an additional 20 years marked the defeat of these hostile forces, permanently as it turned out. Meanwhile the state chartered banks were growing in strength despite their inability to issue bank note currency. This assured the perpetuation of the dual banking system—concurrent state and federal chartering and regulation—as a powerful political and economic force down to the present.

In 1882 there were 2,239 national banks and 704 with state charters. Within a decade, however, national banks were outnumbered. By 1900 there were 5,000 state but only 3,731 national banks. Of total commercial bank deposits held by the public (excluding interbank and federal government deposits), 51 percent were in national banks in 1882, only 45 percent in 1900, and 42 percent by 1913.

Free banking was not only the federal policy but also came to be that of most states. When the National Bank Act became law, eighteen states had free banking. Beginning with Nevada in 1864, the principle was embodied in the constitutions of all new states west of the Mississippi. On the eastern seaboard, a special charter for a new bank was still available in 1913 in North Carolina, Maryland, and Delaware, but only in the latter was special incorporation the exclusive method.

Before 1900, minimum capital requirements for national banks ranged from $50,000 in places with fewer than 6,000 inhabitants to $200,000 in places of over 50,000 population. States commonly demanded only $10,000. As a result, Wisconsin in 1898 had state chartered institutions exclusively in almost 80 percent of the localities with banks, while national banks were found mainly in larger cities. Iowa allowed commercial banks to open with only $25,000 in capital in places with up to 3,000 inhabitants, while $50,000 was required for larger areas. Nevertheless, the stock savings bank (which did a commercial bank business despite its name) became very popular because only $10,000 in capital was needed in towns with a population under 10,000. By 1913 Iowa had 759 out of a United States total of 1,355 stock savings banks.[4]

Capital requirements for national banks in towns under 3,000 population were cut in half in 1900. The new $25,000 minimum continued to be higher than that required by many states. Nevertheless, 2,858 small national banks were added from 1900 to 1913, 55 percent of all new national banks chartered during those years. Almost three-fifths of the national banks with less than $50,000 capital were located in the South and West Central states, predominantly agricultural regions.

Although as many national banks were chartered in the period 1900-1913 as were in 1863-1899, they managed to average a return on total capital of 8 percent a year. State banks were over twice as numerous as national banks by the time the Federal Reserve Act became law at the end of

1913. In many cases, a state bank's capital was below the federal minimum. Others with enough capital found more attractive profit possibilities because state reserve requirements might be lower, or real estate loans important in a locality, or a trust company charter granted greater scope. In such instances, these considerations more than compensated for the generally greater prestige enjoyed by national banks and for whatever earnings the note issue privilege brought. Yet another advantage of a federal charter was its attractiveness to distant investors. Nonresidents owned about one-third of the stock of all national banks in the Prairie and Rocky Mountain states in 1889.

Unlike his predecessors since 1875, Comptroller Lawrence Murray, who took office six months after the Panic of 1907, considered charter grants subject to a test of need. He paid special attention to applications from small towns. He also initiated a policy in 1908 of examining every new national bank before it could open for business, a practice previously adopted by states concerned with verifying the payment in full of capital subscriptions and compliance with the law. Murray added only 650 national banks between 1908 and 1913, while the states issued over 4,000 charters.

Meanwhile the number of banks operating without any charter doubled between 1880 and 1900. As the twentieth century began, there were some 5,200 private banks; they were more numerous than national banks until 1905. Frequently they combined banking with mercantile, commission, real estate, and brokerage operations. In Wisconsin, as elsewhere, private banks opened in small localities that could not support a state bank with the minimum capital specified by law. After a decade in which the average failure rate of private banks was 2 percent a year, Wisconsin offered private banks a choice in 1903 of incorporating or withdrawing from banking. State charters were immediately taken out by 137, 10 went out of business, and 1 was placed in the hands of a receiver.

Texas incorporated no banks from the time the state was admitted to the Union until 1905, except for 18 chartered during Reconstruction (1869-1876). In the 1880's Texas never had fewer than 107 private banks. National banks had become more numerous by 1890, when there were 148 private banks. Anyone having enough to buy a safe and pay office rent could open a bank, and advertise whatever capital he desired, even though it had not been paid in. By 1905 Texas counted 197 private banks.

Wall Street banker Levi Morton remarked in 1895 that "the bank is the general agent of civilization in its advance." The former vice-president of the United States explained that "in the extension of the bank to the remoter districts are carried the same improvements to the every-day business conditions of the community that the water work brings to the sanitary condition, or the public school to the educational conditions." The feverish pace at which banking facilities were expanded reflects that. Several applications for the privilege of the First National Bank might be submitted even before a townsite was ready for settlers. "Two or three banks are started when the first train whistles at the unpainted depot," it was reported in 1908.

Branches and Affiliates

The United States boasted some 27,000 commercial banks at the end of 1913. The large number was related to the rarity of branch facilities in the post-Civil War era. Despite its name, the national banking system consisted of unit banks confined to a single location until 1922.

The debate over the National Bank Act did not consider the branching issue. Although an 1865 amendment permitted converting state banks to keep their branches, the Washington County Bank of Williamsport, Maryland, was ordered to divest itself of its Hagerstown branch. Comptroller Freeman Clarke cited an 1864 law's requirements that the organization certificate specify the particular place where the banking operations would be carried on. Succeeding Comptrollers followed that precedent for many years. Toward the end of the nineteenth century banks began to show an interest in branches. The Comptroller turned down numerous applications for additional offices as contrary to the intent of the law but allowed converting banks to keep existing branches by the early 1900's. In 1910 there were 9 national banks with 12 branches, while 283 state banks had 536 branches. Various Comptrollers recommended statutory amendments to permit national banks to branch in the head office city (1887, 1888), in places with under a thousand inhabitants and without a national bank (1895, 1896), or in places with fewer than 2,000 people (1898). Congress paid no more attention to President Grover Cleveland's recommendation that branches be authorized in "small communities," than to the suggestions of the Comptrollers.

Branching was viewed as antithetical to the principle of free banking. Most bankers shared the sentiment of former Comptroller Charles Dawes that the American banking system had been "built up by protecting the rights and the opportunities of the small man, and the small bank. . . . " As president of the Central Trust Company in Chicago, Dawes told the Pennsylvania Bankers Association in 1903 that branch banking "would certainly not aid in building up our undeveloped country, and the newer sections of the United States."

The reduction in the minimum capital requirement for national banks in 1900 diminished the urgency of branching, at least as a device to bring banking to smaller localities lacking adequate facilities. In 1912 Comptroller

Murray could boast that the United States "gives banking facilities under local control and direction to every little hamlet in this great country."

The number of states specifically authorizing branching decreased from twenty in 1896 to twelve by 1910. Most important for the future was the 1909 law permitting branches throughout California. Following a 1909 ruling of Michigan's attorney general, most Detroit banks and some in Grand Rapids acquired branches. New York modified its 1844 prohibition in 1898 to allow New York City banks to locate offices anywhere in what had become a unified five-county area of over 300 square miles. President Nash of the Corn Exchange Bank, viewed branch banking as "the permanent extension to small institutions of that support that is given to the Clearing House banks when they join together in financial panics and pool their resources for mutual protection." Quick to take advantage of the change in law, Nash's bank had absorbed seven others and opened seven new offices as early as 1902. In 1913, Corn Exchange operated at thirty-three locations in what was by far the largest branch network. Branches were very much the exception in 1900; there were, however, 119, belonging to 87 banks. By 1910 the number increased to 292 banks with 548 branches, half of these in the headquarters city.[5]

As most states prohibited branches, bankers seeking close ties with others were "developing rapidly a system of joint ownership in banks," A. Barton Hepburn of Chase National Bank (a former Comptroller of the Currency) noted in 1902. Many leading nonnational institutions were buying control or an interest in other banks around the turn of the century. Chain banking, involving ownership of several banks, which tended to evolve into group banking where a holding company owned several banks, was found in the Midwest, Northwest, and South. The Union Investment Company of Minneapolis, organized around 1903 acquired a number of rural banks. C. H. Ross of Minneapolis and Charles Davidson of North Dakota controlled 22 banks in that state by 1910. In the early 1900's the president of the Continental National Bank of Salt Lake City organized a chain that spilled over from Utah into Idaho and Wyoming. A Spokane holding company controlled about 25 rural banks in Washington and Idaho by 1910. William Witham built a chain in the South, which became a holding company owning 70 banks by 1906 and 125 by 1911.

Branches, chains, and holding companies were not typical, however. Most banks remained proudly independent. The locally owned, locally oriented single-office institution flourished in unprecedented numbers in the years just before World War I, an important element soon to disappear from the setting of an America of small towns. Nevertheless, the heritage of the 1863-1913 epoch, a dual banking system with unit banks numerically predominant, survives to the present day.

Notes

1. The reserve for national bank notes was eliminated in 1874.

2. He also organized Chase National Bank in 1877, which merged in 1955 with the ancient Bank of the Manhattan Company to become Chase Manhattan.

3. From 1878 to 1882, their share dropped to under half, according to the tabulation in Milton Friedman and Anna J. Schwartz, *A Monetary History of the United States, 1867-1960* (Princeton, Princeton University Press), 1963.

4. The 1935 annual report of the Comptroller of the Currency (the last to report them separately) showed 341 stock savings banks in the entire country, 306 of them in Iowa.

5. U.S. Bureau of the Census, *Historical Statistics of the United States Colonial Times to 1957* (Washington: Government Printing Office, 1960), p. 635.

CHAPTER VII

BANKS AND THE MEANS OF PAYMENT, 1863-1913

National Bank Notes

State bank notes were "heterogeneous, unequal and unsafe," Secretary of the Treasury Chase complained in December 1861. The national banking associations he proposed would establish "one sound uniform circulation, of equal value throughout the country, upon the foundation of national credit combined with private capital." Reluctantly, Congress passed "an Act to provide a National Currency, secured by a Pledge of United States Stocks, and to provide for the Circulation and Redemption thereof" which became law in February 1863. It was superseded by the June 1864 National Currency Act. An enthusiastic Judge Alphonso Taft (father of the later president) wrote to Chase at the time that "if the Civil War resulted in nothing else than providing the country with a uniform currency it would not have been fought in vain."[1]

Congress envisioned the eventual retirement of the Civil War issues of United States notes, and the circulation of national bank notes as the sole paper currency in the United States. At their peak in 1863, $239 million in state bank notes circulated in the North. They disappeared once the punitive tax on them took effect in 1866.

National bank notes exceeded $239 million in 1866, reaching $341 million in 1875. Although the statutory ceiling was eliminated in 1875, that year's national bank note total was not seen again until 1881. In each year from 1882 until 1891 the amount in circulation declined; 1882's $352 million was not surpassed until 1903.

The explanation is related to the fluctuations in profitability of issuing the notes. Budget surpluses in the 1880's were used to retire bonds, the Treasury bidding up their price in the process. United States bonds were selling above par throughout the period while national bank notes could only be issued up to 90 percent of par value. As the bond premium declined in the early 1890's note issue once again became profitable. To encourage an increase in national bank notes, the 1900 Gold Standard Act authorized notes for 100 percent of par value and allowed each bank to issue an amount equal to 100 percent of its capital instead of the previous 90 percent limit. Whereas before 1890 national bank notes outstanding were only about 20 percent of the maximum allowed by law and about 28 percent in 1900, by 1914 they were as much as 80 percent. Until 1905 the maximum was constrained by the capital stock of national banks and thereafter by the total of eligible bonds carrying the circulation privilege. Nevertheless the $300 million of national bank notes circulating in 1900 doubled by 1908.

Per capita, national bank notes reached a peak of $8.22 in 1873, a low of $2.54 in 1891, doubled by 1904, but still only $7.37 in 1912. In 1913, circulating alongside $700 million in national bank notes were $1,000 million in gold certificates (warehouse receipts for Treasury held gold), $470 million in silver certificates, and $337 million in greenbacks. Not even in the pre-Federal Reserve era were national bank notes the exclusive component of the currency.

Domestic and Foreign Exchange

National bank notes circulated at par throughout the country. Remittances could therefore be made to any point in the United States at no more than the cost of transporting the notes, including insurance and forgone interest. Exchange between Chicago, St. Louis, or Cincinnati and New York City was frequently at par, and it rarely exceeded 80 cents per $1,000, whereas before the Civil War the cost had been $10 or $15. Some $19.5 billion in domestic exchange was drawn in 1890 at a total cost of $11 million. The then Comptroller of the Currency estimated that the expense would have been $195 million at the 1859 rate of 1.0 percent. In the early 1900's the usual shipping charge between New York and San Francisco had become 40 cents per $100. The reduced cost reflected, in part, improved transportation and communication, but the par feature of national bank notes was also an important factor.

The money-order business developed by express companies troubled commercial banks in the interior in the 1890's and early 1900's. The American Bankers Association responded with a money-order scheme handled by the American Surety Company, which was in use by almost 900 banks in 1909, and with a travelers cheque plan whereby banks sold drafts on Bankers Trust Company in New York City in their own name.

Foreign bills of exchange continued to be sold mainly by institutions performing both mercantile and financial functions, just as in the antebellum period. Few national banks were in the foreign exchange business until around 1900. While some had "large and successful" foreign departments, as the Comptroller of the Currency reported in 1904, foreign bankers financed most American imports and exports. The National Monetary Commission noted with dismay in 1912 that "though the status of the United States as one of the great powers in the political world is now universally recognized, . . . we have yet to secure recognition as an important factor in the financial world." National banks were authorized to open foreign branches in 1913, but overseas offices did not become significant until the 1920's.

Interest-Bearing Deposits

Banks in almost every city and village in the United States were paying interest on deposits; Comptroller Knox commented in his 1873 annual report that the custom "has done more than any other to demoralize the business of banking." A bank in good condition, the head of the Philadelphia National Bank insisted at the 1884 American Bankers Association Convention, did not make interest payments to depositors. Despite such misgivings, the practice became general in the post-Civil War era. Even the conservative Massachusetts Bank of Boston began to pay interest in 1907 on all except active accounts and those belonging to customers requiring loan accommodation. As of mid-1909 deposits not bearing interest totalled only $1.1 billion; interest was paid on $6.6 billions of non-savings deposits and on $5.7 billion in commercial banks' savings accounts.

By the early 1900's time and savings deposits had become increasingly important to commercial banks. They comprised about one-fifth of the total deposits from 1896 to 1901 and as much as one third by 1913. Commercial bank time deposits equalled those in mutual savings banks for the first time in 1909. About half of all national banks had savings accounts by 1911. Reserves for both demand and time deposits were identical for national banks, whereas states generally had lower requirements for time deposits. This led some national banks to organize a state chartered affiliate, like the First Trust and Savings Bank, which was sponsored by the First National Bank of Chicago and owned by the same shareholders. This Chicago Plan, had the approval of the Comptroller of the Currency and was widely duplicated.

After the hardships suffered in connection with failures around the time of the Panic of 1907, the idea of segregating savings deposits and requiring that these funds be invested conservatively became more popular. New Hampshire had so legislated in 1891, as had Michigan in stages between 1893 and 1909. Connecticut in 1907, Massachusetts and Rhode Island in 1908, and California and Texas in 1909 also took action along those lines.

Policies Regarding Checking Accounts

The American business community's use of checks was so extensive by 1881 that over 90 percent of total receipts of banks took the form of checks, drafts, and bills. By 1910 small checking accounts were growing in numbers, a reflection of the "check habit" of the American people, as Professor David Kinley informed the National Monetary Commission. Small town banks of the period did not have a minimum balance requirement, unlike banks in larger cities. In one eastern city, balances had to average $100.00 to $200.00 a year. Some banks charged $2.00 a month to cover handling costs. By the early twentieth century, up-to-date banks in larger cities were increasingly analyzing the activity of deposit accounts for the purpose of gauging their profitability to the bank. A Kansas banker exhorted his colleagues at the 1884 American Bankers Association Convention not to render gratuitous services "such as making no charges for stationery or blanks, foreign exchange and collections, cashing drafts." In the face of competitive market forces, however, such appeals were in vain. If charges were to be levied, local banks would have to join in cooperative efforts. Uniform collection charges appear to have been instituted first in Buffalo in 1881. In 1899 the New York City Clearing House established compulsory charges for out-of-town items. Similar arrangements existed in ninety-one cities by 1912.

Under a system developed in 1899-1900 in Boston, the clearinghouse forwarded checks written on the country banks of all the New England states to the drawing customer's bank for remittance at par (the face value of the check). Checks drawn on the relatively few New England banks that refused to pay at par, were subject to an exchange charge when a customer deposited them in a Boston bank. The Boston Plan of par collection for banks in their area was adopted by a number of major clearinghouses including those in St. Louis, Kansas City, Detroit, Atlanta, and eventually New York. Boston's regional check clearing system reduced collection costs from $1.25 to .07 per thousand transactions. It served as a model to the Federal Reserve later on.

To avoid the payment of a remittance charge to the bank on which the check had been drawn, banks developed elaborate check-routing arrangements in the pre-Federal Reserve era. The case of a check on a North Birmingham, Alabama, bank deposited in a Birmingham bank four miles away was cited in a Federal Reserve pamphlet distributed at the 1923 convention of the American Bankers Association. Over a 14-day period the check travelled from Birmingham to Jacksonville to Philadelphia, back to Birmingham and finally back to the North Birmingham bank. In that instance, there were insufficient funds, so the check had to go the same route a second time, a total of 4,500 miles.

Currency Versus Deposit Usage

Currency was used for at least half of the payments made in rural districts in 1874, but even in small cities the proportion was no more than one fourth. Around 1882 payments in kind were still being made in many parts of the South and Southwest. As late as the mid-1890's western Iowa farmers used mostly currency and coin. The "great lack of banking facilities in the sections which continually clamored for measures calculated to result in unsound currency" was remarked by former Comptroller Hepburn in his popular *History of Currency*. In the last third of the nineteenth century, bank assets per capita were in the South about one fifth and in the prairie and mountain states, under half the national average. By 1914 the gap had narrowed, though those sections continued to lag behind the rest of the country. In the South the number of inhabitants per commercial bank was 22,772 in 1880 and 5,137 in 1909; nationally the figures were 8,538 and 4,256 respectively.

Smaller agricultural centers found national bank charters unattractive because of high capital requirements (especially before 1900) and the ban on real estate loans. At the same time, state banks were forbidden to provide the currency sought in rural districts. To increase the money supply, rural America proposed further issues of greenbacks and, later, silver purchases. Greenbacks stayed fixed at the $347 million limit set in 1878, but the Treasury did buy over $500 million worth of silver. The $15.65 currency per capita in 1900 represented a growth of 22 percent over the 1870 amount.

An elastic currency, one which responded to variations in seasonal needs, was a concept few understood. When greenbacks became convertible into gold in 1879, it was widely (but mistakenly) expected to produce elasticity.

For decades thereafter, bankers and the public criticized the seasonal inade-
quacies of the system, but inelasticity was inherent in the bond-backed
national bank note. To make matters worse, a bank that reduced its notes
outstanding was precluded from taking out more currency for another 6
months.

Deposits did adapt "to the demand of the moment without visible
effort", as Harvard's Charles Dunbar pointed out in 1887, but the farmer who
distrusted checks or who lived far from a bank could not be consoled by this
economist's argument. Hired hands and local creditors were paid in currency,
hence the farmer demanded currency when he sold his crops. Crop moving
time was an "anxious period in the money market," as Sereno Pratt the
editor of the *Wall Street Journal* noted in 1903. After 1900, as many new
banks opened up to serve the farmer, rural America increasingly developed
the check-writing habit.

Meanwhile nationally the use of deposits as a vehicle of payment had
grown apace. The proportion of currency to money balances held by the
public dropped from 44 to 24 percent between 1867 and 1886. Friedman
and Schwartz estimate that in 1870 there was only $1.53 of adjusted com-
mercial bank deposits for every dollar of currency held by the public. "The
use of coin and currency is almost nothing in proportion to the use of the
modern instrument of checks which we find upon the remotest frontier,"
Comptroller Knox told the New York Chamber of Commerce in 1882. As he
spoke, the deposit-currency ratio stood at $2.21, only half of what it was to
be in 1900. The ratio reached $7.19 in 1913. By 1909 80 to 85 percent of
the nation's business was conducted by means of checks. At $68 per capita in
1900, commercial bank deposits were 3.5 times as great as in 1870 and over 4
times the amount of currency. Yet as late as 1909, banking reform was
discussed mainly in terms of remedying defects in the note issue.

The misunderstanding of the monetary role of commercial bank deposits
was by no means confined to the public at large. No less eminent an economist than Francis A. Walker limited the concept to specie, the (then incon-
vertible) governmental greenback currency, and to bank notes. Bank deposits,
he insisted in his influential 1878 treatise on money, economized on the use
of money but did not serve the function of money—that is "the final dis-
charge of debts, full payment for commodities."[2] The "Walker tradition" was
dominant in this period, as seen for example in the 1914 revised edition of
Joseph French Johnson's *Money and Currency* (Boston: Ginn & Co.).

It was the National Monetary Commission, which "established the idea
that it is *credit . . . primarily in the form of deposits, that must be made
flexible and responsive*," A. Piatt Andrew, a monetary economist who headed

the commission's research efforts pointed out.[3] The Commission's report, submitted in January 1912, was a forerunner of the Federal Reserve Act.

Reserve Requirements and Correspondent Banking

Reserve requirements for deposits somewhat lower than those in effect just before the Civil War were among the 1864 amendments to the National Bank Act aimed at attracting state banks into the system. National banks in New York, the central reserve city,[4] had to carry a 25 percent reserve, just above the 23.8 percent actually held in 1860 but matching the standard adopted by the clearinghouse in 1860. National banks in sixteen additional cities, which also served as redemption centers for national bank notes, could keep half of the 25 percent reserve in New York. Elsewhere, national banks had to hold 6 percent of their deposits as cash-in-vault, while another 9 percent could be placed with national banks in the seventeen cities. This 15 percent requirement was substantially below prevailing usage around 1859-1860. Thus, the federal law, contrary to a widespread misconception at the time, did not call for greater reserves than had been customary. Weak banks, however, would be keeping more than they had been accustomed to.

The concentration of bank reserves in New York City had occurred well before the Civil War. In December 1860 New York City holdings of bank balances were very close to what they could have been had the 1864 law been in effect then. Pyramiding of reserves in Wall Street was not initiated by the National Bank Act. Rather, the law took cognizance of the long-standing position of New York as holder of the underlying reserves of the American banking system.

An 1887 amendment made it possible for three-fourths of the national banks in a populous city to request a change in their reserve classification. Chicago and St. Louis quickly voted to join New York as central reserve cities hoping for a sharp increase in correspondent bank balances. National banks in those commercial centers now had to pay the price of keeping all of their required reserves in their own vaults. In 1914, Chicago's $205 million of interbank balances were almost six times as great as in 1887; St. Louis's $66 million were twelve times as large, but New York's $423 million were only thrice those in 1887. In addition to the three central reserve cities, forty-nine others were eventually classified as reserve cities under the National Bank Act (see Table 2).

Although New York's margin over the other two central reserve cities had narrowed considerably by the time the Federal Reserve Banks opened for business, it remained "the clearing-house of the country," in economist

TABLE 2 *Reserve Cities under National Banking System as of 1913
and their Category under Federal Reserve Act, 1913-1972*

Central Reserve Cities

New York City[abce]
Chicago[abce]
St. Louis[abcf]

Other Reserve Cities

Boston[abc]	Spokane (1 March 1948)[dg]
Philadelphia[abc]	Portland[d]
San Francisco[abc]	Los Angeles[d]
Baltimore[abd]	Salt Lake City[d]
New Orleans[abd]	Brooklyn
Cincinnati[abd]	Fort Worth
Cleveland[bc]	Galveston (1 March 1951)[g]
Pittsburgh[bd]	San Antonio
Louisville[bd]	Waco (1 March 1951)
Detroit[bd]	Columbus
Richmond[c]	Indianapolis
Atlanta[c]	St. Paul
Dallas[c]	Cedar Rapids (1 March 1957)[g]
Minneapolis[c]	Des Moines
Kansas City, Mo.[c]	Dubuque (1 March 1954)[g]
Leavenworth (1872)[bg]	Sioux City (1 March 1957)[g]
Albany (1 July 1929)[bg]	St. Joseph (1 March 1954)[g]
Washington[b]	Lincoln (1 March 1954)
Milwaukee[b]	South Omaha (annexed 1915)
Omaha[d]	Kansas City, Kans. (6 Sept. 1962)[g]
Savannah (1 Oct. 1945)[dg]	Topeka
Houston[d]	Wichita (23 Aug. 1962)[g]
Denver[d]	Pueblo (25 Nov. 1965)[g]
Oklahoma City[d]	Muskogee (15 March 1930)[g]
Seattle[d]	Tacoma (1 Nov. 1923)[g]

Source: Board of Governors of the Federal Reserve System, Supplement to Banking &
Monetary Statistics Section 10, pp. 63-64, for reserve city designations.

[a]Subtreasury city under Independent Treasury System. Charleston, South Carolina, also
served as one, 1846-1876 but was never a reserve city.

[b]Redemption City under 1864 National Bank Act.

[c]Federal Reserve Bank Headquarters.

[d]Federal Reserve Bank Branch.

[e]Changed to reserve city, 28, July 1962.

[f]Changed to reserve city, 1, July 1922.

[g]Termination of designation as reserve city.

O.M.W. Sprague's phrase. The "concentration of surplus money and available funds" in New York City was mentioned by the National Monetary Commission in 1912 as a major defect in the banking system. Under federal law only balances with national banks counted toward their legal requirement, giving them an advantage in correspondent banking over state banks. A small number of national banks carried the bulk of the bankers' balances. These came to have also the greater share of other banking business in the key cities. Thus the seven largest in New York City in 1890 made 26 percent of all loans by national and state banks there; by 1910 the top six made 46 percent. Here was grist for the mill of those who discerned a Money Trust.[5]

The payment of interest on bankers' balances was sometimes offered as an explanation for their concentration in New York City. The House Banking and Currency Committee, reporting out the 1912 Federal Reserve Bill, was only the latest of an ancient line of critics who spoke of the "long standing evil which has drawn funds to places where they were not needed and away from those where they were." Actually, in 1873 and in 1886 only about half of the Wall Street banks paid interest (1 to 2 percent). Others offered various free services such as collection of out-of-town items. By 1891 most banks were paying interest; twenty years later Chemical National Bank was the sole holdout. For that matter, banks outside New York also paid interest on deposits. The commercial and financial pre-eminence of the great Atlantic metropolis was what attracted funds to Wall Street banks.

The success of the correspondent banking arrangements helps to explain why there was no strong branch banking sentiment in the post-Civil War era. Country banks developed "a feudal dependence" on large city institutions for counsel and assistance in the half century before 1913.[6] A bank expected to be able to call on its correspondent for loans, especially to meet seasonal needs, or in times of difficulties. Borrowing took the form mostly of promissory notes; because of certain criticisms from the Comptroller and some adverse public opinion, it was sometimes in the guise of loans to bank directors and officers or of the sale of securities that could subsequently be repurchased. Interbank borrowing averaged below $9 million on any one day from 1869 through 1882, about $16 million from 1883 through 1892, and $38 million from 1893 through 1914. Such loans increased available funds locally, but not to any great extent. According to an 1898 estimate, loans from outside the region were under 5 percent of the total in New England and the Eastern states, 11 percent in the South, and around 15 percent in the Pacific and Western states.[7]

In the early years, national banks held reserves considerably in excess of the legal requirements. By 1873, however, the fifteen smaller redemption cities were only 2 percentage points above the minimum. In New York, the average reserve was almost at the minimum by 1883. Before 1900 national banks carried greater excess reserves than subsequently, a course dictated by fear of panics and unavailability of outside resources. The level and volatility of excess reserves declined around 1900 as the Treasury attempted to assist the banking system during periods of monetary stringency.

The purpose of reserve requirements before 1914 was to provide banks with absolutely liquid assets. Cash components of the legal reserve for national banks included gold and "lawful money" (silver coin, United States Notes, and gold and silver certificates). The supply of these was rather inelastic. A national bank could not make new loans or dividend payments as long as it was deficient in reserves. An increase of bank reserves made necessary by calls from the interior was mainly met by import of gold from abroad.

Certain state laws were the source for the provision in the National Bank Act requiring reserves against deposits, as we have seen. In turn, subsequent state enactments drew on the 1864 federal law. By 1913 reserve requirements were found in all states except Illinois, Indiana, Maryland, Mississippi, South Carolina, and Virginia. Illinois remains the sole holdout to this day. Starting with Nebraska in 1889, six states called for a higher reserve against bankers balances than for other deposits because of their greater instability. The Federal Reserve Act did not place bankers balances in a special category but did include the distinction first made by New Hampshire in 1874 and followed in ten other states by 1911; time deposit reserve requirements (commonly 5 percent, as in the 1913 federal law) were set below those for demand deposits. Banks took advantage of this opportunity to reduce reserves relative to total deposits by encouraging a great growth in the proportion of time deposits after 1913.

The diffusion of banking facilities encouraged vastly increased use of deposit transfers as a means of payment. Commercial bank deposits as a proportion of all money held by the public rose from 55.5 percent in 1867 to 81.3 in 1900 and 88.2 in 1913. Clearing and collection of a growing volume of out-of-town checks from far and near led to a great expansion of correspondent banking. The public at large, slow to recognize the shrinking relative importance of currency, remained much concerned with its adequacy throughout most of the period.

Notes

1. Quoted in A. Piatt Andrew, "The Crux of the Currency Question," *Yale Review* n.s.

2 (1913), p. 609. Andrew commented that Taft's letter "was not a very great exaggeration of the truth."

2. Francis A. Walker, *Money* (New York: Holt, 1878), p. 405. Curiously, many years earlier Walker's father, Amasa, had recognized that deposits were identical with bank notes from the currency standpoint and that deposits represented the most important part of the currency [Joseph Dorfman, *Economic Mind in American Civilization*, Vol. 3 (New York: Viking Press, 1949), pp. 54, 103].

3. A. Piatt Andrew, "The Crux of the Currency Question," *Yale Review* n.s. 2 (1913), p. 608. Italics in original.

4. In 1874 the treasurer of the United States was given the redemption responsibility. Redemption centers came to be called "reserve cities."

5. See Benjamin J. Klebaner, "The Money Trust Investigation in Retrospect," *National Banking Review* 3(1966), pp. 393-403, and Vincent P. Carosso, *Investment Banking in America A History* (Cambridge: Harvard University Press, 1970), pp. 137-155.

6. J. Laurence Laughlin, *The Federal Reserve Act: Its Origins and Problems* (New York: Macmillan, 1933), pp. 146-147.

7. R. M. Breckenridge, "Discount Rates in the United States," *Political Science Quarterly* 13 (1898), p. 138.

CHAPTER VIII

LOANS AND INVESTMENTS, INVESTMENT BANKING, AND TRUST COMPANIES 1863-1913

Short-Term Commercial Loans: Theory and Practice

In the venerable British ideal, reflected in the underlying philosophy of the Federal Reserve Act of 1913, only short-term, self-liquidating loans were proper for commercial banks to make. As Comptroller of the Currency Knox affirmed in 1875, "a bank is in good condition just in proportion as its business is conducted upon short credits, with its assets so held as to be available on brief notice." The American Institute of Banking's 1916 text-book on loans explained that in the case of commercial loans, the means of repayment would be obtained before maturity in the course of producing and marketing the goods. Actually, however, American banks departed more or less frequently from that principle. Comptroller Hepburn's claim that "national banks do a purely commercial business" was more accurate as a description of the 1864 act's conception than of the reality of 1892. State chartered and private commercial banks were likely to stray even farther from the ideal.

Important American writers in the pre-1914 era urged banks to confine their loans to meeting the needs of business and genuine commercial pur-poses. Such a policy was believed to avoid the dangers of speculative overtrad-ing, and overissue, while adjusting bank credit automatically. Banks were also called upon to shun long-term real estate or fixed capital loans and bond investments.[1]

Around 1900, about half of the earning assets of commercial banks consisted of business loans, extended mainly to small and medium size firms in manufacturing and trade on a short-term basis, financing working capital. Long-term business credits (essentially in the form of corporate bond holdings) were no more than a fifth the amount of short-term loans. Insofar as commercial banks were supposed to extend only "commercial credit," however, they were a misnomer. Many long-term loans to agriculture and industry were made, especially in smaller localities. Bank credit was a vehicle of permanent financing of corporations in the large cities and even smaller centers. Only one-third of all bank loans around 1914 were estimated to represent commercial transactions. About half of all loans were for investment purposes; two-thirds of commercial bank credit went for fixed rather than working capital. In brief, unsecured so-called commercial loans did not in fact always represent "genuine commercial operations".[2]

Banks came to look to the excess of their customers' current assets over current liabilities, rather than specific and actually completed business transactions, as the assurance for loan repayment. The average maturity of business loans was 60 days, but renewals as needed were frequent. Under the customary annual "clean-up," outstanding debt to the bank was paid up for a time, often by borrowing elsewhere. The requirement that borrowers keep "compensating balances" with the bank from which they expected loan accommodation had already appeared before the Civil War. It spread afterwards as unsecured single-name paper came to be the basis for loans, as bank operating expenses increased, and as some bank customers resorted to open-market borrowing. The more conservative banks came to limit their lending as much as possible to customers with a continuing deposit relationship.

Loan Limits By Law

National banks were not allowed to lend to any one borrower an amount exceeding 10 percent of the bank's capital. Exceptions were made for "the discount of bona fide bills of exchange drawn against actually existing values" and for discounted business paper. In practice about half, but not always the same, banks saw fit to violate the statute. As the head of the First National Bank of Central City, Colorado, explained to his cashier in 1880, "there are times when we *must* accommodate our most valued customers . . . and in such cases we must break or evade the law and take the chances." In that particular case, the bank gave advances in excess of $5,000. State banks for the most part had higher, or no, lending limits. Successive Comptrollers urged Congress to raise the limit. In 1906 it was set at 10 percent of capital plus surplus accounts. Under this revised rule, there were only thirteen national banks that could lend as much as $1 million as of 1912.

After the law was amended, Comptroller of the Currency William Ridgely was prepared to revoke the charter of any duly warned bank that violated the law. By September 1909 some 15 percent of all national banks reported excessive loans. The next Comptroller, Lawrence Murray (1908-1913), criticized only those banks whose excessive loans were considered unsafe or inadequately secured.

Credit Practices

Larger banks began to perceive the need for a credit department as business became more complex and directors no longer had first-hand knowledge of all borrowers. Mercantile credit reporting agencies such as Dun & Bradstreet antedated the Civil War, but banks found that for purposes of deciding on credit applications, their information was too limited and unspecific. Around 1883 the Importers' & Traders' National Bank of New York City organized one of the earliest credit departments in order to investigate firms whose open market commercial paper it was considering for purchase. In 1892 there were said to be only six in the entire country. There were less than ten by 1899 when the American Bankers Association Convention voted to set up a model credit department in the secretary's office and to provide banks with technical information on how to proceed, Vice President James Cannon of the Fourth National Bank in New York City, a pioneer in the field, promoted the idea vigorously. By 1911 most major banks had a complete credit department.

Endorsements or guarantees for the notes of borrowers continued to be required. Gradually, however, customers came to be considered on their individual merits, and a bank would extend a line of credit on the basis of information contained in the balance sheet submitted with the loan request. First used in the late 1870's, financial statements did not become common even in larger banks for another twenty years. In 1895 the New York State Bankers Association executive committee recommended that members obtained written statements of borrowers' assets and liabilities over their signatures. In 1899 the American Bankers Association adopted a uniform property statement form. Financial statements came to be required in the years of recovery after the Panic of 1893, but thirty years later there were still those who viewed the request for a statement to be a reflection on the borrower's credit standing.

Loans to Agriculture

Unrest in rural America in the 1880's was partly related to the dearth of credit facilities to tide the western farmer over the interval between planting and harvesting. Especially in frontier regions, he had to rely mainly on merchants, implement dealers, and commission men. Thus, Emil Movius operated a farm implement business, general store, furniture store, lumber yard, and flour mill all mainly on a cash basis. In the early 1890's he organized a state bank in Lidgerwood, North Dakota, where customers could obtain financing. Loans were secured by chattel mortgages on horses, crops, and machinery or by a real estate mortgage on the land. Kinsley, Kansas, had two banks in the 1870's and added a third in 1887. They made few real estate loans before 1900, mostly second mortgages. The three Kinsley banks were mainly interested in short-term loans on chattel or personal security. Before 1913, such loans, frequently renewed, were also made by national banks precluded by law from real estate loans. National banks also circumvented the law by establishing loan offices that made long-term funds available. Agricultural credit, particularly the nonmortgage variety, was obtained mainly from local sources. Outside lenders, such as mortgage companies or individual investors, paid a fee to banks for their services as agents.

Banks serving farmers began to sprout in the West in the 1880's. To encourage their increase, the Dakotas, Nebraska, Kansas, Oklahoma, and Wisconsin authorized banks with as little as $5,000 in capital. Other farming states set a $10,000 or $15,000 minimum. By 1910 there was hardly a hamlet with over 200 people which did not have one, sometimes two, banks. Between 1900 and 1914 Oklahoma gained 810 banks and North Dakota, 613. Cass County, Iowa, typical of better agricultural sections, boasted seventeen banks in 1912: the largest of eight Iowa towns (population 4,560) had five, while places with a population ranging from 490 to 1118 had two banks each.

The 1900 reduction in national bank's minimum capital requirement to $25,000 in places with a population under 3,000 stimulated the formation of 2,500 banks in a few years. Both federal and state law moved to make banks more accessible to residents of rural areas. By 1914 short-term agricultural loans reached some $1.6 billion, about 15 percent of all commercial banks' non-real-estate loans. Nevertheless farmers were dissatisfied with the amount and terms of credit available to them. To meet their complaints, federally sponsored institutions were created in the following decade.

Real Estate Loans

The National Bank Act of 1864 forbade loans on real estate; so did the law in the Dakotas until the 1890's; Oklahoma until 1905; and Ohio until 1908. Various authorities on banking opposed the long-term commitment of funds on the part of institutions with liabilities payable on demand, but in practice banks found it impossible to stay away altogether. Nonfarm residential mortgages comprised about 4.5 percent of total commercial bank assets from 1900 to 1910. In 1900, 6.6 percent of new mortgages were being placed with banks and in 1912, 11.9 percent. This was a greater relative increase than for any other financial institution. Commercial banks owned over 9 percent of total nonfarm residential mortgages outstanding by 1913. Faced with competition from state chartered banks, national banks, with the complicity of the Comptroller of the Currency, used indirect methods to evade the ban. Sometimes a mortgage and trust company would be organized which shared the premises and management of the national bank.

Farmers were hostile because national banks were not allowed to lend on real estate securities, Comptroller William Trenholm explained in his 1888 annual report that national banks were "exclusively devoted to the collection, the safekeeping and the employment in temporary loans of the floating capital of the country." The fact remained that the ban on real estate lending restricted the ability of national banks to serve "farmers and other borrowers in rural communities," as the National Monetary Commission recognized in 1912. Despite the absence of direct participation by national banks, commercial banks held almost $700 million of the $4.7 billion in farm mortgages outstanding at the end of 1913. In the 1910-1914 period, banks financed between 17 and 18 percent of farm mortgage recordings.

Call Loans

Call loans payable on demand, with stock exchange securities as collateral, grew rapidly after 1863. National banks in New York City made about one-third of their total loans in this form in the 1870's and almost half in the 1880's and 1890's; they reduced the ratio to one-third by 1913. During the period 1904-1913, when security prices were in a downtrend, an amount just about equal to all deposits placed by correspondent banks with New York national banks (after the required reserve was set aside) went into the call loan market.

Rates, normally between 2.5 to 6 percent per annum, soared in periods of stringency. As a rule, collateral had to be worth 20 to 30 percent more than the amount of the loan. Call loans were made by certain investment banks and by commercial banks both in New York City and elsewhere, the latter usually through their New York City correspondents.

Commercial Paper

In the sale of goods by the manufacturer to the wholesaler, and by the latter to the retailer, long-term credit evidenced by a note was the rule before the Civil War. As the war proceeded, the arrangement was replaced by discounts for immediate cash settlement; a 30-day limit on accounts receivable became widespread. With this change in credit practices, the trade acceptance, already waning before 1861, lost further ground, becoming negligible by 1900. Concomittantly, the commercial paper market, dealing in unsecured promises-to-pay of well-known, sizeable firms, developed to a far greater extent than outside the United States. By 1860 banks in some of the larger cities of the South and Midwest had begun to place surplus funds in the commercial paper market, though even in 1876 most of the paper continued to be held by banks in New England and the Middle Atlantic States. During the next 25 years the practice spread rapidly, except in the capital-poor South. By 1900, at least some banks in virtually every larger city had begun to buy this paper from dealers, while small country banks were discovering this investment medium. Favorable experience during the 1907 Panic encouraged more banks to hold commercial paper. All large cities had offices of commercial paper dealers or their representatives by 1913, through whom some 2,500 to 3,000 firms offered their short-term obligations for sale.

Call loans made in the open market and commercial paper were two of the assets banks acquired in the interest of diversification and liquidity. To round out their portfolio, they turned increasingly to investments in securities issued by governments and the corporate sector.

Security Investments

Among Secretary Chase's arguments for the national banking system was "the improvement of the public credit." He was pleased to report at the end of 1863 that the establishment of the system "at once inspired faith in the securities of the government and more than any one cause, enabled the Treasury to provide for the prompt payment of the soldiers and the public creditors." A national bank had to buy $30,000 of federal bonds, or an amount equal to one-third of its paid-in capital if that was greater, before opening for business. By the end of the war, $128 million worth had been sold to national banks, one-twentieth of the growth in the federal debt in the preceeding four years. Ever since 1874 national banks with over $150,000 in capital could have as little as $50,000 in United States bonds. Smaller banks were authorized minimum bond holdings amounting to only one-fourth of their capital in 1882. Compulsory purchase of United States bonds by national banks ended in 1913.

National bank holdings of federal bonds (almost entirely for note issue purposes) actually dropped by more than half from 1873 to 1893. However, over half of the $1 billion of the outstanding interest-bearing federal debt was owned by commercial (mainly national) banks in 1900 and 77 percent of the slightly smaller total by 1913. United States bonds comprised 5.2 percent of all commercial bank assets in 1900 but only 3.5 percent in 1913.[3]

Holdings of other types of bonds, corporate and "municipal," increased dramatically; in 1893 Comptroller Hepburn remarked on the large amount of securities owned by commercial banks. Securities other than those of the United States Treasury, which were only 1 percent of total national bank assets in the 1860's, were 4 percent around 1890, 8 percent by 1903, and over 9 percent a decade later. National banks invested less heavily in such securities than did other commercial banks. For all commercial banks, the ratio of nonfederal bonds to total assets was 12 percent in 1903 and 13 percent in 1913. These bonds were bought for current income, anticipation of capital gains, and sometimes in the hope of attracting the business of firms and government units whose securities were held. They were not considered liquid assets for seasonal or cyclical purposes.

Obligations of state and local governments, while only about 2 percent of the assets of all commercial banks were 10 percent of the total amount outstanding in the early 1900's. Banks owned over 13 percent of the larger and even more rapidly growing category of corporate bonds, which comprised 6.7 percent of total commercial bank assets in 1900 and 9.3 percent by 1912. About half of the corporate bonds were promises of railroads and other public service corporations. Perhaps one-fourth of the railroad bond issues between 1860 and 1914 were bought up by commercial banks.

Banks were demonstrating an increased interest in securities in the latter part of the period. In mid-1896 investments comprised 13.3 percent of bank assets, but 18 years later they were 16.7 percent. Meanwhile loans declined from 60.7 percent to 57.9 percent of assets. When "all other" loans than those on real estate or on collateral are compared with the aggregate of nongovernment securities held by banks, the ratio shows a drop from 5.5 to 2.8 during the period 1896-1914.

Investment Banking

Many commercial banks became partners in underwriting syndicates probably in order to obtain newly issued bonds at favorable prices. Acquisition of securities for the bank's own portfolio led to purchases on behalf of customers, particularly correspondent banks. In a few cases, that eventuated in a full range of investment banking activities. The First National Bank of New York was a large-scale seller of United States bonds from its inception in 1863, and it remained active after the Civil War. Under George F. Baker's leadership, the bank came to be allied with J. P. Morgan's operations, as was the National City Bank under James Stillman. Several Chicago banks also carried on investment banking functions. By 1891 the First National Bank of Chicago took over an entire $1,276,000 issue of that city's bonds.

After the Comptroller of the Currency ruled that national banks were forbidden to act as full-range investment banks, James Forgan, with a "well-organized and profitable" bond department now unable to deal in bonds secured by mortgages on real estate, formed a security affiliate, The First Trust and Savings Bank in 1903. It was a state bank owned by the identical shareholders as the First National Bank of Chicago. Two major New York City banks emulated the Chicago Plan; First National Bank established The First Security Corporation in 1908 and The National City Bank established The National City Corporation in 1911. Security affiliates, destined to play a major role in the 1920's, thus had their beginnings before World War I.

By the early 1900's, then, the bond department of certain commercial banks offered services that were available from the traditional investment banking firms. The lines separating the latter from commercial banks became increasingly indistinct. The private banks also carried deposit liabilities, on which they paid interest, that were usually confined to corporate customers rather than a wider public. J. P. Morgan, with over $160 million in deposits in 1912, averaged about 10 times the liabilities of his main Wall Street rival, Kuhn, Loeb and Company. At this time the largest commercial bank, National City, had deposits of $252 million.

Trust Companies and Commercial Banking

Early trust companies specialized in the management of property placed in their care. By the late nineteenth century, the range of financial services they offered increased until, apart from their fiduciary function, they became indistinguishable from commercial banks. Probably the first American corporation to act as trustee was the Farmers' Loan and Trust Company.[4] Incorporated in 1822 as the Farmers' Insurance and Loan Company, this New York City firm was empowered to execute lawful trusts. But it was forbidden to engage in the banking business. First to be chartered exclusively as a trust company was the United States Trust Company in New York City, a leader in the field to this day. Its 1853 charter became the model for others and for New York's general trust company incorporation law of 1887, which was enacted 4 years after Minnesota's. A number of states waited until the early twentieth century to enact general laws for trust company incorporation. Pre-Civil War legislatures had objected to the combination of banking and trust functions. However, trust companies took advantage of the ambiguities surrounding the "proper boundaries" of banking to invade fields previously occupied by commercial banks. Depositors were writing checks against their balances with trust companies no later than 1857. The United States Trust Company, the Buffalo Trust Company, and the New York Life Insurance & Trust Company[5] handled almost 9,000 checks, totalling nearly twice the amount they held on deposit at the end of 1856.

While already engaging in some banking activities before the Civil War, trust companies did not make their competition felt until the years 1873-1875. After several trust companies failed in the 1873 Panic, New York, in 1874 required them to make regular reports to the State Banking Department. There were no statutory restraints on the activities of their trust company rivals, much to the irritation of state and national banks.

By 1887, the Superintendent of Banks in New York confirmed, there was very little difference between the business of banks and trust companies. The latter, however, continued to deny this. A trust manual published in 1898 by the Colonial Trust Company of New York explained:

A bank receives the deposits of the business community without interest and in consideration therefore agrees to distribute its funds among its depositors as their several needs may require, and the available funds permit. The right to a discount is the compensation which a depositor receives for giving the bank the use of his deposits, and is to a certain degree, at least, dependent upon his average balance.

On the contrary, the very idea of a trust company presupposes the payment of interest upon its deposits, and while therefore it is under no direct obligation to extend credit to its depositors, it is at all times ready and willing to extend such credit as is consistent with conservative, prudent banking. . . . While banks discounted notes, trust companies usually required collateral security. The trust company can support larger enterprise, and for a longer time. It can loan directly upon real estate which a bank is prohibited from doing.

At the same time that legal reserve requirements were nonexistent or low, trust companies kept little cash on hand. Thus they could put a greater proportion of their funds out at interest than banks. Beginning in May 1903, the New York City Clearing House began to require a 10 percent reserve of trust companies that wanted their checks cleared by a member bank. Rather than hold double the amount of reserves required by state law, the trust companies gave up the clearing privilege. In 1903 commercial bank opponents of the trust companies organized the Bankers Trust Company, a firm boasting an eminent board of directors (including a Morgan partner) which would not compete with banks the way existing trust companies did.[6]

New York State raised the reserve requirements for trust companies in 1906 and again following unfortunate experiences in the Panic of 1907. Under the 1907 law they had to keep 15 percent cash in their vaults but only on demand deposits. In 1911, the New York City Clearing House voted to admit to regular membership those trust companies willing to keep an additional 10 percent in balances with clearinghouse banks. Most larger trust companies joined, ending decades of conflict with the traditional commercial banks.

The number of trust companies in the United States more than tripled between 1900 and 1913. The more than 1,800 in existence had deposits greater than the total in state chartered commercial banks. The diversity of their financial activities, largely unhampered by legal restraints, undoubtedly contributed to their success. Until 1913, only the states chartered corporations with trust powers. A national bank like Riggs in Washington, D. C., directed trust business to the nearby American Security and Trust Company, while the latter sent commercial bank business to Riggs under a gentleman's agreement. In 1910, on the basis of then existing tendencies, a trust officer forecast that "we shall have but one kind of financial institution, which will combine all the functions of the commercial bank, savings bank, and trust company." This became increasingly the case after 1913, when the Federal Reserve Act made it possible for national banks to expand their services by applying for trust powers.

Notes

1. Lloyd Mints, *History of Banking Theory* (Chicago: University of Chicago Press, 1945), especially pp. 206-207. This is sometimes called the "real bills doctrine."

2. Harold G. Moulton, "Commercial Banking and Capital Formation," *Journal of Political Economy* 26 (1918), pp. 644, 729.

3. For national banks alone, the proportions were 15.7 in 1900 and 10.1 in 1913.

4. Acquired by National City Bank in June 1929, it was finally consolidated by the bank in 1963.

5. Founded in 1830, it merged with the Bank of New York in 1933. The Buffalo Trust Company opened for business in 1855 but lasted only 8 years.

6. In 1917, it, too, moved into commercial banking. For a number of years, Bankers Trust Company has been one of the ten largest commercial banks in the nation.

CHAPTER IX

FAILURE AND PANIC

Bank Failures

Though far from panic-proof, the national banking system could boast a relatively low failure rate, 6.5 percent from 1863 through 1896, compared with 17.6 percent for nonnational banks. Creditors of national banks recouped 75 percent of the amount owed them; other banks repaid only 45 percent of their debts.[1] By the end of 1913, after over 50 years, 538 of 10,472 chartered national banks had suspended operations; 19 were subsequently restored to solvency. Dunbar's evaluation of the first quarter century of the national banking system is appropriate for the second as well: "It carried note issue and deposit banking side-by-side throughout the greater part of the country, under the management of a class of remarkably sound institutions, giving to the community many of the benefits of free banking with the minimum of its risks."[2]

Before 1863, suspension had meant that a bank was unable, or unwilling, to redeem its circulating notes in specie; the notes might still circulate, though at a discount. This ceased to be a problem when state banks stopped issuing notes; holders of national bank notes would be paid in full by the United States Treasury, whatever the financial condition of the bank. With the disappearance of state bank notes after 1865, suspension involved a bank's inability to meet its depositors' demands in currency. Thus, during the

1893 depression, national banks were forced to close their doors because they could not secure cash rapidly enough to satisfy their frightened customers, except at ruinous sacrifice of values. Comptroller James Eckels distinguished between institutions he considered insolvent, which he turned over for liquidation, and those capable of resuming their activities and paying all creditors in full.

Reviewing the factors responsible for national bank failure from 1865 through 1911, the Comptroller of the Currency considered adverse business conditions responsible for relatively few, only 13 percent. Fraudulent management and other criminal violations of the law accounted for over 36 percent. Loans in excess of the legal limit were found in 20 percent of the cases, while "injudicious banking" was assigned as the cause of 23 percent.

Interbank Cooperation and Association

While the downfall of specific banks was often due to internal weaknesses, the interdependence of all banks in a trade area became apparent in the periods of financial crises that recurred with unpredictable but embarrassing frequency. The clearing house loan certificate, invented by George Coe, head of the American Exchange Bank, was a notable instrument of mutual assistance. The New York Clearing House used it for the first time in November 1860, when a crisis arose in connection with Lincoln's election. Banks deposited securities as collateral for an interest-bearing loan; the large-denomination certificates received in exchange could be used to settle balances due at the clearinghouse. New York again resorted to the loan certificate in the 1873 crisis, as did Philadelphia, which had already used it in 1861, Boston, Baltimore, Cincinnati, St. Louis, and New Orleans. In 1893, $100 million in clearinghouse loan certificates were issued, including small amounts in such places as Buffalo, Pittsburgh, Detroit, Atlanta, and Richmond. Chicago did not use certificates in 1873 or 1893.

From time to time, the clearinghouse members would come to the rescue of a failed bank's depositors to prevent a general loss of confidence locally. When three Chicago banks under common control failed at the end of 1905, James Forgan persuaded the clearinghouse to assume the losses. Chicago thereupon pioneered in the clearinghouse examination of member banks, establishing a special bureau for the purpose. By 1913, nineteen other clearinghouses had followed suit at the urging of Comptroller Murray.

Cleveland had the only clearinghouse west of the Alleghenies before the Civil War. Chicago's dates from 1865, St. Louis's from 1868, and San Francisco organized one in 1876. In the entire nation there were 51 by 1890 and

242 in 1912. As clearinghouses evolved they added other functions to the original one of arranging check settlements. At various times and places they also restricted competition by agreements regulating the interest paid on deposits and the charges made for clearing out-of-town checks. Concerned with depositor safety, they set minimum reserves that were sometimes above the legal requirements for national banks. They collected trade credit information and rendered technical assistance to members. They played an important role in periods of panic.

Clearinghouses were organizations of banks located in a limited geographic area, generally a city. A permanent organization on a national level was formed in 1876. Bankers met in October at the Philadelphia Centennial Exhibition, following an earlier convention in Saratoga Springs, New York, in July 1875, to establish the American Bankers Association (A.B.A.). Subsequently, in state after state, banks formed association to further mutual interests in legislation and public relations, starting with Texas in 1885. Rhode Island in 1915 completed the roster for the forty-eight states;[2] Alaska's dates from 1949 and Hawaii's from 1961.

With the A.B.A.'s encouragement, the American Institute of Banking (as it was renamed in 1907) was organized in March 1901. Local chapters were opened to further the training of bank employees. In October 1934 the A.B.A. approved a Graduate School of Banking, which meets annually on the campus of Rutgers University.

Panic of 1907

National banks located outside reserve cities, "country banks," were permitted to keep as much as 9 of the 15 percent reserve required by statute against deposit liabilities with national banks in any of the larger centers, then numbering 43. By 1907 half of the reserves of the national banking systems were in reserve city banks, almost a third of these interbank balances being in New York City alone. The balances owed country banks would be mostly loaned out after reserve city banks had set aside the reserve required of them. This pyramiding of reserves proved to be a source of instability when westerners demanded currency each fall to move crops. Call loans were first to be affected, and interest rates would rise in the money market. "The system has produced disturbance and stringency every autumn for forty years, and panic after panic," the Comptroller of the Currency noted in connection with the events of 1907. All four deep depressions in the years between the Civil War and World War I—1873, 1884, 1893, 1907—followed a panic. Only in 1890 was panic not the prelude to a severe downturn in business.

The panic of 1907 came as a great shock to bankers, who felt that the significant growth of the nation's economy and of the banks over the years would prevent the recurrence of another 1893. The 1907 depression was worldwide, but imperfections in the banking mechanism made it particularly acute in the United States. Real net national product declined 11 percent between 1907 and 1908. On 22 October 1907, the Knickerbocker Trust Company, third largest in New York City, suffered a run. The second largest was hit the very next day. Theodore Roosevelt's Secretary of the Treasury quickly deposited $36 million in New York national banks. Beyond insisting that the private financial interests act in unison, he did not assume any role.

Led by J. P. Morgan, then 70 years old, prominent Wall Street figures met until the early hours of the morning in "Jupiter's" palatial Renaissance library in late October 1907. Morgan would have been pleased to see the smaller trust companies, long a thorn in the side of bankers, go under; James Stillman of National City Bank persuaded him to extend aid to them. To alleviate the stock market call-loan situation, Morgan organized a $25 million pool with funds from leading banks on 24 October and another pool of $10 million the next day.

Just as the situation in New York City was calming down, country banks made large demands for currency on their reserve correspondents. On 26 October, New York banks restricted the convertibility of deposits into currency, and the clearinghouse began to issue loan certificates. Cash payments were more or less restricted by banks in two-thirds of the cities with a population exceeding 25,000. Thus, on 30 October, the Atlanta Clearing House adopted the following resolution:

In view of the action taken by the New York Clearing House, and subsequently adopted by Chicago, St. Louis, Philadelphia, Cincinnati, New Orleans, Nashville, Birmingham, Baltimore, Louisville, Memphis, Montgomery, Mobile, and many other principal cities throughout the country restricting the shipment of currency, and the restriction of other business to its proper channel, the Clearing House; therefore, be it

RESOLVED by the Atlanta Clearing House Association—

1. That until further notice collections and bank balances be settled in exchange or clearing-house certificates.

2. That checks drawn on the members of this association be paid through the Atlanta Clearing House, and correspondents and customers be requested to so stamp their checks.

3. That payments against all accounts, including certificates of deposit, be limited to $50 in one day, or $100 in one week (Monday to Saturday).

4. That exception shall be made to the above in case of payrolls, which shall be paid as follows: All denomination of under $5 to be paid in cash as desired.[4]

In early November the premium on currency over deposits rose to as much as 4 percent and remained above 1 percent until mid-December, vanishing at the end of 1907.

The banking system had become more vulnerable over the years to shifts in the public's preference for cash. For every dollar in currency there were $6.00 in deposits by 1907, compared with $2.00 in 1879. The 1907 ratio of deposits to vault cash was double the 4.4 of 1879. The great rise in these ratios made banks increasingly sensitive to possible runs and quick to seek additional cash as a precaution. Conditions leading to the panic "were not due to the lack of confidence of the people in the banks, but more to a lack of confidence of the banks in themselves and their reserves," the Comptroller of the Currency commented at the time.

A contemporary economist, Wesley C. Mitchell, agreed that the payment restrictions and consequent premium for currency were due to "timidity in using bank reserves" rather than their actual lack. Had the New York banks tried to meet all demands in full, Mitchell suggested in 1913, there probably would not have developed a great scramble for cash, and banks in smaller cities would have been in a position to avoid restriction. This eminent scholar of the business cycle criticized national banks for having made "a fetish of the reserve requirements ... Just at the moment of hesitation when timidity ... spreads fear among businessmen and when boldness inspires confidence, the banks have been timid."[5] Suspensions in 1907 affected 1.22 percent of total commercial bank deposits (three to six times as great as from 1900 to 1906), dropping back to 0.65 percent in 1908. Depositors lost 18 cents per $100 in 1907, (three or more times the experience earlier in the century), and 14 cents in 1908.

The restrictions on currency payments did enable many illiquid banks to survive. Once the restrictions were in effect, however, public distrust of banks was reflected in an 11 percent rise in currency holdings between September 1907 and February 1908, while deposits declined by 8 percent, according to calculations by Friedman and Schwartz. Early in 1908, when the danger of further runs appeared over, the restrictions on cash payment were eliminated.

In late 1907, then, the United States suffered "what was probably the most extensive and prolonged breakdown of the country's credit mechanism since the establishment of the national banking system."[6] A record number of some sixty clearinghouses, including every major city except Washington, resorted to the issue of loan certificates. The total of $256 million was two and a half times the 1893 volume. In addition to the loan certificates, over twenty clearinghouses sponsored small-denomination certificates. These "clearinghouse checks," endorsed by all the member banks, were sometimes as low as $1.00. As an example, Harrisburg, Pennsylvania's, clearinghouse certificates of indebtedness carried the legend, "This check may be deposited but will not be paid in cash," translated into Polish, Hungarian, and Italian. New York refused to issue such "checks" as that clearinghouse feared they would circulate far from home. Major firms filled the gap by issuing printed payroll checks, usually in $5.00 denominations. Standard Oil's, drawn on the National City Bank, enjoyed a considerable circulation. The public at large used over $250 million of these various currency substitutes.

The Aldrich-Vreeland Act of 30 May 1908 was a product of the 1907 debacle. National currency associations, each comprising at least ten national banks, were permitted emergency note issues. These could circulate, subject to a tax that escalated for every month they were outstanding. Conceived as a stopgap measure to expire in mid-1914, the authority was extended for an additional year by the Federal Reserve Act of 1913. The usefulness of the extension was made apparent when, following the outbreak of World War I, almost $400 million in emergency currency was issued by November 1914.

As in earlier crises, almost $212 million in clearinghouse loan certificates were made available throughout the country. 1914 was the tenth occasion when the New York Clearing House had to appoint a loan committee. From 1860 through 1914, New York issued a total of $394 million in loan certificates.

The banking situation in 1907 had been less serious than in 1873 or 1893. Yet the country suffered "the most complete interruption of its banking facilities" since 1861.[7] The Comptroller of the Currency remarked trenchantly in reporting on the events of 1907 that

> if the experience of the country in the bank panics from 1857 to 1893 needed any further confirmation, the panic of 1907 has demonstrated beyond the possibility of denial that perfectly solvent banks—if independent, isolated units with no power of cooperation except through such voluntary association as their clearing houses—cannot protect themselves in a panic and save themselves from failure with such a suspension of payments as to produce disorder and demoralization in all the business of their customers.[8]

Under the Aldrich-Vreeland Act, Congress established a national monetary commission, whose studies and report provided the springboard for the debate that finally produced the Federal Reserve Act. By this measure, Congress hoped to prevent the recurrence of another panic like that of 1907. As it turned out, 1933 was far worse.

Notes

1. Over the 22 years ending in mid-1913, 1702 nonnational banks with liabilities of over $622 million failed, contrasted with 367 national banks having $182 million in liabilities.

2. Charles Dunbar, *Economic Essays* (New York: Macmillan, 1904), p. 182.

3. For dates in the first forty-eight states, see Fritz Redlich, *Molding of American Banking: Men and Ideas*, Vol. 2 (New York: Hafner, 1968), pp. 301-302, n. 268.

4. *Commercial and Financial Chronicle*, 9 November 1907, p. 1182; quoted in O. M. W. Sprague, *History of Crises under the National Banking System* (Washington: Government Printing Office, 1910), p. 288.

5. Wesley C. Mitchell, *Business Cycles and Their Causes* (Berkeley: University of California Press, 1941), reprint of part III, pp. 127-128. The original appeared in 1913.

6. A. Piatt Andrew, "Substitutes for Cash in the Panic of 1907," *Quarterly Journal of Economics* 22 (1908), p. 497.

7. Sprague, *Crises under National Banking*, p. 319.

8. Comptroller of the Currency, *Annual Report 1907*, p. 79.

CHAPTER X

BANKING, THE GOVERNMENT, AND THE ECONOMY, 1863-1913

Government Supervision

A total of five New England states (all except Rhode Island) examined banks regularly in 1863 while certain others examined banks under suspension. Soon after its establishment, the office of the Comptroller of the Currency instituted the policy of examining each national bank annually. Most states, however, subjected banks to "very little interference and scarcely any espionage on the part of officials," the Comptroller pointed out in 1884, concerned as he was with federal-state rivalry under the dual banking system. Not until 1884 did New York examine its banks regularly. By then only Indiana, Minnesota, and California had joined the five pioneering New England states in the practice of official "espionage." By the time of the next Comptroller's survey in 1895, an additional twenty-one states had instituted regular examinations, and fourteen more did so between 1897 and 1908. Between 1912 and 1914 Arkansas, Kentucky, Mississippi, and Tennessee became the last four of the forty-eight contiguous states to introduce examinations.

In 1895 only fifteen states had distinct banking departments; twenty-one others gave an official with other functions (for example, secretary of state or treasurer) responsibility for supervising banks. By 1913 there were twenty-nine banking departments. North Carolina, in 1931, was the last of the forty-eight states to establish a specific agency for bank regulation.

Examinations tended to instill public confidence in banks, as Wisconsin's bankers recognized. At their 1894 convention, they urged the state to assume this function. Federal supervision originally had the two-fold purpose of protecting the public from loss resulting from improper use of the bank notes issued, and the government from loss in connection with deposit of inland tax revenues. Already in 1865 the Comptroller was writing to banks requesting the correction of weaknesses revealed by the examiners. Comptroller Knox in 1878 proudly contrasted "the excellent system now in operation" with the "generally lax system of bank supervision" found in the states before 1863.

Comptroller Henry Cannon extended the role of supervision in 1884 to include the elimination of management difficulties at an early stage. By studying causes of bank failures he suggested to national bank examiners "such methods of examination as seemed to be best calculated to prevent repetition of such disasters, and to expose violations of law which led to the same." At the same time Cannon admonished national bank shareholders to "be more careful to elect men as directors and trustees who are competent and who will exercise proper care and supervision over the management of the affairs intrusted to them, who will select competent and honest officers, provide suitable rules and regulations for the conduct of the bank . . . and appoint regular committees of examination . . . not only to verify the accounts, but to keep a watchful eye over the association and the officers. . . . "[1] In short, despite government supervision, the soundness of a bank was primarily the responsibility of its owners and managers.

National bank examiners were remunerated by a fee for each examination, based on the bank's capital. This encouraged superficiality. After over twenty years in national banks, an Ironton, Ohio, banker told the American Bankers Association convention in 1887: "I found Examiners to be gentlemen of high character, yet they have one great fault. They are too fast. One might think that . . . the Furies were driving them on, *on*, ON, without rest." Twenty years later, many bankers complained to Comptroller Murray that "the first question that an examiner asked was what time the next train left town." By visiting banks along a regular route, examiners would economize on travel expenses. Banks alerted as to the examiner's whereabouts could prepare themselves for his visit. The element of surprise, so essential to a meaningful bank examination, would be lacking.

Selection was not necessarily based on merit. James B. Forgan complained to the National Monetary Commission in 1908 about "the political influence at present almost controlling the appointment of national bank examiners. . . . " Comptroller Murray admitted before the commission that "the supervision we have been able to give banks under the law as it stands has been ineffectual and inefficient and disastrous." He proceeded to institute more effective examinations than before by removing incompetents, rotating examiners, and insisting on thoroughness. In 1909 Murray also brought about cooperation between state and national bank examiners in arranging joint examinations where national banks were allied with state chartered institutions.

The "more effective supervision of banking in the United States" was one of the purposes specified in the Federal Reserve Act of 1913. Examiners were placed on a salary basis, as all examining states except Delaware and Illinois had already done by 1910. A career system was established and the field force organized under twelve chief national bank examiners who exchanged ideas, which they passed along to the men under their jurisdiction. This contributed to a greater uniformity of procedures and practices throughout the nation. The act also made national banks subject to examination twice a year.

Federal Statutory Restraints

The free banking system of the United States meant that "any persons, however unfamiliar with [banking] principles, who have the necessary capital" could be in the business, as the 1898 Report of the Monetary Commission of the Indianapolis Convention of Boards of Trade pointedly remarked. However, a number of prohibitions incorporated in the National Bank Act served as safeguards to the extent that they were obeyed. Among them were bans on lending on real estate, on lending an amount in excess of 10 percent of the bank's capital to any one borrower, on investing in stocks, on allowing reserves against deposits to fall below the prescribed minimum, and on borrowing an amount in excess of the bank's capital stock. However, the deputy comptroller of the currency estimated that one-third of all national banks managed to violate the law in one way or another.

Federal Treasury and the Banks

The federal government's relationship with commercial banks was not confined to the examination and regulation of national banks. In August 1861, Congress authorized Treasury deposits of loan proceeds in banks, which sometimes reached $40 million. Refusing to accept inconvertible state bank notes, Washington issued its own during the Civil War; first, Treasury notes, and, later, United States Notes (the famous greenbacks). National bank notes could be used in payment of all dues to the United States Treasury except customs.

Though the Independent Treasury system lingered on until 1921, the federal government dispensed with commercial banks for deposit purposes only from 1847 to 1863, when the national banking system was established. National banks were eligible to serve as internal revenue depositaries. Tariff receipts, the bulk of federal revenues, continued to be held in the sub-treasuries, located in major port cities (See Table 2, p. 70, designation a).

After the Civil War, successive secretaries of the treasury viewed the deposit of public monies in national banks as something to be done only in emergencies. In the 1870's, except during the 1879 bond refunding, deposits were generally around $10 million and only somewhat higher in the early 1880's. Faced with surplus revenues that could not be used to retire Treasury bonds, Secretary Charles Fairchild made deposits that amounted to $54 million by 1888.

On the occasion of several nineteenth-century crises, the Treasury came to the aid of the banks. In the early 1900's Secretary Leslie Shaw enlarged its role to anticipate and eliminate recurring autumnal stringencies even in ordinary times. Congress subsequently gave statutory recognition to Shaw's actions. A 1907 law empowered the Secretary of the Treasury to decide what collateral to require of depositary banks; previously only United States government bonds in an amount equal to the deposit were eligible. Moreover, customs receipts could now be deposited in national banks.

In May 1908 the reserve requirement for federal deposits was eliminated. By 1913 these government balances rarely fell below $50 million. The Secretary of the Treasury had developed a paternalistic attitude toward the banks in the matter of government deposits, opening the government to a charge of discrimination and favoritism. The Treasury, however, understood the need to seek ways of minimizing the disruptive impact of its cash holdings on the money markets and the national economy in the pre-federal reserve era.

Banks and the Economy

Large-scale extension of banking facilities to every corner of the Union marked the half century ending with the passage of the Federal Reserve Act in 1913. The number of banks rose five times as rapidly as total population. Over 7,000 communities enjoyed the services of local banks in 1900.

Although the banker played a central role in the economy, he was unpopular in many quarters. The mayor of Cedar Rapids, Iowa, reminded the 1889 convention of the Iowa Bankers Association that in the eyes of many the banker "is considered cold and repellent, grasping and unsympathetic, anxiously seeking opportunity to hold as his own that which belongs to another. . . . " Bankers, along with saloon-keepers, lawyers, and physicians, had the dubious distinction of being ineligible to join the all-embracing Knights of Labor.

If bankers were often considered aloof and forbidding, it was no accident. The first instruction Governor William Larrabee gave the man who took charge of the First National Bank of Elkader, Iowa, in 1883 was not to solicit business from anyone, lest he put the bank under obligation, making it more difficult to refuse the customer when he requested a loan. The Merchants National Bank of Boston forbade employees to solicit deposits, discouraging the notion that a depositor was entitled to a line of credit. Frederick Haven, who served as its president until 1883, deemed it an honor for someone to open an account with Merchants.

By the end of the century, however, bankers were actively soliciting correspondent business by mail and, in some cases, by sending traveling representatives. No longer was it beneath their dignity to seek out new deposit and loan accounts. New York and Philadelphia banks were "soliciting business from our Chicago merchants on wide open principles," Forgan of the First National Bank of Chicago complained in 1906. Banks in large cities were beginning to open new business departments around 1912, and within a few years every large bank had one. Local solicitation was considered unethical, as young Percy Johnston (later to head the Chemical Bank in New York) learned when he visited another Louisville bank's clients. There had always existed "a nice gentlemanly relationship" among the Kentucky city's banks.[2] Bankers reasoned that nothing would be gained by going after each others customers. And financial advertising now also made its appearance. The staid First New Haven, the second national bank in the country to receive a charter, retained a Cleveland expert for $25.00 a month in an effort to develop and increase the bank's business.

As late as 1890 most of a bank's work was performed manually. Not until 1888 was the adding machine developed to the point where it was practical. New York's Hanover Bank got its first adding machines around 1900, "but it was not infallible, and bookkeepers footed their columns by hand to verify its results."[3] Various types of machines became available shortly before 1900, leading to changes in office procedures. By 1914 a truly up-to-date bank might use adding machines, punched card tabulators, automatic typewriters, duplicating machines, and check-writing equipment. After 1914 improved models were offered from time to time but no really new machines appeared until the electronic computer began to be installed in the mid-1950's.

The "business of banking" as defined in the 1864 National Bank Act went well beyond certain early nineteenth-century notions of an instrumentality for bank note issues, extending to "discounting and negotiating . . . evidences of debt, . . . receiving deposits; . . . buying and selling exchange, coin and bullion; . . . loaning money on personal security. . . . " Increased diversification of lending and investing marked the pre-1914 era. As trust companies became significant competitors, banks responded by emulating their broad range of activities, taking on time deposits and investment banking as well as trust functions. To describe this comprehensive diversification the phrase "department store banking" was already in use in the early 1900's.[4]

Leading banks of the period were managed by "businessmen of the highest caliber," according to Redlich. A striking proportion of Comptrollers of the Currency filled important positions following their Washington service. Hugh McCulloch, the first, rounded out a distinguished career as partner in the London branch of Jay Cooke. John J. Knox resigned after 12 years in office to lead the National Bank of the Republic in New York City. Henry Cannon became head of Chase National Bank, as did A. Barton Hepburn subsequently. Important Chicago banks were led by Charles Dawes, James Eckels, and Edward Lacey.

In 1913 the real gross national product of the United States was seven times the level of the late 1860's; on a per capita basis, it was almost three times as great. On the eve of World War I, American bank assets, including central banks and savings banks, were equal to 16 percent of the United States' national wealth, compared with 12 percent for the United Kingdom's and 14 percent for Germany's. In 1912 commercial banking's share of total assets of all American financial intermediaries reached a peak for the twentieth century of 53.5 percent, slightly above 1900's 52.8 percent. Life insurance companies had 13 percent of assets of all intermediaries, having grown significantly in the preceding 50 years. Mutual savings banks, confined to the Northeast, with a 12 percent share had lost ground; savings and loan associations, formidable rivals after 1950, were a mere 3 percent of the 1912 total.

Lending and investing activities of commercial banks were responsible for the greater part of the United States' money supply. As defined by Friedman and Schwartz, the concept includes the public's holdings of government and bank-originated currency plus all types of commercial bank deposits. From 1867 to 1879 the money supply grew very slowly, averaging 1.3 percent a year and actually declining in 5 of the 12 years. From the resumption of specie payments in 1879 to the election of William McKinley in 1897, money increased very unevenly at an average of 6 percent annually. Widespread clamor for government action to expand the money supply accompanied the price decline, which averaged under 1 percent a year from 1879 to 1897, though this represented an improvement over the 3.5 percent yearly decline estimated for 1867-1879. By contrast, in the 1897-1914 period, money growth averaged 7.5 percent and prices rose over 2 percent a year. The acceleration was traceable in good measure to the great increase in the world's gold output, which added to the reserves of the banking and monetary system. With this turn of events, agitation for special inflationary measures dwindled.

National bank notes, unlike state bank notes, had never sustained any losses. Depositors' losses in closed national banks represented a minute fraction of total deposits of the system. Yet, as the events of 1907 had clearly revealed, the mechanism was unsatisfactory. As Carter Glass, then the leading member of the House Banking Committee, insisted in 1913, "the failure of the system in acute exigencies has caused widespread business demoralization and almost universal distress." In the same year, Wesley C. Mitchell the outstanding American authority argued in his monumental study of the business cycle that "banking reform is both the most needed and the easiest of all the changes that promise to increase our control over the workings of the money economy." On the basis of his analysis of United States experience, he was convinced that panics *could* be avoided; their recurrence was due to defects in banking law and practice. "Elasticity of lending power is needed more than elasticity of currency," Mitchell suggested. The Federal Reserve system set out to provide both kinds of elasticity.

Notes

1. Comptroller of the Currency, *Annual Report 1884*, p. 49.

2. Frank W. Nye, *Knowledge is Power: The Life Story of Percy H. Johnston, Banker* (New York: Random House, 1956), pp. 64-65.

3. William S. Gray, *The Hanover Bank* (New York: Newcomen Society, 1951), p. 12.

4. Sereno Pratt, "New York's Financial Institutions," *The Independent*, 22 Dec. 1904, p. 1435.

CHAPTER XI

FORMATIVE YEARS OF THE
FEDERAL RESERVE SYSTEM, 1914-1920

Deficiencies in the Old Order

American banking's individualism struck Paul Warburg on his arrival in New York City in 1902 to join the outstanding investment house of Kuhn, Loeb & Co. Centralization was seen as a threat that would either bring politics into banking through complete governmental control or, alternatively, banking into politics through Wall Street domination. As a consequence, banks in the United States had remained "individualistic in the highest degree," as the Banking Committee of the House of Representatives noted in 1913.

Before 1914, other institutions were performing certain central bank functions, albeit inadequately. Banks could borrow from correspondents in major cities, but just when country banks faced the greatest need, the reserve city institutions had a diminished capability of lending. Clearinghouses, unlike these city correspondents, were in a position to expand reserves by resorting to loan certificates on certain critical occasions, but this palliative functioned only on a local basis. The United States Treasury, by placing deposits with national banks, as in 1907, added to their reserves; regular operations with commercial banks were not within its powers.

Reformers' energies had mainly been devoted to the problem of making the currency elastic. Already on 10 December 1865 a Congressional resolution called for a flexible paper currency "increasing and decreasing according to the requirements of legitimate business." However, an elastic currency by itself would not "meet the need for a more effective supply of deposit credits," the House Banking Committee stated, recognizing that in periods of stress banks suffered from an "inability to convert good assets into a medium that can be used in making payments." Accordingly, part of the long title of the Federal Reserve Act read "to afford means of rediscounting commercial paper," just after "to furnish an elastic currency." The 1913 act represented the first attempt to deal directly with the "long recognized rigidity of our credit system," as J. Laurence Laughlin pointed out at the time. The University of Chicago economist stressed that "wider and deeper than the inelasticity of our currency has been the inelasticity of our credit system." Provision of "a sound and elastic supply of both currency and credit" was thus a major purpose of the act.[1] The main ends sought in 1913 were clearly stated in the majority report of the Senate Banking Committee:

> to give stability to the commerce and industry of the United States; prevent financial panics or financial stringencies; make available effective commercial credit for individuals engaged in manufacturing, in commerce, in finance, and in business to the extent of their just deserts; put an end to the pyramiding of the bank reserves of the country and the use of such reserves for gambling purposes on the stock exchange.

The national banking system had failed to "afford any safeguard against panics and commercial stringencies or any means of alleviating them," the House Banking Committee stated. The one point on which there was general agreement among bankers and the public was that the measure would "render a recurrence of financial panic impossible," as the Denver *Rocky Mountain News* editorialized at the time the Federal Reserve bill was enacted. An optimistic Comptroller of the Currency asserted in 1914 that because of the Federal Reserve Act, panics "seem to be mathematically impossible." And Federal Reserve Board Chairman Charles Hamlin assured the Western Economic Society in November 1915 that "we will never have any more panics."

Indeed, there was no panic in the first major business downturn after the establishment of the Federal Reserve System, despite the sharp 44 percent drop in wholesale prices and a 32 percent shrinkage in industrial production. At the business cycle peak, January 1920, deposits were 7.05 times currency holdings of the public; at the trough, July 1921, 7.0. There was no scramble for cash on the part of commercial banks; they contracted their loans as the Federal Reserve Banks reduced their credit.

Discount Facilities

Banks belonging to the system, "member banks," could now obtain funds outright at an interest rate known in advance and uniform for all, whereas correspondent banks charged what the traffic would bear when lending on secured collateral. The Federal Reserve rediscount rate was to be fixed "with a view of accommodating commerce and business," according to a phrase of the statute attributed to Woodrow Wilson. H. Parker Willis, the banking expert who had worked on the measure for Carter Glass, explained that "credit will be more simply available, cheaper and more equitably open to all."[2]

The Federal Reserve Board defined credit for "productive use" in its famous 1923 annual report as "credit in the service of agriculture, industry, and trade." Rediscounts were originally limited to short-term paper "issued or drawn for agricultural, industrial or commercial purposes." By relating rediscounts directly to the volume of goods bought and sold, Federal Reserve notes and commercial bank deposits would "adjust themselves to the needs of trade," Laughlin, Willis's teacher, reasoned. The board was confident that "there will be little danger that the credit created and contributed by the Federal Reserve banks will be in excessive volume if restricted to productive uses."

Correspondent Balances and Reserve Centralization

The forty-nine major national banks in the central reserve cities (New York, Chicago and St. Louis) feared that the new system would result in very substantial declines in their correspondent bank balances, which represented about half of their total deposits. However, required reserves constituted less than half of the bankers' balances. Country banks had become accustomed to receiving 2 percent on balances they left with correspondents, some $930.00 a year on average, representing 7.7 percent of their net income. For the typical reserve city bank, this income from central reserve city banks came to $15,250, over 12 percent of their net. To ease the adjustment, the law provided for a gradual transfer of reserve deposits to the Federal Reserve Banks over a 3-year period ending 16 November 1917.

The national banking system's classification of central reserve city, reserve city, and country banks was retained as the basis for differential reserve requirements for demand deposits until 1972. Federal Reserve Banks paid no interest on member bank deposits. By way of compensation, the required reserve ratio was reduced, enabling banks to earn interest on the released funds. The system's ability to provide member banks with liquid funds was thought to make the previous higher requirements unnecessary.

Federal Reserve Banks and Member Banks

Multiple Federal Reserve Banks were intended to assure "local control of banking, local application of resources to necessities," the House Banking Committee reported. Member banks of the particular Federal Reserve District, the sole shareholders, selected six of the nine directors of the Federal Reserve Bank. The stock would pay no more than a 6 percent dividend, appropriate to the Federal Reserve Banks' role as "great public utility banks," as the Senate Banking Committee described these "guardians of the public welfare."

While confining their dealings to commercial banks, reserve banks would "do for existing banks what an ordinary bank does for its customers," the House Banking Committee explained. The Federal Reserve Banks would serve member banks by holding their surplus funds, lending to them, handling their deposits, and providing them with facilities for making remittances. The Federal Reserve Banks would not deal directly with the general public, thus avoiding the charge made against the government-sponsored First and Second Banks of the United States that they were private institutions engaged in general banking business.

At the start, the Federal Reserve Banks' operations were largely in the hands of men with previous experience in commercial banking. The system's early days reflected "a great deal of commercial banker mentality, as distinct from direct banker influence."[3] Even the system heads cultivated the view that the Federal Reserve Banks had been created primarily to serve the interests of the member banks; certainly the latter thought this was the case.

Multiple Reserve Banks

Three of the twelve Federal Reserve Banks were inevitably located in what had long before been designated central reserve cities. Only nine of the forty-nine localities that had been recognized by the Comptroller of the Currency as reserve cities by 1914 were privileged to serve as headquarters of a Federal Reserve Bank; sixteen others had a branch of the district bank (see Table 2, page 70). Branches were also opened in nine places that had not previously been reserve cities: Buffalo, Birmingham, Charlotte, El Paso, Helena, Jacksonville, Little Rock, Memphis, and Nashville.

The purpose of establishing a number of reserve banks was to avoid "a very high degree of centralization," so greatly feared by William Jennings Bryan and his followers, and to assure "really independent institutions, likely to look to one another for aid only under emergency conditions." The system "is not a central bank. It is a regional system," the Federal Reserve Board insisted in its 1921 annual report. Similarly, Willis saw that the Federal Reserve bill "would not create a central bank but only a series of reserve holding agencies."[4] Each reserve bank's operations, as well as policies, were independent, subject only to general supervision by the board in Washington.

The Federal Reserve Banks were intended to serve as a source of emergency assistance to commercial banks rather than as an agency for the execution of monetary policy. The discovery that uncoordinated purchases of United States government bonds by the twelve Federal Reserve Banks, in quest of income, had disruptive effects on the securities market led to the setting up of a coordinating committee in May 1921. A year later, the Open Market Investment Committee for the Federal Reserve System was placed under the supervision of the Federal Reserve Board.

Clear-cut, centralized decision-making authority for the renamed Board of Governors of the Federal Reserve System came only with the Banking Act of 1935. As the Federal Reserve evolved into a monetary policy-maker, the individual reserve banks inevitably lost their basic independence. Nevertheless, the 1913 conception of "a cooperative enterprise among bankers for the purpose of increasing the security of banks and providing them with a reservoir of emergency resources" survived the decades that followed.[5]

The Federal Reserve Act and the Aldrich Bill

Paul Warburg, soon to be appointed to the first Federal Reserve Board, and possibly more than any other man responsible for the basic features of the 1913 law, wrote triumphantly to Carter Glass that the Federal Reserve Act embodied long-sought fundamental objectives. The national bank note would gradually be eliminated, as would "scattered reserves, . . . immobilized commercial paper, and pyramiding of call loans on the stock exchange." Warburg argued that the Aldrich bill proposed by the National Monetary Commission, though denounced in the 1912 Democratic platform for attempting to establish a central bank, provided the substance as well as various technical provisions of the Federal Reserve Act. The chief difference, as he understood, was that the Federal Reserve Board would have federal government representatives on it, whereas Aldrich contemplated banker domination of the National Reserve Association. The latter would have been "an evolution of the clearing-house idea, extended to include an effective central organization," in the view of the National Monetary Commission. The most fundamental concept of the 1913 act, uniting the banks of the nation, had been taken from the clearinghouse practice of emergency pooling of reserves, as Willis recognized.

Bankers fought hard against those features that were departures from the Aldrich bill. The Federal Reserve Board had no banker representation and they feared that presidential nominees would turn the board into a political instrumentality; legal reserves would be transferred from correspondents to the Federal Reserve Banks; and if checks were collected at par, country banks would lose an important source of income.

Membership in the Federal Reserve System

That the Federal Reserve legislation was evolutionary did not make it any more palatable to the banking community; a measure limited to providing relief in emergency situations of credit stringency would have satisfied them. An American Bankers Association committee complained that banks would have "a very limited voice." National banks had to subscribe to stock in the federal Reserve Banks on penalty of forfeiting their charter if they did not join within a year. Compulsory membership was denounced, but by 2 April 1914, a total of 7,471 banks had agreed to join. Only 15 relinquished their national charter, while another 13 failed to become members by the deadline. State chartered banks stayed away. Out of the 8,500 eligible, only 53 had seen fit to join the system by June 1917, when the law was amended to make it more attractive for them, but only 36 more became members that summer.

At least as important as the 1917 amendment were fears of a drain on bankers' resources related to America's participation in World War I and calls to patriotism from high-level officials. In October 1917 President Wilson admonished the state bankers that they could "best measure up to their duties and responsibilities through membership in the Federal Reserve System." By the end of 1918, 930 state banks had heeded the call, but almost ten times that number failed to do so. Nevertheless, the system could boast that member banks had 63 percent of all commercial bank deposits, whereas between 1914 and 1916 their share had been only 42-43 percent. A record 1,600 state banks were members in 1922. The vast majority preferred to remain outside, collecting interest on their reserves with correspondent banks (until 1933) and charging exchange for clearing checks, while keeping fewer required reserves.

The Federal Reserve and the Role of Banks in World War I

War broke out in Europe 4 months before the Federal Reserve Banks were ready to open. During the ensuing panic, banks did not suspend cash payments because of the emergency currency issue under the Aldrich-Vreeland Act. Almost 2,200 national banks joined national currency associations. At the peak on 24 October 1914, $384 million of their notes were outstanding, about one-fourth of the total amount of currency in the hands of the public before the war began. Within 2 months, $217 million was redeemed, and all but $200,000 by July 1915.

United States government bonds represented only one-thirtieth of all commercial bank assets in mid-1914. Banks reduced their holdings slightly from 1913 to 1916, at which time they had over 78 percent of the outstanding total. Newly organized national banks no longer had to buy government bonds after 1913. However, a 1916 amendment, in what developed into a significant departure from the "real bills" approach of the original Federal Reserve Act, authorized the discounting of paper secured by federal government bonds. At the time, the amendment is said to have been viewed as "a technical alteration of no great importance."[6] In 1916 there were only $300 million of United States bonds that were not serving as collateral for national bank notes.

Banks added an amount equal to three times their 1916 portfolio in the next 2 years. By mid-1919, United States government bond holdings were at a peak of almost $5 billion, comprising over one-ninth of all bank assets. Though over half of their entire investment portfolio consisted of federal securities, this represented only 23 percent of the total outstanding in 1919. Commercial banks further assisted the Treasury's war requirements by making large advances to finance acquisition of United States securities by others responding to the slogan "Borrow and buy."

When Congress declared war in April 1917, the Federal Reserve Banks established a preferential rate on member bank borrowings secured by federal bonds, which was kept for over a year following the Armistice at the urging of the Treasury. Member banks were encouraged to borrow from the Federal Reserve at little or not net cost. Banks thus overcame their longstanding aversion against rediscounting. In October 1920, a record $2.8 billion of borrowings from the Federal Reserve (not reached again until mid-1973) exceeded by almost $1 billion the total reserves of member banks.

Between 1914 and the peak in 1920, total loans made by commercial banks more than doubled in dollar amount, but wholesale prices rose even more. Short-term bank loans to agriculture reflected the sharp wartime rise in the demand for American farm output. From $1.6 billion in 1914-1915 they soared to a high of $3.9 billion in late 1920 through early 1921. Meanwhile banks had over $1.4 billion in farm mortgages by the end of 1920, twice as much as 6 years earlier.

Measured in current (inflated) dollars, banking grew rapidly. In 7 years to mid-1920, the Comptroller of the Currency noted, total national bank assets increased by as much as in the half century preceding June 1913. Total assets of all commercial banks increased 115 percent as current dollar gross national product rose 128 percent, and wholesale prices soared 121 percent from 1913 to 1920.

Gigantic financial transactions could now be executed smoothly and simply with the assistance of the Federal Reserve Banks. "War finance on our present scale could hardly have been carried on by the old machinery," Benjamin Anderson noted in 1920. That bank economist considered this "a supreme vindication of the federal reserve system."

Notes

1. Quoted in *Federal Reserve Bulletin* 26 (1940), p. 280.

2. "The Federal Reserve Act," *American Economic Review* 4 (1914), p. 19. Willis headed the division of research at the Federal Reserve Board 1915-1922. He launched the *Federal Reserve Bulletin*.

3. Emanuel A. Goldenweiser, *American Monetary Policy* (New York: McGraw Hill, 1951), p. 296. Goldenweiser served as chief economist to the Federal Reserve Board for many years.

4. Lloyd W. Mints, *History of Banking Theory* (Chicago: University of Chicago Press, 1944), p. 281.

5. Quoted in Commission on Money and Credit, *Report on Money and Credit*, (Englewood Cliffs, N. J.: Prentice-Hall, 1961), p. 85.

6. Benjamin H. Beckhart, *The Federal Reserve System* (New York: Columbia University Press, 1972), p. 111.

CHAPTER XII

BANKING IN THE 1920'S

Decline in Business Lending

The Armistice in November 1918 was followed by vigorous speculation in inventories and rising prices. The ensuing collapse of prices (40 percent in the year ending July 1921) brought heavy losses. Hand-to-mouth buying became an ideal, while improved transportation and techniques of inventory control and accounting facilitated greater efficiency in managing inventories. After 1922 inventories and accounts receivable, both traditionally financed by bank loans, declined while fixed assets became relatively more important to business.

Bank credit was curtailed in 1921-1922, but only after prices tumbled. Even then, business loans in 1922 were almost twice as large as in 1915. Many firms, unable to renew or pay off their loans, came under the control of bankers in the early 1920's. Businessmen viewed this as a lesson in the desirability of attaining independence from bank financing. Earnings retained out of sizable net profits served as an important source of funds. The boom on Wall Street facilitated bond and, especially in 1927-1929, stock flotations for working capital purposes.

The trend toward borrowing from the investing public rather than directly from the banks was especially noticeable on the part of large firms. Not uncommonly the leading corporations in an industry had no outstanding bank loans. Current assets of 729 mostly successful larger companies rose 32 percent from 1922 through 1928, but their bank loans declined 37 percent. By paying off bank indebtedness, firms hoped to avoid the risk of insolvency during a sharp cyclical drop in earnings.

Despite the Federal Reserve Act's encouragement, short-term commercial bank lending declined in relative importance during the 1920's. Loans eligible for rediscount at a Federal Reserve Bank fell from 32 percent of the 1920 national bank loan total to just over 20 percent by the end of the decade, declining from 24 to 12 percent as a proportion of total bank loans and investments. Commercial loans, 47 percent of all bank loans and investments in 1922, were only 33 percent by 1929. In the face of the reduced demand for commercial loans from creditworthy borrowers bankers turned to other lending areas. By 1923 security and real estate loans combined exceeded the commercial ("all other loans") category. The $15.5 billion commercial loan total of 1920 was not surpassed until 1929.

Small and medium enterprises, not in a position to reinvest as great a proportion of their profits or to sell securities, received about three-fifths of the 1920 commercial loan total and three-fourth's of the 1930 total. Unlike large borrowers who could shop around for the best terms, smaller ones were expected to keep an ample deposit balance and have their entire line of credit with a single bank on a permanent customer basis. Banks wanted customers to secure their explicit permission before going to the commercial paper or general acceptance market. Some businessmen complained that banks were meddling excessively in the affairs of borrowers who were neither insolvent nor likely to get into any kind of trouble.

In most large cities, especially those where the booming industries of automobiles, steel machinery, and electrical equipment were located, bankers bemoaned the disappearing large borrower. In smaller centers, the number of good quality industrial and commercial borrowers shrank as they merged into larger firms. In rural localities the withering impact on local merchants made by chain stores, mail-order houses, and shoppers who motored to larger cities for sizable purchases also affected banks adversely.

Business indebtedness to banks had increased as a fraction of total funds used by business from 1900 to 1920, only to drop in the next 15 years. Commercial banks became less important as a source of short- and long-term funds to corporations, with 32.1 percent of net corporate debt at the end of 1920 but only 23.3 percent 9 years later. Nevertheless business loans and securities combined represented 37 percent of total commercial bank assets in 1928, 1 percent above the 1900 share.

Banks responded to their relative decline as direct lenders by increasing their investments acquired in the open market. The upsurge of time deposits encouraged banks to add to their security holdings as well as to make larger loans based on security collateral. Unsecured loans, 60.8 percent of the 1920 total, were down to 45.9 percent by 1928 as loans secured by stocks, bonds, and mortgages on real estate expanded greatly. Yet the United States remained "par excellence the land of the unsecured loan based on a showing of a financial statement and other evidences of financial capacity and integrity."[1]

Credit Departments

Credit departments, a rarity in 1913, were opened by most of the large and medium banks in the 1920's and 1930's. One factor was that the Federal Reserve Banks insisted that a bank's files contain financial statements for the firms whose paper it was rediscounting. The federal corporate income tax, first imposed in 1913, was even more important in inducing better record keeping. The old-fashioned banker had kept his credit file in his head. When First Bank Stock, a Minneapolis holding company, asked subsidiary banks to install credit files in the 1920's, many country bankers balked but had to yield in the end. Such information could no longer be viewed as trade secrets for the exclusive use of the senior bank officials. Loan officers reviewing business balance sheets and earnings reports tended to focus on a small number of financial ratios. This led to some degree of standardization of credit policy among banks.

Credit information was now being exchanged on a larger scale. The Wisconsin Bankers Association sponsored countywide credit bureaus that consolidated information about borrowers in a given area; fourteen were organized or under way by mid-1927. It was discovered that, on average, one out of seven Wisconsin borrowers had been receiving credit from more than one bank, without the banks being told about this.

Farm Mortgages

Individual lenders, historically the major source of farm mortgages, still provided around 40-50 percent of the total in the early 1920's. The bank share, under one-fifth before 1915, was closer to one-fourth during most of the 1920's. Farm mortgage debt was at a peak of $10.8 billion at the beginning of 1923 as certain short-term bank credits were consolidated in this form. Banks held one-tenth of 1930's $9.6 billion total while the life insurance companies' share was more than twice as great.

The federal government entered the field of systematic cash lending for the first time in July 1916 with an act authorizing the establishment of 12 Federal Land Banks to provide first mortgage loans. Privately owned, joint-stock land banks could also be chartered under the 1916 law, which aimed to furnish capital for agricultural development. Federal Land Banks' holdings surpassed those of commercial banks by 1927 and in 1930 amounted to over 12 percent of all farm mortgages.

Joint-stock land banks, at their peak at the end of 1927, had less than 7 percent of all farm mortgages outstanding. The successful California Joint Stock Land Bank, started in 1919 by the predecessor of the Bank of America, made long-term credit available at 6 percent. Many of the 83 organized before 1930 failed; others had to resort to drastic measures to avert failure.

Land banks organized under the 1916 law obtained loanable funds by selling bonds secured by first mortgages. They were separate from commercial banks and, unlike the colonial and pre-1861 land banks, were not associated with currency schemes. The federal government's investment in the Federal Land Banks reached a peak of $314 in 1939; they were converted to private ownership in 1947. The joint-stock land banks made no further loans after 1933 and were liquidated completely by 1951.

Short-Term Agricultural Credit

Agricultural loans expanded by $1 billion from 1914 through 1918 and by a further $1.2 billion in the next 18 months. By May 1920, farm prices were two and a half times the 1913 level, only to tumble by more than half in the next 13 months. By mid-1923, short-term bank loans dropped over 20 percent from their peak of $3.9 billion in mid-1920. Even so, commercial banks had about $2.6 billion on their books in the late 1920's, an amount not seen again until 1952.

Farmers had experienced difficulties in arranging loan renewals in periods of credit stringency. The farm price collapse was (erroneously) blamed on lack of credit accommodation. The 1920-1921 depression in agriculture thus brought forth agitation for new sources of intermediate credit, with up to 3 years' maturity. The Agricultural Credits Act of 1923 established 12 federally owned intermediate credit banks, whose service boundaries were identical with those of the Federal Land Banks, to rediscount notes of commercial banks, agricultural credit corporations, and livestock loan companies, as well as to lend directly to cooperative marketing associations.

Urban Real Estate Lending

After 1913 national banks could make real estate loans, but only on "improved and unencumbered farm lands" for up to 5 years. Nonfarm property was made eligible for 1 year first mortgages in 1916, increased to 5 years in 1927. Although other commercial banks continued to have the bulk of real estate loans, by 1930 national banks had five times as much as in 1921.

Bank real estate loans of all types doubled in the aggregate between 1920 and 1929. A real estate boom, which began in Florida in 1920 and California in 1921, spread to most of the nation in the later years of the decade. Urban construction activity was one of the major forces behind the prosperity. Bank holdings of nonfarm mortgages on one- to four-family dwellings were 11.7 percent of the 1929 total; on dwellings for more than four families, their share was 8.4 percent.

The commercial bank share of the sharply rising nonfarm residential mortgage total increased from 8.8 percent in 1920 to 10.7 percent in 1929, when these mortgages represented 8 percent of bank assets, which was double the 1920 proportion. The duration of mortgages extended by banks was 2 to 3 years in the early 1920's and 3½ years by 1930. As the amount loaned was equal to about half of the value of the property, home buyers supplemented these with second and sometimes third mortgages from other sources.

Consumer Loans

Banks began to establish personal loan departments in 1918. Symbolically, the first Richmond bank to offer consumer loans, in 1927, located the department in the basement. National City Bank of New York, the largest in the nation, took the step in 1928, and 200 others followed within a year. Though many departments were discontinued in the next few years of depression, some 157 operating in 1938 had been opened by 1930, over half before 1925.

Bank installment loans to consumers, a mere $19 million in 1920, were ten times as great a decade later; noninstallment loans grew from $285 to $837 million. By 1930 consumer loans amounted to 3 percent of all commercial bank loans, and banks supplied almost one-sixth of all consumer loans. Most of the upsurge in personal loans was from sales finance companies, making mainly auto loans, consumer finance companies; and the Morris Plan "industrial banks," started in 1910 and concentrating on the wage earner.

The satisfactory experience of these lenders, themselves heavy borrowers from banks, taught bankers that personal loans were both safe and profitable. In the 1930's an increasing number of banks consequently changed their attitudes about the appropriateness of consumer loans.

Bankers Acceptances and Commercial Paper

National banks were authorized to issue bankers acceptances for transactions arising out of foreign trade, in 1913, and out of domestic trade, in 1916. London banks had previously been the main source for bankers acceptances, whereby a bank that put its name on a draft agreed to make payment if the firm that was expected to do so failed to meet its obligation. To encourage the use of this credit instrument, Federal Reserve Banks maintained a preferential buying rate, progressively lowered standards of eligibility for purchase, endorsed acceptances sold to foreign central banks, and entered into repurchase agreements with dealers.

The framers of the Federal Reserve Act had hoped that markets would develop in all twelve Reserve Bank cities, but only New York had an active one in the 1920's. The several hundred accepting banks in the early 1920's dwindled to some 164 by the end of 1930. Most of the business was done by 40-50 major banks. The $1 billion of bankers acceptances outstanding in 1920 was not surpassed until 1927. The peak of $1.7 billion in 1929 rivalled London's volume.

The Federal Reserve Banks bought from 26 to 60 percent of the bills drawn between 1916 and 1924, and 20 to 50 percent in the next 7 years, owning 22 percent at the end of 1929. Subsequently the Federal Reserve's buying rate was held slightly above the market rate. Commercial banks acquiring bankers acceptances could sell them to the Federal Reserve Banks when necessary. Accepting banks came to hold over half of the shrunken volume after 1932—$400 million were outstanding in 1935 and only $210 million in 1940—whereas in 1929 they had only 11 percent.

Commercial paper was at a peak of $1.3 billion in 1920, used by about 4,400 borrowers. Beginning in the mid-1920's, more financing was done through the upstart bankers acceptance market than in the venerable commercial paper market. Volume was down to $334 million by 1929. In the slack conditions of the 1930's, few borrowers found it worthwhile to sell dealer-placed commercial paper—only 734 firms in 1940, aggregating $218 million.

Brokers' Loans in the Great Bull Market

Before 1914 the call loan had served as the main type of secondary reserve for banks. As war loomed and European investors sold vast quantities of securities, the New York Stock Exchange closed on 31 July 1914. Until trading was partially resumed 4½ months later, call loans secured by investment securities could not be liquidated, creating a prejudice against relying on call loans as secondary reserves. This was dispelled by experience during 1920-1921, when bankers could turn stock market loans into cash. Deposits held with correspondent banks, on the other hand, were unavailable for a time, and supposedly self-liquidating commercial loans turned out to be frozen.

The sponsors of the Federal Reserve Act hoped that banks would devote less of their funds to financing the security markets. Instead, loans on security collateral, 27.5 percent of total national bank loans in 1915, were 28.8 percent in 1925 and came to be 34.6 percent in 1929.[2] The 50 percent rise in common stock prices between 1923 and 1926, and again from 1926 to 1928, was climaxed by a further gain of 25 percent in the first nine months of 1929. Member firms of the New York Stock Exchange required a minimum margin of 20 percent for most of the 1920's, raising it to 25 percent in mid-1929. With a 25 percent margin, a customer trading for a rise could borrow three-quarters of the purchase price of a stock. Call loan rates, a sensitive barometer of money market conditions, had been as high as 20 percent earlier in 1929 but were only 6-12 percent by August.

Nonbank lenders, mainly nonfinancial corporations, became very important sources of funds in the call loan market toward the end of the 1920's, providing 70 percent of the $9.2 billion total of loans to brokers and dealers in late October 1929. Member banks in New York City reported, in mid-October, brokers' loans of $1.1 billion for their own account, $1.8 billion for out-of-town banks, and $3.9 billion placed "on account of others." These nonbank sources had financed 85 percent of the increase in the preceding year. In the last week of October 1929, nonbank lenders recalled over one-third of their funds in the wake of the sharpest price drop in Wall Street's history. New York banks filled the gap created by this withdrawal. Lenders suffered few losses as the call loans had been amply secured, and enforcement of a good margin was easy.

One of the main responsibilities given the Federal Reserve, was to prevent speculation "from making undue inroad upon the preserves of legitimate business finance. Accordingly in 1929 the system was concerned that the absorption of funds in stock speculation would raise the cost of credit for legitimate uses. Member banks seeking discounts at the central bank—over half were doing so at one time or other in 1929—were admonished if they held collateral loans while in debt to the Federal Reserve.

Brokers' loans made by member banks had ranged from 9 to 14 percent of total loans in the late 1920's. As a share of total loans and investments of member banks, brokers' loans reached a peak of 7.2 percent at the beginning of 1929, dropping to 4.3 percent by the end of 1930.

Actually, loans secured by stock collateral did not diminish funds available for other uses or raise interest rates levels. Already in March 1920 the New York Federal Reserve Bank had explained to the Senate that call money rates "do not determine and have not exerted an important influence on the rates for commercial borrowings; it is the universal custom of the banks to satisfy first the commercial needs of their customers." As long as call loans were important, however, they aroused doubts and misgivings among a wide public.

Federal Funds

A new money market instrument, federal funds, made its appearance in the 1920's.[3] Depending on a commercial bank's reserve position and needs, these balances at the Federal Reserve Bank might be bought (borrowed) or sold (loaned out). In the early summer of 1921 some New York City member banks had excess reserves because of depressed conditions, while others were borrowing at the discount window of the New York Federal Reserve Bank. Borrowers found it to be less troublesome to buy federal funds instead.

Local markets also developed in Boston, Philadelphia, Chicago, and San Francisco. Volume averaged $40-$80 million a day, rising to a minimum of $100 million in the late 1920's and sometimes to as much as $250 million. Despite this sharp growth, the federal funds market was quite small compared with what it was to become a generation later and with other open market instruments in the 1920's. In 1928-1929 the federal funds rate was often above the Federal Reserve discount rate, as some borrowers lacked eligible paper and others wished to avoid criticism at the Federal Reserve for borrowing. During the Great Depression, the federal funds market almost disappeared, reviving somewhat for a time during 1937-1942, and enjoying a resurgence in the 1950's.

Rediscounting

Banks had learned to use the Federal Reserve as a source of funds during World War I. Rediscounts reached a peak of $2.8 billion in October-November 1920, an amount well in excess of the total member bank reserves, despite a record of 7 percent rate on such loans. By the end of January 1922, rediscounts dropped below $1 billion for the first time since June 1918. Borrowing next exceeded $1 billion in May 1928 and in most months thereafter until the end of 1929.

System officials did not dispute the appropriateness of borrowing for seasonal, temporary, or emergency needs. The Federal Reserve did, however, oppose banks' taking advantage of the generally prevalent differential between money market rates and the rediscount rate, or remaining continuously indebted to the district bank. Meanwhile during the 1920's the system succeeded in sharply reducing seasonal stresses in the money market, and the corresponding seasonal movements which had earlier characterized interest rates.

Security Investments

"Bonds for secondary reserves" was a popular slogan of the 1920's. Conservative country bankers, seeking to diminish their dependence on local loans, invested in marketable corporate bonds, viewing them as a source of liquidity. When all types of medium- and long-term debt of nonfinancial corporations are combined, commercial banks held 8.4 percent of the $19 billion outstanding in 1920, and 9.5 percent of 1930's $30 billion.

Between 1922 and 1929 the corporate bond portfolios of the banks grew by $1.3 billion, more than any other type of investment. The increase was especially notable in public utilities and manufacturing bonds, yet bank holdings of 12.4 percent of all outstanding corporate bonds were a slightly lower proportion than in 1912. Corporate bonds, 8 percent of total bank assets in 1920, were over 11 percent in 1930.

Despite a 36 percent decline in the federal debt outstanding between 1919 and 1930, bank holdings of United States government bonds in 1928 again equalled 1919's $4.9 billion, remaining at that level until the latter part of 1930. Banks owned almost 29 percent of the outstanding federal debt in 1929, whereas in 1912 they held 65 percent of a very much smaller total. At 7 percent of total bank assets in 1929, holdings were double the 1912 proportion. Among national banks the proportion not held for the purpose of securing national bank notes rose sharply, from 3.2 percent in 1913 to 30.3 percent in 1930, evidencing the increasing popularity of federal bonds.

Total state and local government bonds increased from 2.4 percent of bank assets in 1912 to 3.1 percent in 1929. Nevertheless the bank share of all municipal bonds outstanding was the same at both dates, 12 percent.

In the 1920's New York became a center of international finance, rivalling London in importance. A flood of new foreign issues were now being offered on Wall Street, over $1 billion worth in each year from 1924 through 1928.

Foreign government and private securities were held in negligible amounts before World War I, representing 2.3 percent of total national bank investments in 1913. By 1929 all commercial banks had almost $1 billion worth, 1.5 percent of their assets and about 7.7 percent of all national bank investments. Many of these issues went into default as international trade collapsed in the early 1930's.

The expertise developed by large banks in the securities field was applied to the underwriting of new issues. Commercial banks' investment affiliates came to surpass the regular investment banks' volume by the late 1920's.

Banks as Department Stores of Finance

The concept of banks as financial department stores antedates 1914, but only after 1920 did the practice become widespread, especially in urban centers. By diversifying their services, banks aimed to increase their usefulness to customers and to achieve more rapid growth of earnings.

Beginning in 1915 a national bank could open a trust department after securing permission from the Federal Reserve Board. In 1920 a total of 1,294 national banks had such permits; and almost twice that number had permits by 1930, about one-fourth of all national banks and including most of the sizable ones. Safe deposit boxes were offered by some national banks even before the 1927 law specifically authorized this activity. The same was true of underwriting activities. Thus an up-to-date bank of the late 1920's was "equipped to render any form of financial service . . . a composite of the old commercial bank, savings bank, trust company, bond house, insurance company, safe deposit company, and mortgage house."[4]

Par Collection of Checks

Cartel agreements, or "business ethics," had earlier imposed high if not excessive check collection charges on American business.[5] Banks called upon to make payment through the mail generally deducted an "exchange charge." The Federal Reserve was expected to change this. In June 1915, member banks were asked to remit checks at par (face value), but only one-fourth of them agreed to it. A year later, compulsory par remittance was instituted. By the end of 1916 some 16,000 banks, including a great proportion of non-members, were on the par list. The Federal Reserve Banks eliminated all charges for check collection in 1918 to encourage maximum use of their clearing facilities.

There were 10,000 nonpar banks at the end of 1918 when a vigorous drive to make par collection universal got under way. Within a year the number had shrunk to 3,996, and by the beginning of 1921, to 1,755 (out of 30,253 commercial banks). Uncooperative banks were confronted with demands for payment in currency at face value over their counter, as required by common law.

Nonmember banks triumphed in 1923, however, when the Federal Reserve Board instructed the Federal Reserve Banks to discontinue over-the-counter collection. By the end of 1925 the nonpar list had expanded to almost 4,000. The earlier expectation of the Federal Reserve that before long almost all banks would remit at par was not realized because of political interference on behalf of the nonpar banks.

Service Charges on Checking Accounts

The slogan "pay by check and have a receipt" popularized small checking accounts among households, including industrial workers. Bankers then discovered that such business could be unprofitable. Half of the accounts in nine Minnesota country banks had balances of less than $50.00 in 1930.

Analysis of customers' accounts and imposition of service charges had already been proposed in the late nineteenth century. The practice became important only in the 1920's. A guide intended to instruct smaller banks in particular was published by the American Bankers Association in 1925, at a time when some 100 cities throughout the country were known to be imposing service charges. By 1929 over 500 localities were doing so, and many more would have, were it not for severe competitive conditions. At least some banks in 40 states were usually collecting $.50 cents or $1.00 when the balance fell below $50.00 or $100.00.

Interbank Deposits

The feared loss of correspondent bank deposits materialized to a considerable extent within a few years after the opening of the Federal Reserve Banks. Member bank deposits held in other American banks represented 14.4 percent of their total deposits in 1915, falling to half as much in 1920, and to 6.2 percent by 1930. For all commercial banks combined, interbank deposits dropped from 15 percent of total deposits in 1914 to slightly over 10 percent in 1920, remaining near that proportion during the decade.

Government Deposits and the Independent Treasury

Public monies were received and disbursed by 850 regular national banks depositaries in 1913, twice as many as in 1908. As late as mid-1920 there were 587. Not until January 1916, over a year after the opening of the Federal Reserve Banks, did the Treasury Department make much use of them for business previously handled by the depositary national banks.

Federal Reserve Banks were not originally intended as a substitute for the subtreasury system. As events unfolded, however, the superfluity of the old arrangement became apparent. The nine subtreasuries were finally closed down between October 1920 and February 1921, and most of their monetary and depository functions were turned over to the Federal Reserve Banks. The role and significance of the Independent Treasury System had been diminishing gradually ever since the Civil War, but it lingered on for 75 years. Even after 1921, the Treasury Department found it necessary to use several hundred national bank depositories in localities with considerable federal government business but no Federal Reserve Bank or branch.

War loan depositaries were used in 1917 but declined sharply after 1918, becoming important once again in 1943. In 1950 the War Loan Accounts with commercial banks were renamed Treasury Tax and Loan Accounts, to hold income and retirement taxes as well as bond receipts. What had been originally an emergency measure thus developed into a permanent instrument, the Treasury wishing to avoid having a disruptive impact on money markets.

Time Deposits

The Federal Reserve Act of 1913 explicitly authorized national banks to assume time deposit liabilities. The 5 percent reserve requirement, reduced to 3 percent in 1917, was much lower than for demand deposits. Already by 1912 time deposits had become almost one-third of the total deposits, excluding those owing to banks and the United States government. The proportion was 34 percent in 1920 and over 40 percent by 1930, with national banks showing the greatest gain.

The Federal Reserve Board expressed concern in 1927 over "the constantly growing tendency to transfer what are in effect demand deposits into so-called time certificates or savings accounts." Commercial banks, interested in benefiting from the lower reserve requirement, encouraged the transfer. Banks advertised heavily for "savings deposits"; some, especially in large cities, allowed customers to write checks against time deposits.

Between 1921 and 1929, time and savings deposits held by individuals at commercial banks doubled. Mutual savings banks' deposits grew only 60 percent, while the then small savings and loan industry tripled in size. The $15 billion of these deposits at commercial banks in 1929 equalled the combined claims on the latter two specialized savings institutions.

Clearinghouse Agreements and Competition

It was not a legitimate function of a clearinghouse to compel members to pay identical interest on deposits, the manager of New York's had testified in 1912 before the Pujo Committee. By 1918, however, the New York Clearing House had fixed maximum rates, varying from 1 to 3 percent depending on the 90-day commercial paper note, without objection from the Federal Reserve Board. Disagreements among the banks prevented the Baltimore Clearinghouse from regulating interest rates before 1927. Detroit, like most other clearinghouses, had a maximum somewhat above New York and also enforced uniform charges for small deposit accounts and for collection services.

Banks in Cleveland and New York had gentlemen's agreements not to encroach on an area already dominated by another bank. In Detroit, which lacked such an understanding, excessive branching brought low profits or even losses in several locations. Clearinghouse regulation of interest paid on deposits and on minimum exchange charges had sought to eliminate cutthroat competition. Notwithstanding the uniform schedules and regulations, the situation in most cities was said to be one of "wholesome competition."[6] Large banks reached out for the business of significant customers in other major centers. In 1922 about twelve of the larger New York City banks had offices in such places as Chicago, Detroit, Boston, Cleveland, and Buffalo.

Position of New York

With but 1.2 percent of all the commercial banks in the nation, New York

City had 25.4 percent of their resources in 1900; the shares in 1929 were 0.5 percent and 22.6 percent respectively. The sponsors of the Federal Reserve Act sought to diminish the power of Wall Street, and to a lesser extent of other financial centers; they did not have much success. In 1930 eight of the twelve largest banks in the country were located in Manhattan. Indeed, New York became slightly more important after 1914 relative to other centers as holder of bank balances. A study found that as of 1932 the New York money market had actually increased in importance.

New Bank Formation

By 1920 there was a bank for every 3,500 Americans. This was the culmination of a movement that saw Wisconsin, for example, adding 684 state banks by 1921 to the 143 already there in 1900, while its population grew by a mere 30 percent. Only a fourth of the 827 in 1921 had as much as $50,000 in capital. Rockland, Wisconsin, with 120 inhabitants, boasted 2 banks in 1920. Sometimes feuding groups would create "spite banks." Americans were known to erect spite fences and even spite towns. Banks chartered for reasons of pique, though, could be a source of failure, as the Study Commission for Indiana Financial Institutions argued in 1932.

The office of the Comptroller of the Currency issued only 21 percent of the 6,109 charters granted from 1921 through 1929; he rejected 30 percent of the applications before him. There was a marked tightening after 1925, Comptroller Joseph McIntosh being of the view that "there is too often a desire to organize banks in localities where the communities are amply served and which would not support new institutions with a likelihood of any fair measure of success." Altogether from 1926 through 1929 the number refused was only 30 less than the 518 national banks approved. Another barrier was erected when some states banned the organization of any new private banks, while permitting existing ones, some 3,500 in 1919, to continue. Texas took this step in 1923, Georgia, in 1960.[7]

The 1920's saw a reversal in the trend toward lower capital requirements which had come to a climax around 1900, though Congress did not eliminate the possibility of opening national banks with $25,000 in capital until 1933. The entry deterring effect of higher minimum capital was recognized by the Economic Policy Commission of the American Bankers Association, but the bankers also sought legislation requiring a demonstration of need before new banks could open. In 1927 this commission called for recognition once and for all of "the damaging consequences of an excessive number of banks."

Need had been incorporated as a criterion in Pennsylvania's bank charter law as early as 1889 and in New Jersey's a decade later. New York's "public convenience and advantage" provision was an aftermath of the Panic of 1907; five more states added such a test by 1909. The wisdom of such a policy was increasingly urged after 1920, but such measures were usually realized only slowly. Thus Virginia's Banking Division recommended the needs test in 1911 and the Virginia Bankers Association, in 1912; not until 1928, however, was the chief bank examiner empowered to refuse a charter application. By 1938 the need criterion was the law in thirty-eight states, most of which also considered the purpose or integrity of the applicants. New bank formation did slow down in the 1920's. Combined with the closing of unsuccessful banks, this brought the population per bank in 1930 to 30 percent above the 1920 level.

Mergers

Despite the organization of over 6,000 new banks in the decade, by 1930 there were 6,600 fewer banks. Failures and mergers account for the decline. Many combinations, especially in the South and the West were prompted by the desire to avert outright failure. Acquisition of branches was another powerful motive. Urban banks aiming to expand their range of services would take the merger path as commercial lenders sought out specialists in savings business or trust activities. On average, about 60 to 75 banks were acquired each year from 1900 through 1909, and twice as many from 1910 through 1918. The annual average for 1919-1920 was 180; for 1921-1925, 330; and for 1926-1930, 550.

The great merger activity in the industrial sector was thus matched by a parallel increase in banking combinations in the 1920's. Indeed some acquisitions reflected a drive for greater size to enable banks to better serve larger business customers. In May 1930, after merging with two New York City trust companies, Chase National Bank became the largest bank in the world. Half a year later two California banks owned by A. P. Giannini were combined to form the Bank of America National Trust and Savings Association. The Bank of Italy, the larger component, had become the largest bank west of Chicago within 16 years of its founding in 1904 in a San Francisco immigrant neighborhood.

In 1920 the 100 largest banks in the United States had about one-fourth of all bank assets and a decade later, around one-third. By 1929, the 2 to 4 largest banks controlled over half of the bank assets in most metropolitan areas and an even greater proportion in smaller cities. This concentration of assets was largely a consequence of mergers.

Branching at Home and Abroad

Branches represented 4 percent of all commercial bank offices in 1920 and 13 percent a decade later. Despite this growth, just over 3 percent of all banks had any branches in 1930, and most of these but a single one.

Intracity branches tripled between 1920 and 1930. Indeed a majority of all branches were in places of 100,000 or more inhabitants. New York, Detroit, Los Angeles, and Philadelphia between them had over one third. Two-thirds of all the branches in the nation at the end of 1929 were in the states of those metropolises plus Ohio. Out-of-town branching grew more rapidly than in-city after 1925. Still, by 1930 fewer than a third of all branches were outside the head-office city, with California having half of the national total.

When the Federal Reserve Board suggested in 1916 that a national bank be allowed to open branches in the city or county of its head office, the American Bankers Association was aroused to vote against any form of branch banking, reiterating this position in 1922. By 1930, however, the membership was prepared to accept "community-wide branch banking in metropolitan areas and county-wide branch banking in rural districts where economically justifiable." At that time, ten states allowed city or contiguous territory branching, and nine others allowed statewide branching.

To meet the challenge of state branch banks, in 1921 Comptroller Daniel Crissinger authorized national banks to open tellers windows limited to accepting deposits and cashing checks where a state permitted its banks to branch. Full-power branches were authorized for the first time in 1927, but these were confined to the head-office city in those states that allowed it for their banks. Chairman Louis McFadden of the House Banking Committee and ex-president of the First National Bank of Canton, Pennsylvania assured his fellow representatives that the measure was really "anti-branch banking ... severely restricting [its] further spread."

Opponents considered branch banking as "monopolistic cream-skimming," in the phrase of Andrew Frame of Wisconsin's Waukesha National Bank. Comptroller Dawes in 1924 echoed the view that branch banks would secure the "easiest obtainable and most desirable business ... leaving the unit bank to take care of the enterprises of the town which have not already reached a condition of independence." Like many others, Dawes was convinced that "the rapid economic development of America has been largely due to the policy of the pioneering unit banks which recognized the principle of service." President Hoover reaffirmed in 1929 that "one of the fundamentals of the American credit system [was that bank credit] be subject to the restraint of local interest and public opinion."

The prevalent hostility precluded Giannini from realizing one of his fondest dreams. After buying a large Wall Street bank in 1928, his holding company was renamed Transamerica (today's Western Bancorporation) as indicative of its objective. In 1930 Giannini urged nationwide branch banking before the House Banking Committee. Though his goal was not to be achieved, he could boast the largest branch system in the country. Such was the bustle in Giannini's branches that Californians used to tell the story of a stranger who saw large numbers entering and leaving and concluded, erroneously, that a run on the bank was under way. At the end of 1929 the Bank of Italy had 287 branches while the Corn Exchange Bank, the largest network in New York City, comprised only 67.

Meanwhile the first overseas branch of an American bank was opened in 1887. There were only 26 by 1914, half of these in the Far East. National banks were empowered to open branches outside the United States in 1913. By the end of 1920, American banks had 181, a number not attained again until 1965; 122 of these were in Latin America. Overseas branches totalled only 107 in mid-1926; and in 1939, 110. For decades New York's National City Bank has had the largest number of foreign branches.

Chain and Group Banking

Chains, uniting several banks under common ownership or direction, already existed in the 1890's but became particularly notable in the 1920's. As Illinois held fast to unit banking, Chicago has been the largest city whose banks are precluded from branching. However, by 1930, 94 of its 206 banks (representing about half of Chicago's banking resources) were associated with chains or, in a few cases, holding companies. Dozens of banks opening in new sections of Chicago in the years following World War I were more or less closely linked to the downtown giants.

Chain banking declined in relative importance in the late 1920's while holding companies, "group banking," became more popular as a device for linking banks. The stock market boom facilitated the financing of acquisitions; pressures felt by rural banks made them eager to join. Most of the major holding companies that were to be important in the next 35 years were organized in the late 1920's in states with limited or no branching. Some group banks, like the Minneapolis-based Northwest Bancorporation and First Bank Stock Corporation, bestrode many states along the northern tier;

others, also founded in 1929, like the Marine Midland Corporation in New
York and BancOhio, confined their bank subsidiaries within the boundaries
of the state.

Dual Banking System

The advantages previously enjoyed by banks with state charters in fiduciary
activities, time deposits, and real estate loans were reduced in 1913. Nevertheless, by 1919 the national banks' share of total commercial bank assets fell
below 50 percent for the first time since 1865, sinking to 44.4 percent by
1926. The 1927 McFadden Act was intended "to put new life into the
national banking system," the House Banking Committee explained. Federally chartered banks were given increased powers to invest in, and underwrite, securities; to make real estate loans; to branch; and to lend more than
had previously been permitted any one borrower. The Senate Banking Committee was satisfied that the measure modernized the National Bank Act
"along the lines of conservative banking, and without any deviation from the
high standard which has been set by the national banking system."

Defections continued, however, as the 1927 act did not remove all of the
competitive disadvantages suffered by national banks. By 1929 the national
bank share—43.7 percent of all commercial bank assets—was slightly less than
in 1926. Regretfully the Comptroller of the Currency listed 127 national
banks with assets of at least $5 million ("large" in an era when the median
size was less than one-tenth as great) that had converted to state banks in the
decade ending October 31, 1929.

From 1900 through 1920, 2,828 state and private banks had converted
to national charters, many seeking to escape from the burdens of deposit
guaranty schemes instituted by several states. After 1920, though, there were
no new schemes to frighten away state banks. During the decade every state
was trying "to build up its own banking system."[8] That problem did not
concern the Federal Reserve as much as it did the Comptroller of the Currency; many former national banks continued their membership in the system. Indeed, member banks had 64.3 percent of all commercial bank deposits
in mid-1920 and 69.8 percent a decade later. The Federal Reserve's success,
important for effective monetary policy making, occurred despite the reduction of reserve requirements in some states after 1913.

Bank Examinations

With the abolition of the fee system in 1913, examiners were now required to spend as much time as was needed "to acquire a thorough knowledge" of a bank's condition, the Comptroller of the Currency reported in 1915. "Constructive guidance" was offered, in addition to verification of the bank's condition. In 1931, Comptroller John Pole noted that "his primary function is that of a bank supervisor." Federal supervision in the 1920's reflected "a reasonable degree of intrusion into the affairs of banks."[9]

The 1920's saw a marked upgrading in the quality of state banking departments. Overall, state examinations had not been as effective as federal in protecting depositors and bank shareholders. Yet the 1920's and 1930's saw a "progressive improvement," much of the credit for which belonged to the high standards of the national banking system."[10]

Failure

Notwithstanding improved government supervision and general prosperity from 1921 to 1929, except for two minor downturns, almost one-fourth of the banks operating in mid-1920 had to suspend operations by the end of the decade. On average, at least one bank closed every day of the year. In 1926, as many as 2.7 banks failed each day. The annual rate of bank failure, 1.97 percent, contrasted with 1.06 percent in commercial enterprises, whereas from 1892-1920 businesses had failed relatively more frequently than banks. One consequence was a great increase in banking by mail, as depositors sought out banks they considered safer than the local one.

From 1921 through 1929, over 5.400 banks, holding in excess of $1.5 billion in deposits, suspended, a total far in excess of the aggregate for the preceding 56 years. The suspension rate from 1898 through 1920 was never as high as 1.0 percent; from 1921 through 1929 it was as low as 1.3 percent only in 1922.

The situation did not arouse much concern at the time. The disappearance of small, weak banks would only strengthen the banking system, it was thought. National banks averaged profits of 8 percent on total capital from 1919 through 1929. Failures, in the Federal Reserve view, resulted from bad management and dislocations brought about by World War I. Few suspected that worse was to come.

Notes

1. Ray B. Westerfield, *Money, Credit, and Banking* (New York: Ronald, 1938), p. 297.

2. Member banks decreased the proportion of loans on securities from 39.3 percent at the end of 1928 to 38.1 percent in mid-1929. It should be noted that not all such loans were for Wall Street speculation.

3. An antecedent was the Boston Clearinghouse's unique arrangement during the period 1880-1910. Balances would be borrowed and lent at the morning exchanges and settled the same day by orders of the clearinghouse.

4. George W. Dowrie, *American Monetary and Banking Policies* (New York: Longmans Green, 1930), p. 25.

5. H. Parker Willis, "The Federal Reserve Act," *American Economic Review* 4 (1914), p. 21.

6. Dowrie, *Monetary and Banking Policies*, p. 69.

7. As recently as mid-1963 there were 55 private banks operating in Georgia; 22 of these had been organized since 1949. A 1966 law ordered the incorporation of all private banks by the start of 1968. See William Sherard Rawson, "Entry, Exit and Structural Evolution of Markets: A Case Study of Georgia Banking, 1900 to 1964," Ph.D. Diss., Duke University, 1967, pp. 178-180.

8. Charles S. Tippetts, *State Banks and the Federal Reserve System* (New York: Van Nostrand, 1929), p. 2.

9. Dowrie, *Monetary and Banking Policies*, p. 117.

10. Charles O. Hardy, in *Government and Economic Life*, Vol. 1, Leverett Lyons et al. (Washington: Brookings, 1940), p. 163.

CHAPTER XIII

BANKING COLLAPSE 1930-1933

Rising Tide of Failures 1930-1932

Small rural banks dominated the failure records for the decade ending in the fall of 1930. November 1930 saw the closing of more than twice as many banks as in any previous month since data began to be collected in 1921. December was even worse: 352 banks with over $370 million in deposits, about three-fourths of 1 percent of total United States bank deposits. Half of the deposits were in New York City's Bank of United States, ranking twenty-eighth in the nation at the end of 1929, the largest bank to fail up to that time.[1] The early months of 1931 saw an encouraging drop in failures, but in March they turned up again. After a June high, they declined in the summer.

Britain's abandonment of the gold standard in September 1931 set off a wave of uncertainty and a large outflow of gold to Europe. Just a few months prior to January 1932, United States government bonds declined 10 percent in price, and high grade corporate securities shrank 20 percent as a consequence of a selling wave by banks anxious to strengthen their cash position. The winter of 1931-1932 was marked by "the most desperate scramble for liquidity we have ever experienced."[2] Over 1,800 banks, with $1.4 billion in deposits, some 4 percent of the total, suspended in the half year ending 31 January 1932.

The 1931 suspensions were four times the average number for

1921-1929; deposits involved exceeded the aggregate for those 9 years. Beyond the direct losses and frozen deposits in failed banks, the policy of restricting credit that many banks adopted as a defensive measure generated serious problems for the economy. As banks sold bonds and reduced loans, deposits contracted by 16 percent in the second half of 1931 alone.

After prompting from President Hoover, large banks established a National Credit Corporation in October 1931. To his disappointment and dismay, the cooperative venture fizzled after a few weeks of lending $135 million against security collateral not usually acceptable. Hoover's memoirs recall that "the business world threw up their hands and asked for governmental action." The president responded with two important measures. January 1932 brought forth a new major federal lending agency, the Reconstruction Finance Corporation (RFC). Late in February the Glass-Steagall Act authorized the Federal Reserve Banks to use government securities as collateral for Federal Reserve Notes and permitted rediscounts to be made, at a penalty rate, on ineligible assets.

Federal Reserve open market purchases—an unprecedented $1 billion of government securities between April and August 1932—came none too soon. Bank loans had shrunk by one fourth in the year ending in mid-1932. Secretary of the Treasury Andrew Mellon advised President Hoover that what was called for at the time was to liquidate labor, stocks, the farmers, and real estate. Mellon and other liquidation advocates might not be displeased by the sharp deflationary trend, but it was accompanied by massive, rising unemployment.

The Federal Reserve authorities saw themselves as lenders of last resort, their chief responsibility being to keep the Federal Reserve Banks, holders of the ultimate reserves of the nation, liquid and solvent. Money supply regulation was distinctly not a primary objective. As their then chief research economist, Emanuel Goldenweiser, wrote years later, "commercial bank concepts were simply being applied to a central bank." Until amended in February 1932 meticulous statutory rules of 1913 may have prevented the Federal Reserve from lending to otherwise sound banks. In Goldenweiser's judgment, the law was being interpreted "rather liberally in efforts to help out member banks known to be fundamentally sound but in difficulties."[3]

Yet many member banks found credit more readily available at a correspondent bank than from the Federal Reserve. Clark Warburton, a Federal Deposit Insurance Corporation (FDIC) economist, argued that the Federal Reserve Banks had "discouraged rediscounting almost to the point of prohibition."[4] Except toward the end of 1931, member bank borrowings were a fraction of the 1928 and 1929 volume, amounting to 5-10 percent of eligible paper, excluding Treasury bonds, and 2-3 percent if they are included. Low short-term money market rates deceived the Federal Reserve Board into believing that an easy monetary policy was being pursued.

The RFC strengthened the confidence of depositors and succeeded in holding down suspensions for almost a year. From February to the end of 1932, the RFC authorized almost $900 million in loans to assist over 4,000 banks striving to remain open. Congress hampered its usefulness in August by ordering the release of the list of borrowers each month. Many banks sorely in need of help stayed away from the RFC because of pride or fear or both.

Local moratoria had already been declared in 1932 in a number of communities in the Midwest, many on the pretext of celebrating the bicentennial of Washington's birth 22 February 1932. Nevada proclaimed the first statewide moratorium on 31 October 1932. The 1,453 suspensions in 1932 were 37 percent below 1931's swollen numbers; more important, deposits involved were 60 percent below 1931's. Yet Hoover's description of the 1932 record as the "normal" failure rate hardly seems appropriate.

Tragic Holiday

Scene 1 of the final act of the banking collapse drama took place in the automobile capital of the world. The sharp slump in sales had seriously affected mortgages on local homes and Detroit's municipal obligations. Hoover's emissaries had explained to Henry Ford that failure of the Guardian Union group's banks would topple the other major Detroit holding company, First Wayne, and force the closing of other banks in Michigan and neighboring states. Ford, however, refused to assist the Guardian Union group further by subordinating his deposits so that the RFC could make additional loans. He was quite prepared to "let the crash come." Ford as the largest taxpayer in the country could see no reason why he "should bail the government out of its loans to banks."

Michigan's governor declared a statewide bank holiday, originally from 14-22 February 1933, that had to be extended. The two Detroit giants never reopened, but on liquidation depositors received back everything owed them plus 5 percent interest.[5]

Panic reached a peak in the first three days of March 1933. Over the nation, deposits were being withdrawn at the rate of 10 percent a week—in excess of $800 million on March 2 and 3. The Federal Reserve Banks lost $425 million in gold in 9 days ending March 3. In February their gold holdings had dropped below $3 billion for the first time in years.

Hoover rejected the advice of his Secretary of the Treasury and the

Federal Reserve Board to order a nationwide bank holiday. The governors of New York and Illinois waited until the eve of inauguration day to declare a bank holiday, thereby shutting down most of the nation's correspondent banks. As Roosevelt took the oath of office on 4 March 1933, almost every bank in the country outside of Pittsburgh was either closed by state order or restricting payments to depositors. The new president declared a 4 day moratorium, later extended to 9, on Sunday March 5.

Americans had been led to believe that the elastic currency feature of the Federal Reserve Act had solved the problem of panics.[6] Yet less than two decades later, all the commercial banks of the country, as well as the Federal Reserve Banks, were ordered to close for what turned out to be 6 to 8 business days. During this period, withdrawals were allowed only for routine purposes, but depositors were philosophical. The emergency measures to deal with the banking crisis had the support of all segments of the population.

In a nationwide radio address on 12 March 1933, Roosevelt announced the reopening schedule: the next morning for licensed banks in the twelve major centers where Federal Reserve Banks were headquartered, March 14 for banks in some 250 other cities with recognized clearinghouses; and the March 15 for licensed banks in all other localities. Every member bank had to apply for a license attesting to its soundness. Despite the haste with which examinations had to be made, only 221 licensed banks (15 of which were member banks), with $152 million in deposits, suspended by the end of 1933.

In the first ten weeks of 1933, of the 17,796 commercial banks previously in operation, 447 suspended, merged, or liquidated. Some 11,878 of the 17,349 in existence 11 days earlier were licensed to reopen at the conclusion of the bank holiday on March 15. As of 12 April, 4,215 banks, with about $4 billion in deposits, were unlicensed. There were still about 1,900 without licenses at the end of 1933, but their deposits of $1.25 billion amounted to less than 4 percent of all deposits in commercial banks.

In his March 12 speech, the president appealed for a return of currency hoards to the banks, assuring the public that unsound banks would not be permitted to reopen. Doubt concerning a bank's solvency was resolved in its favor. Years later Jesse Jones, former head of the RFC, wrote that it could be charged that a fraud had been perpetrated when the nation was given to understand that only sound banks would be licensed. Jones argued that not until 14 months later, after massive infusion of RFC funds could all the operating banks be considered solvent. Yet who is to say that Roosevelt was wrong when he assured his audience that it was "safer to keep your money in a reopened bank than under a mattress."

In January and February 1933 the public's desire for currency took the form of a specific preference for gold for the first time since the stock market collapse. As compared with the end of 1932, coin holdings rose by $100 million to reach $284 million (the highest level since April 1918), while gold certificates rose 8 percent. This development "represents something more than the hoarding of currency which reflects a distrust of banks; it represents in addition a distrust of the currency itself and it is inspired by talk of devaluation of the dollar and inflation of the currency," George Harrison, head of the Federal Reserve Bank of New York, noted privately.[7] As various state holidays were declared, time-honored substitutes for unavailable currency were resorted to. Perhaps $1 billion in scrip was in circulation through the federal bank holiday.

Roosevelt's soothing words and bold actions put an end to the panic. By April 5, over $1.2 billion in currency had been returned to the Federal Reserve Banks. In mid-May only about $250 million of the currency withdrawn by the public between February 7 and March 4 was still outstanding.

At the time of the bank holiday, Congress would have agreed to transfer the banks to public ownership, Rexford Tugwell, a member of Roosevelt's brain trust, noted, regretting that the president had not asked for it. Instead "capitalism was saved in eight days," as Raymond Moley, an influential adviser to Roosevelt at the time, later boasted. The policies followed had indeed been "thoroughly conservative" and their execution was marked by "swiftness and boldness," as Moley claimed. A leading conservative financial journalist considered the resolution of the banking crisis "the greatest single achievement of the Roosevelt administration."[8] Yet, at the time no fundamental reform of the banking system was undertaken other than deposit insurance, and this measure had been opposed by the president.

RFC Rescue Efforts

Deposit insurance was a tangible bulwark for a badly shaken public in need of more than verbal reassurances. Even earlier, the Emergency Banking Act of 9 March 1933 (passed by Congress in exactly one day) authorized RFC investment in the preferred stock and capital notes of commercial banks. By mid-1935, when this program ended, almost half the banks in the country— 7,115 in all—had been strengthened to the tune of $1.1 billion. RFC investments were equal to one-third of the capital of all banks in mid-1932. Losses and chargeoffs turned out to be insignificant. The same was true of the $1.1 billion in RFC loans to 4,922 open banks.

Loans to closed banks for the purpose of providing depositors with funds came to $80 million during the Hoover administration. In the first 7 months after the bank holiday, the RFC disbursed over $900 million more to depositors in 2,421 closed banks. To speed up these operations, the Deposit Liquidation Board was set up in October 1933.

Shareholders in national banks had always been liable for an additional amount up to the par value of their stock to pay off creditors in the event of failure.[9] By 1930, all but ten states had similar provisions, usually in the form of "double liability," as in the federal law. To encourage investment in bank stock after the collapse, the banking acts of 1933 and 1935 eliminated double liability on newly issued stock. Instead, national banks were to accumulate a surplus at least equal to the par value of the capital. The states followed suit.

Traditionally, bank capital had consisted of common stock supplemented by retained earnings. By the end of 1934, however, preferred stock comprised almost 11 percent of the capital funds of member banks and subordinated notes and debentures another 2.5 percent. The RFC bought $782 million of preferred stock from 4,202 banks and $434 million of capital notes or debentures from 2,913 banks. These emergency devices to restore depleted capital funds were retired over the next quarter of a century. They had a revival under more auspicious circumstances after Comptroller James Saxon authorized their issue on a permanent basis in 1962, and many states followed his example.

The FDIC looked for a minimum of net sound capital, after adjusting the nominal capital for poor assets, equal to 10 percent of the appraised value of a bank's assets. In 1939, of the nation's 13,589 insured banks, 2,884 fell below this standard. Another 3,000 did not have adequate capital in light of such factors as the nature and quality of their assets, in the judgment of the FDIC. World War II earnings brought about a marked improvement in the capital position of commercial banks.

Deposit Insurance

Between 1886 and 1933, 150 deposit insurance proposals were introduced in the Congress. Meanwhile Oklahoma set up the first state scheme in 1908, followed by Kansas, Nebraska, and Texas in 1909; Mississippi, 1914; South Dakota, 1915; North Dakota, 1917; and Washington, 1917. Only Kansas and Washington did not compel their banks to join the deposit guaranty system. All eight succumbed to the heavy losses in the failure wave of the 1920's and early 1930's, starting with Oklahoma in 1923. This lack of success experienced by the states was used as an argument against federal legislation. The vice president of Cleveland Trust Company pointed out that "there is scarcely any sort of legislation, except that of national prohibition, with which we have had more thorough experience or a more sweeping record of unbroken failure." [10] Bankers also felt that well-run institutions should not have to pay for the bad, dishonest, incompetent ones.

Public clamor for deposit insurance won the day, however, in the Banking Act of June 1933. To restore public confidence, banks were admitted to insurance on a showing of bare solvency, based on intrinsic rather than prevailing market value of assets. The RFC helped the FDIC realize its objective for insured banks of "net sound capital" equal to at least 10 percent of deposits. [11]

Deposit coverage took effect 1 January 1934, limited to the first $2,500 in an account. The limit was raised to $5,000 in August 1934, to $10,000 in September 1950, and to $20,000 in December 1969. At the start of 1934, 87 percent of all commercial banks, holding 97 percent of all deposits, became insured. Bankers were troubled, however, by their liability to further insurance assessments (beyond the one quarter percent of covered deposits they had to pay in) in the event the fund dropped below one quarter percent. This provision was eliminated when the Banking Act of 1935 set a premium of one twelfth percent of total deposits.

Only 7 percent of the commercial banks, with an even smaller proportion of deposits, were not insured when permanent arrangements took effect on 23 August 1935. For most of the years since 1934 the fund has equalled about 0.8 percent of total deposits in insured commercial banks and, after 1940, about 1.5 percent of total insured deposits. Insured deposits represented about 42 percent of total deposits in insured commercial banks in 1936, climbing to 56 percent at the end of 1950, the same proportion as in 1972.

Through the end of 1972, the FDIC was called upon to make disbursements of $716 million to depositors in 496 insured commercial banks, whose deposits totalled $1.1 billion. The net loss to the corporation was about $74 million. Previously, depositors experienced long delays, and the drawnout liquidation process often consumed a large part of the failed bank's assets. Though the FDIC may wait for years to realize on the assets it takes over, insured depositors are paid off quickly.

Federal deposit insurance was enacted against a backdrop of some 4,000 suspensions in 1933, involving deposits of $3.6 billion and eventual losses of over $540 million to depositors. Over half of the $3.5 billion losses from 1865 to 1935 occurred in the 13 years preceding the formation of the FDIC. From 1934 through 1945, a total of 493 banks failed, 97 being noninsured, with deposits of about $540 million and losses under $10 million, which were suffered mostly by depositors in the failed noninsured banks.

Speaking at the December 1931 convention of the American Economic Association, Professor Walter Spahr exclaimed that

> we cannot afford to perpetuate our system of little unit banks, with its amateur bankers, with its inability to cope with modern business problems satisfactorily, and with its tremendous number of bank failures which have caused unmeasured losses and untold misery for millions of depositors, borrowers, stockholders, officers, and directors, who have striven valiantly to accumulate a little surplus which will afford them security in the evening time of their lives.

Deposit insurance took the edge off the losses and misery aspect of this argument. Small unit banks got "a new lease on life," as Yale's Professor Ray Westerfield noted ruefully. As intended by Chairman Henry Steagall of the House Banking Committee in 1933, the FDIC has served to "preserve independent dual banking in the United States."

Deposit Rate Ceilings

The spirit of reform engendered by the spectacle of a tottering banking system affected the long controversial practice of paying interest on interbank deposits. After the panic of 1857, the New York Clearing House suggested a ban, arguing that otherwise a bank would be compelled to "expand its operations beyond all prudent bounds." [12] The Comptroller of the Currency, in the aftermath of the panic of 1873, urged clearinghouse members to agree *not* to pay interest. For a time after the panic of 1884, the banks belonging to the New York Clearing House limited payment on bankers' deposits to 2 percent.

The hope that the establishment of the Federal Reserve would lead to a rechanneling of funds away from the Wall Street call loan market was not realized. Though bankers balances no longer counted toward a member bank's legal reserve requirement, they were convenient for making investments and loans outside the immediate locality of banks in the interior, and they continued to serve as a highly liquid, income yielding asset. Banks in other cities followed suit when Wall Street raised the rate on bankers' balances to 3 percent in March 1918. The Federal Reserve's denunciation of this type of competition led to a conference and an agreement by the New York

Clearing House to reduce the rate to 2.5 percent and to link it to the rediscount rate, as was the practice in London.

There was a widespread but erroneous impression that "the payment of interest on demand deposits has resulted for years and years in stripping the country banks of all their spare funds, which have been sent to the money centers for stock speculation purposes," as Senator Glass alleged. Accordingly, the Banking Act of 1933 forbade the payment of interest on every type of demand deposit. In June 1933, this provision had little practical significance because the New York Clearing House members had earlier reduced their rate to one quarter percent. In the long run, however, the statutory ban on demand deposit interest affected interbank and business deposits adversely.

The eight states with a guaranty scheme had placed a limit on interest payments on time deposits to forestall anticipated aggressive rate competition, which might push paying banks into risky, unsound assets. Willis, a leading authority, was convinced that "payment of higher interest rates has been the cause for the making of speculative loans and the purchase of doubtful securities which have in turn contributed so largely to bank failures" during the decade preceding 1933. As earnings fell during the early 1930's, bankers advocated a reduction in interest payments. Total deposit interest had averaged around 2.0 percent of member bank deposits in the 1920's, declining to 1.5 percent by 1932; apparently banks sought further reductions.

The 1933 law empowered the Federal Reserve Board to set a ceiling on time deposit rates offered by member banks "in order to put a stop to the competition between banks in payment of interest, which frequently induces banks to pay excessive interest and has many times over brought banks into serious trouble," said the chairman of the House Banking Committee, expressing a widely held belief that persists despite lack of supporting evidence.

Since 1935, time deposit rate ceilings applicable to all insured commercial banks (Regulation Q) have been set by the Board of Governors working harmoniously with the FDIC. Until around 1950, Regulation Q had no operational significance for banks. Subsequently, rate ceilings have had important consequences for the growth of commercial banking vis-à-vis other financial intermediaries.

Separating Commercial From Investment Banking

The separation of business investment security underwriting from commercial banking was another reform that grew out of the banking collapse of the early 1930's. The booming new issues market of the 1920's attracted a number of sizable banks in leading financial centers to engage in investment banking activities. Security affiliates were usually established in the way pioneered by the First National Banks of Chicago and New York before World War I.

The $10 billion new issue volume of 1927 was twice the level of the early 1920's, and in 1929 the business reached $11.6 billion. Commercial banks originated 22 percent of all new security issues in 1927 and more than twice that proportion by 1930. Bank participation in new issues represented 37 percent and 60 percent of the dollar total in those 2 years. By 1930 the greater part of the new issue business was in the hands of commercial banks. Five of the 8 leaders were in New York—Guaranty, National City, Chase, Bankers Trust, and Equitable Trust. Chicago's Continental Illinois, Boston's First National, and Detroit's Union Trust completed the list.

Although the 1932 convention of the Investment Bankers Association affirmed that "the existence of affiliates of banks is necessary for the distribution of securities and the financing of corporations," the sharp decline in volume and the heavy losses sustained after the stock market collapse prompted commercial banks to rid themselves of the operation. The newly appointed head of Chase, Winthrop W. Aldrich, the Senator's son, was convinced that "the spirit of speculation should be eradicated from the management of commercial banks." The National City Bank, also under new leadership, disaffiliated in March 1933. Impressed by the speed with which the two largest American banks accomplished their severance, Congress ordered the divorcement of investment from commercial banking to be completed within a year of the passage of the Banking Act of 16 June 1933. The House of Morgan's investment banking functions were turned over to the newly organized partnership of Morgan, Stanley, and Company, while the firm's commercial banking operations retained the historic name J. P. Morgan and Company, until the 1959 merger which created the Morgan Guaranty Trust Co. The former affiliate of the First National Bank of Boston became the separate investment house, First Boston Corporation. Commercial banks could continue to act as underwriters of general federal, state, and local government obligations. And over the years, they have played an active role in these markets.

Reformers chose to ignore those like Eugene Meyer—in May 1933 he resigned from the Federal Reserve Board over the issue—who feared that divorcement would diminish the availability of underwriting facilities at a juncture when encouragement of business investment was so urgently needed. The elimination of banks as corporate security underwriters had the effect of hindering business recovery to some (unknown) extent. At the same time, the divorcement did not put an end to the dependence of investment banks on commercial banks for financing their operations.

Overbanking and Other Factors in the Collapse

Overbanking contributed to the failures of the 1920's and early 1930's. "There were too many banks, and competition among them was too sharp," the then chairman of the FDIC testified in 1955. His agency was pledged to work to prevent the recurrence of such a state of affairs.

Within the city limits of Chicago, 318 new banks were launched between 1921 and 1935; 263 of these failed or disappeared by merger by 1935. In the early 1900's it cost less to start a bank than to buy a good farm. Brunswick County, Virginia, exemplifying the rural situation, got its first bank in 1890. By 1921 there were 6; 4 in the county seat and 2 in towns with under 400 inhabitants. Of the 9 established since 1890, only three were still open at the end of 1933.

Virginia's Senator Glass, for decades the most powerful congressional figure dealing with banking legislation, said in debate in March 1933: "Little banks? Little corner grocerymen who run banks, who get together $10,000 or $15,000 . . . and then invite the deposits of their community, and at the very first gust of disaster topple over and ruin their depositors!" Leading local businessmen had traditionally seen the role of bank president as the pinnacle of their careers. Senator Glass had the support of scholars when he argued that the lack of "real bankers" had been an important factor in failure. "We have had too many banks and too few bankers," the head of New York's Chemical Bank testified before Glass's committee in March 1932.[13] Earlier in a 1930 report on failure to Idaho's governor, the Commissioner of Finance argued "there were too many banks and an insufficient number of real bankers."

Yet Milton Friedman and Anna Schwartz have insisted that deterioration in the quality of loans and investments, measuring their quality at the time they were added to the bank's portfolio, was not a major cause of bank failure, at least after 1930. Between mid-1931 and mid-1932 bond prices tumbled as deposit withdrawals compelled banks to liquidate securities in a demoralized market. Federal Reserve policies, they argue, failed to provide the commercial banks with the additional reserves which would have prevented a multiple contraction of deposits in the face of the clamor for additional currency.

Most Federal Reserve officials apparently did not understand how to use open market operation properly in the crisis. The March 1933 crisis could have been averted if only the Federal Reserve Banks had bought large amounts of United States government bonds in the last half of February, a recent re-examination suggests.[14] Whatever the reason, the universal expectation of an earlier generation that the Federal Reserve Act meant an end to financial panics proved to be wrong.

The sharp business contraction that began in mid-1929 affected few industries more adversely than banking. Certainly no other had a comparable deleterious impact on the rest of the economy. Deposits had expanded by $18 billion between 1921 and 1930 only to decline by $19 billion in the next 3 years. Suspended banks accounted for $7 billion of this total. The severe business downturn brought down countless banks. Their failure in turn spelled disaster for the overall economy, as the main monetary medium diminished in availability.

The nightmare of the early 1930's was to haunt the supervisory agencies for a quarter of a century. Viewing the debacle as a banking rather than a monetary phenomenon, they followed a "policy of keeping banks and banking practices within the bounds of rightful competition," as the FDIC explained in 1955. Both the authorities and the bankers became cautious.

Notes

1. The misleadingly named bank, founded in 1913, was a member of the Federal Reserve System. Although its assets, a large proportion being real estate loans, were liquidated during the poor market of the 1930's, depositors and other creditors got back 83 percent of the amount due them, all but 2 percent in 8 years. A background article appeared in *Fortune*, March 1933, pp. 62-65.

2. Lauchlin Currie, *The Supply and Control of Money in the United States* (Cambridge: Harvard University Press, 1934), p. 124.

3. Emanuel A. Goldenweiser, *American Monetary Policy* (New York: McGraw Hill, 1951), p. 160.

4. Clark Warburton, *Depression, Inflation and Monetary Policy* (Baltimore: Johns Hopkins Press, 1966), p. 340.

5. To meet the banking needs of the fourth largest city in the United States, General Motors sponsored the National Bank of Detroit. It took over the assets of the First Wayne and the Guardian National banks and opened on 24 March 1933. In August 1933, Ford opened the Manufactures National Bank. Neither auto maker intended to remain in banking.

6. The 1931 edition of the *Encyclopedia of Banking and Finance* stated "this country is now thought to be panic-proof."

7. Quoted in Milton Friedman and Anna J. Schwartz, *A Monetary History of the United States, 1867-1960* (Princeton: Princeton University Press, 1963), p. 350, n. 60. Both devaluation and currency expansion did occur.

8. Alexander D. Noyes, *The Market Place: Reminiscences of a Financial Editor* (Boston: Little Brown, 1938), p. 366.

9. The Comptroller of the Currency actually collected $180 million dollars from stockholder assessments of $329 million in 2,822 receiverships handled by his office since the first failure in 1865.

10. Leonard P. Ayres, *Economics of Recovery* (New York: Macmillan, 1933), p. 58.

11. Nevertheless, in 1940 over one-fifth of insured commercial banks holding almost two-thirds of deposits in all insured banks had net sound capital of less than 10 percent of the appraised value of their assets.

12. In March 1858, forty-two of forty-six member banks agreed to abolish interest payments on correspondent deposits.

13. Frank W. Nye, *Knowledge is Power* (New York: Random House, 1956), p. 182. Two years earlier Idaho's Commissioner of Finance complained that in his state "there were too many banks and an insufficient number of real bankers." Idaho Department of Finance, *Annual Report 1929*, pp. 5-6.

14. Elmus R. Wicker, *Federal Reserve Monetary Policy, 1917-1933* (New York: Random House, 1966), p. 195.

CHAPTER XIV

BANKING OPERATIONS IN THE AFTERMATH OF THE COLLAPSE, 1933-1945

An Industry in Trouble

A Cleveland banker complained in mid-1932 that sarcasm directed at the industry had become a favorite indoor sport. Banking was described by Willis in late 1933 as "a discredited, hampered, and governmentally henpecked . . . occupation."[1] Public opinion held bankers mainly responsible not only for depositors' losses, but for the depression as well. Half of those polled in the summer of 1936 thought banks were not doing their part to assist business and employment.[2] The passage of time and the contribution of banks in World War II helped to restore them in the eyes of the public.

At the depression low, bank credit (loans plus investments) was 38 percent below the 1929 level in the United States, compared with 18 percent in Canada and, on average, decline of 20 percent in thirty-eight countries. Banking fared worse in the United States than in any other major industrialized economy.

The upheaval of the 1930's was reflected in sharp changes in the relative importance of certain key bank balance sheet accounts. As a proportion of total assets, cash combined with United States government obligations, which were less than 23 percent in 1929 and 39 percent in mid-1933, comprised over 61 percent in 1940. Capital accounts declined from 14 percent to less than 10 percent of total assets between 1929 and 1940, while total loans shrank from almost 58 percent to less than 26 percent of total assets.

Commercial bank loans were cut in half in little more than three years after mid-1929. Not until 1948 was 1929's $36 billion volume reached again, at a much higher price level. Although total assets of all commercial banks increased by 175 percent in the decade ending in mid-1940 and real GNP was over one-sixth higher, total loans were half the 1930 level. Indeed, for a decade beginning in 1938, cash assets exceeded total loans.

Loans to Business

For the period from March 1933 to September 1934 two eminent economists reported for the Chicago Federal Reserve District "a genuinely unsatisfied demand for credit on the part of solvent borrowers, most of whom could make economically sound use of working capital." Banker reluctance to make risky loans was a subject of frequent private criticism at board meetings of the New York Federal Reserve Bank in the early 1930's. RFC chairman Jesse Jones, previously a Houston banker, publicly denounced bankers conservatism on many occasions.

A survey of manufacturing firms for the years 1933-1938 found fewer than 9 percent (mostly smaller ones) experiencing difficulties: 5.1 percent reported loan refusals, and 3.7 percent, restrictions. The banks' adverse decision was "fully justified" in a substantial number of cases according to the National Industrial Conference Board, but in other situations the earnings and capital of the applicant were said to have merited a loan.

Large banks complained of a lack of demand from sound borrowers in 1935, when loans of all banks reached a low point of $15 billion, which was 31 percent of total assets. Firms with assets under $5 million received about three-fourths of business loans. Over 80 percent of the dollar amount of commercial and industrial loans was unsecured.

By 1940 the total of loans and corporate securities owned by banks came to 30 percent of earning assets, contrasted with 43 percent in 1930. Business loans and securities together comprised 18 percent of all bank assets in 1940, half the ratio prevailing in 1928 and in 1900. Commercial banking's share of net corporate long- and short-term debt dropped from 23.3 percent at the start of 1930 to 14.0 percent a decade later.

Around 1900, about half of bank earning assets consisted of "business loans" financing working capital requirements of mainly small- and medium-sized firms engaged in manufacturing and trade; by 1940, not quite 25 percent were of this type. Approximately one-fourth of 1940's total earning assets comprised loans to agriculture, consumers, security dealers, and non-profit institutions. The remaining half consisted of federal, state, and local government securities.

As short-term money market rates fell sharply in the 1930's, the prime rate, the interest charge for bank loans to corporations with the highest credit standing, came to the fore. The Committee on Credit Practices of the prestigious Association of Reserve City Bankers advocated in June 1935, and again two years later, a minimum loan rate equal the interest on bankers' acceptances plus the selling charge then, altogether 1 11/16 percent. However, the prime rate stayed at 1 1/2 percent from the time of its introduction in 1934 through 1947. The competition of abundant funds prevented bankers from getting the additional 3/16 percent.

Innovations in Business Lending

A far-reaching "technical revolution in debt financing" began in the 1920's and accelerated after 1933.[3] Banks devised new ways of meeting the needs of small and medium firms for short- and intermediate-term credit, adopting business lending techniques developed earlier for consumer installment purchases.

The range of acceptable collateral was widened. Accounts receivable financing by banks exceeded $800 million in 1940, 40 percent of the total from all sources. This lending was almost entirely on a basis where the customers whose accounts provided the security for the loan were not notified by the bank about the borrowing, contrary to the practice of factoring firms, which earlier had the receivables field to themselves.

Field warehouse receipts were the basis for 2 percent of commercial and industrial loans by the end of 1941, slightly less than commercial bank loans secured by receivables. About one out of eight banks was making the former type of loan around 1940 while one out of four offered accounts receivable financing. In both types, the borrower paid interest only for funds actually used, unlike the traditional loan where a definite amount was borrowed for a specified period.

Installment financing of commercial and industrial equipment was successfully pioneered by commercial finance companies. Banks overtook them by 1940 with $200 million of such loans.

The term loan, far more significant quantitatively than those innovations in collateral, had an original maturity of more than 1 year and generally incorporated provisions for amortization. Negligible in 1933, $2.2 billion were outstanding by the end of 1940, nearly a third of banks' commercial and industrial loans and about 12 percent of all their loans. More and more term loans in the late 1930's were being made in smaller amounts to lesser businesses. By 1941, over half of the number went to firms with less than $5 million in assets.

In time the supervisory authorities came to approve the lengthened maturity. A joint bank examiners conference agreed in September 1934 not to criticize as "slow" loans whose payment was reasonably certain, whatever their maturity. However, many examiners continued to raise the traditional objection. The Banking Act of 1935 recognized that changes in business finance had significantly shrunk the short-term, self-liquidating paper eligible for rediscount privileges under the Federal Reserve Act. By broadening the class of eligible paper, Congress wished to encourage longer-term lending, in the hope of stimulating business recovery. The "slow" classification, previously used in supervisory examination of bank loans, was finally discarded in 1938. Banks were now free to establish policies appropriate to their circumstances, as the federal banking agencies encouraged less liquid loans.

The development and spectacular growth of term loans accelerated the trend toward longer average maturities, already under way in the 1920's with bank purchases of large amounts of corporate bonds. In 1913, 57 percent of all loans matured in 90 days or less, but in 1940 only 30 percent did. Almost half of bank credit to nonfinancial business, excluding agriculture, had by 1940 an initial maturity exceeding 1 year. On the eve of World War II, banks held 3.1 percent of the total short-term debt of nonfinancial business and 3.5 percent of their debt due in a year or more. Term loans comprised 53 percent of the latter.

The demand for short-term business loans weakened as the proportion of total business assets in the form of current assets declined after 1920, especially from 1929 to 1935. Firms were anxious to retire short-term debt. Long-term bonds were refinanced at prevailing lower rates, term loans avoiding the delay and registration expenses involved in meeting Securities and Exchange Commission requirements for public offerings. Even in the sharp business downturn of 1937-1938, there were no serious defaults on term loans. Banks found them to be satisfactory, profitable, and safe. Yet as late as 1945 a majority of experts continued to hold that only short-term loans were appropriate for banks.

Farm Loans

Federally sponsored, short-term Production Credit Associations (PCAs) chartered by the twelve federally owned Production Credit Corporations came into existence in 1933. Together with Commodity Credit Corporation loans and various other emergency programs to deal with the 63 percent decline in farm prices between August 1929 and March 1933, direct and sponsored federal agencies provided 30 percent of all short-term, non-real-estate farm loans outstanding by January 1935 and over 50 percent 2 years later. The commercial bank share of all institutional loans of this type fell from 97.8 percent in 1930 to 58.1 percent by 1940, when Federal non-mortgage loans to agriculture amounted to $750 million.

Mortgage loans were made available to farmers at lower interest costs, with more liberal maturities and loan sizes through the Federal Land Banks. Their peak mortgage volume was $2.15 billion in 1936, 30 percent of the total outstanding. Commercial banks had 10.1 percent of the 1930 farm mortgage aggregate, and only 8.4 percent in 1940.

Combining all types of agricultural loans, the various federal agencies had an amount equal to 4.7 percent of the total held by all private institutions in 1930 but had 58.2 percent by 1940. Holdings of the federally sponsored agencies amounting to 26.0 percent of the private total in 1930 and 87.9 percent by 1940.

Bank lending to agriculture increased by over $300 million between 1935 and 1940 but remained below the 1911 total. The $3.5 billion of 1930 was not seen again until the late 1940's. Commercial banks, source of 29.7 percent of all agricultural credit in 1913 and 23.9 percent in 1930, provided only 15.0 percent of the 1940 total.

Government Loans to the Private Sector

Direct loans from the federal government came to 0.1 percent of 1930's $112 billion net business debt, a remnant of World War I's War Finance Corporation. In 1940 the federal share was 1.1 percent of the $81 billion outstanding.

RFC loans to business aggregated $3.2 billion from 1934, when the agency was first authorized to lend in this field until 1953, when it was superseded by the Small Business Administration. One-third of this total was made available before 1941. Commercial bank participation through sharing the loan or the device of a federal guarantee was encouraged. Although these RFC loans were restricted to firms unable to obtain credit from private sources, federal activities did compete with and restrict the markets of private lenders. In the words of the RFC Act, agency loans had to be "so secured or of such sound value as reasonable to assure repayment," but they represented more than ordinary risk, while rates were below what was necessary to cover full costs. Government loans went mainly to medium-sized manufacturers for a 1- to 10-year period. These amortized term loans stimulated commercial banks to expand in this field.

Another federal financial instrumentality, the Export-Import Bank, was opened in 1934 to encourage American foreign trade. It had outstanding over $130 million in direct business loans by the end of 1940.[4] Unlike the RFC, the Export-Import Bank is still operating.

Federal agency loans reached a high point in relative importance in 1940, when they amounted to 4.8 percent of the combined total of net private and state and local government debt, contrasted with 0.3 percent a decade earlier. Agencies sponsored by the federal government, mostly in agriculture and housing, already had 1.0 percent of the combined total in 1930 but grew much less rapidly, to 2.2 percent, by 1940. Federal loans and loan insurance combined, 9 percent of the depression shrivelled gross national product in the peak year 1934, were down to 3.2 percent of 1940's gross national product.

Federal Mortgage Activity

The system of Federal Home Loan Banks, established in 1932 with government supplied capital (repaid by 1951), served to buttress faltering savings and loan associations. The Home Owners Loan Corporation, set up in 1933 to refinance defaulted mortgages (and liquidated without loss in 1951), not only enabled over a million families to retain their homes, but also strengthened financial institutions with $3.1 billion in bad loans previously on their books. The Federal National Mortgage Association was created in 1938 to establish a secondary, resale, market for mortgages guaranteed by the Federal Housing Administration (FHA).

The FHA, organized in 1934, was by far the most significant New Deal housing measure. By 1939, over one-third of all private nonfarm housing starts were FHA insured—37 percent of all one- and two-family homes, and 21 percent of the amount of all nonfarm mortgages under $20,000. Commercial banks made one-third of all FHA insured home mortgage loans from 1935 to 1952. The federal agencies popularized amortized mortgages, which called for periodic repayment of part of the principal. They also stimulated the lengthening of maturities and an increase in the loan-to-value ratio.

Urban housing mortgage loans from the federal agencies, $2.4 billion at the end of 1940, were $600 million below the mid-1936 peak. Federal farm mortgages at $2.5 billion were $400 million below their high at the end of 1936. Commercial banks had $600 million more than the federal government agencies in urban mortgages by 1940 but were far behind them in farm mortgages.

Real Estate Loans

Bank holdings of nonfarm residential mortgages fell by almost one fourth between 1929 and 1934 before climbing to a record $3 billion in 1940, one-eighth of the total amount outstanding. These mortgages comprised 4.6 percent of all commercial bank assets in 1930 and 4.2 percent in 1940.

Increasingly, banks financed residences rather than business real estate. Dwellings were the basis for 42 percent of total bank mortgages for three decades until the mid-1920's, 56 percent by 1930, and 74 percent by 1940. In mortgage lending on one- to four-family houses, commercial banks had overtaken mutual savings banks by 1940; the gap between the two subsequently grew.

Consumer Lending

Of the 1,222 personal loan department banks operating at the end of 1938, 1,065 were opened after 1929. In the case of consumer instalment paper, commercial banks had only 2-3 percent of the 1929 total but 10 percent in 1936 and over 26 percent by 1941.

Many banks gained their first experience with consumer loans by financing home repairs and modernization under the National Housing Act of 1934. Even after FHA coverage on these loans was reduced from 20 to 10 percent of a bank's portfolio, most continued to make these Title I loans. Banks had over 42 percent of the total held by all institutional lenders in 1941.

Banks broadened their activities to take in other types of consumer lending as well. The Bank of America, which offered San Franciscans low-cost loans in small sums at the time its predecessor Bank of Italy opened in 1904, used radio, billboards, and newspapers to publicize its willingness to finance autos beginning in 1935. The *American Banker*, the daily in the field, doubted whether there was a single literate Californian who had not heard about this by 1939. Commercial banks' auto instalment loans in 1940 were fifteen times the 1930 volume but still under one-third of the total.

In 1940, banks had fifteen times as much in all types of consumer instalment credit as in 1930. Nevertheless, only about one-tenth of the nation's banks were in the field to an important extent, including over a fourth of those with over $10 million in loans and investments.

Over half of the banks' personal loans carried an endorser's signature. Single name, chattel mortgage loans remained the specialty of personal finance companies. Bank personal instalment loans grew greatly during the 1930's, but single payment loans to consumers in 1940 were $200 million below the 1930 bank total of $836 million. Other financial institutions increased their loans in this area from $118 million to $164 million during the 1930's.

Brokers Loans

The Federal Reserve Board's strong desire to encourage "productive" and discourage "speculative" loans in the late 1920's was hampered by insufficient legal authority. Member banks not seeking discount accommodation, nonmember banks, and nonbank lenders in the call loan market were outside the Federal Reserve's jurisdiction until 1933. "The appearance of excessive security loans," in the view of the Senate Banking Committee, had been "an outstanding development in the pre-panic period." Brokers loans were erroneously suspected of channeling short-term funds to the financing of capital improvements and depriving business of its due proportion of credit. Accordingly, the Banking Act of 1933 sought "to prevent the undue diversion of funds into speculative operations," calling upon the Federal Reserve Banks to ascertain whether bank credit was being used excessively for speculative purposes. Moreover, the 1933 law forbade member banks to place loans "for the account of others," that is, for nonbank lenders.

Those measures affecting the supply of funds for security loans were less significant than a 1934 provision in the Securities Exchange Act which empowered the Federal Reserve to set margin requirements for all lenders, not merely for member banks. Stockbrokers and security dealers came under Regulation T in October 1934. Since May 1936 all commercial banks, including non-member banks, have had to follow Regulation U when making loans for the purpose of buying and carrying securities.

By the 1930's call loans dwindled into insignificance, usually amounting to less than $1 billion. Brokers loans ceased to be an open market instrumentality used to adjust a bank's reserve position. After 1933 brokers made face-to-face arrangements with money market banks, which treated them like other borrowers.

Bank Investments

The commercial bank ratio of loans to security holdings was 2.6 in 1929, 1.0

in 1934, and only 0.7 in 1940. Bank holdings of United States government obligations surpassed the commercial, industrial, and agricultural loan total by 1933; in 1940 they came with 5 percent of total bank loan volume. State and local government bond holdings increased by more than 70 percent during the 1930's. The $3.6 billion 1940 total exceeded bank owned private sector bonds for the first time; the difference grew greatly in subsequent decades.

The 1920's had been marked by "overinvestment in securities of all kinds," according to the Senate Banking Committee. The maximum amount banks could invest in nongovernmental obligations of any one borrower was reduced in the Banking Act of 1933 and lowered further to 10 percent of the bank's capital and surplus by the Banking Act of 1935. Previously, the Comptroller of the Currency had required only that investments be marketable. In 1936 he began to control their quality, ruling out "predominantly speculative issues."

Bank holdings of private corporation bonds were, by 1940, half of 1930's $7.4 billion. When term loans are combined with bank investments in business securities, however, the decade showed a growth of 50 percent. Bank ownership of medium- and long-term debt of nonfinancial corporations actually rose from 9.5 percent to 13.1 percent of the total outstanding in 1940.

Craving safety and liquidity, banks had over half of all their investments in United States government obligations by 1933 and almost 70 percent by 1940. Bankers generally disliked the New Deal and opposed government deficits, but they esteemed highly the bonds that financed much of the Roosevelt program. Federal bonds had been only 18.5 percent of all bank assets at the World War I peak in mid-1919. Twenty years later they were 25.6 percent, having been as high as 27.6 percent in 1936. In mid-1930, banks owned 30.0 percent of all United States government bonds outstanding and in 1940, 38.6 percent of a very much larger total.

Treasury bills, government obligations maturing in less than 1 year (generally in 90 days), were first introduced in 1929. Within a few years they had become the dominant money market instrument. At times, banks held half or more of the total bills outstanding. The same was true of Treasury notes. Banks also owned around 30 percent of longer term bonds.

Heretofore, as in the second half of 1932, open market operations had been used to influence the level of bank reserves. In December 1934, however, the Federal Reserve Banks were authorized to make maturity swaps in their portfolios to help maintain stability in the government bond market or to assist the Treasury's financing operations. Some long-term bonds were bought in the following spring in an effort to keep the market orderly.

Transactions necessary "to preserving an orderly market" were authorized in April 1937. A year later, the Federal Reserve sought to avoid too rapid or great a rise in bond prices. The Federal Reserve thus developed a concern for a stable government bond market. Aggregate Federal Reserve Banks' holdings of government bonds remained around $2.5 billion for most of the time from late 1933 to the end of 1939.

Swollen Excess Reserves

Increased holdings of cash equivalents, as well as of short-term United States government securities, manifested heightened commercial bank demand for liquidity in the 1930's. Over and beyond the reserves that member banks were legally required to hold at the Federal Reserve Bank, vault cash, cash items in process of collection, and balances with banks constituted 13.5 percent of their assets in 1929 and 17 percent in 1933. Enormous gold inflows into the United States pushed excess reserves of member banks to $2.8 billion at the end of 1935.

Alarmed at the inflationary potential of the swelling excess reserves after 1933, the Federal Reserve secured authority in the Banking Act of 1935 to double reserve requirements from the previous ratio. The original Federal Reserve Act had incorporated the nineteenth-century concept of fixed reserve requirements for the purpose of providing a liquid safeguard of deposits. Twenty-two years later, ratios were made flexible "to prevent injurious credit expansion and contraction." By May 1937, the requirement was at the new limit, only to be reduced in April 1938 as monetary policy was eased to cope with a sharp decline in gross national product. At the end of 1939, member banks excess reserves were over $5 billion, and a year later they reached $7 billion, over 11 percent of their total assets.

The abundance of reserves brought down short-term rates. By the spring of 1934, the annual yield on Treasury bills was 0.05 percent. Until 6 May 1942, bills did not offer a return of more than 0.35 percent, except in May 1937, when it was as high as 0.74 percent.

Currency and the Banks

National bank notes at various times in the 1920's exceeded the $715 million level of 1913. In the early 1930's, over $650 million were outstanding, and 1933 saw an all-time peak of $900 million. There were still upwards of $700 million in national bank notes when on 1 August 1935 the Treasury

Department retired the United States bonds that served as their backing. Long after the provision of currency ceased to be an important commercial bank function, a century and a half of their activity as banks of issue came to an end in 1935.

Circulation of Federal Reserve Notes had surpassed national bank notes by 1918 and in 1933 were over three times as great. Yet these issues had not realized Willis's goal "of a single uniform currency, provided by federal reserve banks, resting upon an adequate gold reserve issued only for commercial paper, and expanding and contracting as business requirements made it needful."[5]

As gold left the United States in 1931-1932, the rigid collateral requirements of the 1913 law had "prevented the Reserve System from adopting a monetary policy that was clearly in the interests of combating the prevailing deflation," the House Banking Committee reported. After untoward delay, United States bonds owned by the Federal Reserve Banks were made eligible in February 1932, but only temporarily because of misgivings about this departure from principle. The arrangement became permanent in 1935. Subsequent modifications in the law eliminating gold reserve requirements altogether in 1968 at long last made Federal Reserve notes truly elastic.

Time Deposits in Relative Decline

Currency held by the public rose over 34 percent from 1930 to 1933 while deposits held by individuals, partnerships, and nonbank corporations, declined sharply: almost 38 percent in the case of demand deposits and over 42 percent for time. In 1933 demand deposits comprised 58 percent and by 1940 over two-thirds of the total, excluding interbank and government deposits. Demand deposits more than doubled; commercial bank time deposits increased by only a third from 1933 to 1940. Not until early 1944, amidst the high savings of wartime prosperity, was 1930's $20.2 billion attained again. During the depression years, banks developed a disinterest in time deposits—by 1940 some 400 did not accept them at all. Rates offered savers dropped from an average of 3.2 percent in 1930 to 2.4 percent in 1934 and to 1.3 percent by 1940.

The FDIC, the outstanding positive result of the banking collapse, was called upon to protect some 1,300,000 depositors in the 398 insured banks with aggregate deposit liabilities of about $500 million which had closed from 1934 through 1945 (mostly before 1941). Only 2,000 depositors, with accounts in excess of $5,000, suffered any losses.

Service Charges on Demand Deposits

In 1936 demand deposits held by individuals, partnerships, and corporations other than commercial banks surpassed the previous peak of mid-1930 and were over 31 percent greater by 1940. This substantial growth occurred in the face of a prohibition of interest payments by banks after June 1933. Deposits under $5,000 in insured commercial banks represented over 90 percent of the total number of accounts since the end of 1935.

The Bank Management Commission of the American Bankers Association's lamented in 1935 that "it is difficult to free public thinking of the old idea that banks are institutions for 'free service' "; perhaps half of all the accounts in banks were being carried at "an actual loss." The movement for service charges on demand deposits received a great impetus from the National Recovery Act (NRA). By 1935 all but 6 percent of the banks responding to an American Bankers Association questionnaire had adopted service charges. As the decade ended, few well-managed banks failed to levy them.

Just as the minimum balance requirements became widespread, special checking accounts, which did not call for any minimum balance, made their appearance. By 1950, over one-third of the nation's banks offered this service on a fee basis.

Persistence of Nonpar Banks

Despite numerous failures and mergers of nonpar banks, over one-fourth of all nonmember banks did not remit checks at face value in February 1933. On the eve of World War II, 18 percent of all commercial banks, mainly located in the Midwest and South, still were not on the par list.

Checks from nonpar banks have always been ineligible to use the clearing facilities of the Federal Reserve. In 1966, half a century after par clearance was made compulsory for member banks, there remained over 1,400 nonpar banks, over one-tenth of all commercial banks. Several states subsequently outlawed the practice, bringing the number of nonpar banks down to fewer than 200 by the end of 1972. Over the decades this vestige of an almost universal pre-1913 practice has unnecessarily complicated check clearing, imposing an avoidable cost on the economy.

Cooperation Through Clearinghouses

City clearinghouses numbered some 362 in 1925; 391 in 1931; and 351 in the years preceding 1940. Smaller towns and country districts organized regional clearinghouses under American Banker Association guidance beginning in the late 1920's. Regional clearinghouses increased from 56 in 1931 to 233 in the late 1930's, at a time when the NRA inspired the organization of trade associations in many other industries as well.

Thus the code of sound banking practices adopted by the Arkansas Bankers Association in 1931 was left to the fifteen regional clearinghouses for interpretation; service charges within each region would be uniform. Wisconsin regional groups had begun to do the same even earlier, in addition to agreeing on uniform charges on small loans and on a reduction of interest paid on time deposits. The state banking department began to work with these regional groups in the 1930's; by 1945 most of the banks in a particular Wisconsin district had a uniform schedule of service charges.

New York's Position and Correspondent Balances

New York gained notably in deposits held by the public (excluding federal government and interbank accounts) in the years after the banking collapse, as corporate balances found their way to the Wall Street giants. Between 1933 and 1940, member bank deposits gained 114 percent in New York, 84 percent in all reserve cities, and 78 percent in country banks. New York City banks had around 20 percent of the nation's total deposits in the 1920's, 23.6 percent in 1933, and surpassed the 1900 position of 25.4 percent in 1939 with 27.4 percent. However, by 1945 New York's share was down to 22.0 percent.

Some of these changes were due to shifts in correspondent balances. As large excess reserves came to be held in the 1930's, the proportion of interbank deposits to total deposits, 10.0 percent in 1930 and 10.8 percent in 1933, rose to 16.8 percent by 1940. Interbank deposits in New York City member banks were 38.4 percent of the national total in 1930, 40.0 percent in 1934, and 51.6 percent 5 years later; they dropped sharply to 33.1 percent by 1945.

New Banks

Free banking lasted less than a century. It was officially interred by the Banking Act of 1935, which incorporated standards already used by several states as well as by the office of the Comptroller of the Currency at times. The latter, in chartering a new bank (and the FDIC in insuring a state non-member bank), must now consider, among other factors, "its future earnings prospects [and] the convenience and needs of the community to be served by the bank." The FDIC welcomed the 1935 law as an aid "to prevent a recurrence of the evil which is to be greatly feared ... the return of the overbanked condition of the early twenties." In the 1936-1945 decade, 535 new banks opened, less than one-fifth the number that would have been formed had the average pace of 1921-1935 been maintained.

The chartering of new national banks in the quarter century beginning in 1936 went "to the extreme of unduly restricted approval," according to a study prepared at the direction of the office of the Comptroller of the Currency. By the late 1930's and well into the 1940's the United States was "seriously underbanked," suggested a monograph sponsored by the American Bankers Association. Between 1930 and 1935 the number of commercial banks declined by one third. The further net decrease of 934 in the next 4 years brought the total to the lowest level since 1903. The 7,400 average population per banking office in 1940 was more than double 1920's.

Mergers

The desire to avert failure prompted many mergers in the early 1930's. Combinations of operating banks reached an all-time high of 1,567 in the years 1930-1931. In the next 2 years, half as many mergers occurred. These figures do not include numerous takeovers of suspended banks by sound ones.

Mergers abated further after 1933, averaging under 200 a year for the rest of the decade and under 100 a year from 1941 through 1945. From 1935 through 1945, 153 mergers were arranged with the financial aid of the FDIC, thereby giving complete protection to over $395 million in deposits.

Spread of Branching

Between 1931 and 1935, twelve of the twenty-two states that had earlier banned branching abandoned the unit bank principle. Actual and prospective failures prompted mergers, and the operation of acquired banks as branch offices appeared desirable. In a number of other states the permissible territory for branching was expanded, thereby affording facilities to communities which would otherwise be bankless.

New York, where only citywide branches had been previously allowed, set up nine districts in 1934, each comprising several adjacent counties. Wall Street banks however remained confined within New York City's five counties from 1898 until 1960, when adjoining Westchester and Nassau were opened to them.[6]

National banks were at last authorized to branch to the same geographic extent as state banks in 1933. However, onerous capital requirements for branches were not eliminated until 1952.

Between mid-1930 and the end of 1933 there was a net reduction of 736 offices, the only decline in branch offices in the twentieth century. This was offset by an increase of 741 in the following 7 years. Head-office city branches fell by a third during the 1930's, while out of town offices increased 70 percent. Commercial banks with at least one branch grew by 200 and represented almost 7 percent of all banks by 1940.

Unit banks remained numerically preponderant. Until the mid-1930's, they also had the bulk of all commercial banking assets. By the eve of World War II their share was down to 47 percent.

Chains and Holding Companies

In 1931 there were 176 chains, each controlling at least 3 separately chartered banks, with 908 affiliates and about 2 percent of the United States deposit total. About the same deposit share was held in 1939 by 96 chains with 424 affiliates. Most chain banks were located in unit banking states.

Group banking declined in the early 1930's, a number succumbing to failures. By the late 1930's and for a decade thereafter, holding companies with at least three banks had 7 percent of all banking offices and 11 percent of all deposits. The first federal effort at their regulation, the Banking Act of 1933, covered only holding companies with member bank subsidiaries. To obtain a permit to vote its member bank stock, a holding company was subjected to examination by the Federal Reserve Board. Few, only twenty in 1948, actually came under the board's supervision.

The American banking system in 1929 was "a multiplicity of local banks, exhibiting extreme diversity in size, in character and experience of management, and in the surrounding economic conditions of the communities to be served."[7] A decade later, even after the upheaval in banking, much the same could be said. Deposit insurance, after all, helped to perpetuate "our Tom, Dick and Harry type of banking with its thousands of small, independent establishments."[8]

Dual Banking System Survives

The dual banking system was permitted to continue after the debacle of the early 1930's. The sharply higher failure rate of state nonmember banks resulted in an increase in the member bank deposit share, from 70 percent in 1930 to 80 percent in 1933, but President Roosevelt had no inclination to compel all banks to belong to the Federal Reserve System.[9] Though membership remained voluntary, the drift of deposits to larger banks brought 85 percent of commercial bank deposits under direct Federal Reserve control at the peak in 1942. Thereafter, member bank deposits stayed above 80 percent until 1971.

One-fifth of the new banks chartered from 1936 through 1945 managed to open without FDIC protection for their depositors. After World War II, the proportion of uninsured new banks became negligible, giving the federal authorities almost complete de facto control over entry, despite formal continuation of the dual banking system. FDIC insurance induced almost 90 percent of the state banks to submit to federal jurisdiction. The corporation's bank examination policies had the effect of raising standards among nonmember banks.

Supervisory Examination Reforms

Before the Great Depression, supervisors evaluated banks in terms of the ideal of self-liquidating loans to commerce, industry, and agriculture; liquid open-market paper; and marketable securities. In September 1931, however, Comptroller Pole instructed national bank examiners not to charge off bonds rated in the top four grades, regardless of their market price, unless there had been a default. This pioneering approach in the direction of "intrinsic" valuation was hailed at the time by the Senate Banking Committee. In October 1931, Pole instructed examiners "to exercise extraordinary discretion in their work and to use every effort to encourage and sustain the morale in banks examined." He understood that "present conditions demand sympathetic treatment." The following July, Pole complained that some examiners did not "fully appreciate the extremely abnormal business conditions and the weakened condition of the securities market at this time."

The 1939 convention of the American Bankers Association opposed the proposal of Chairman Marriner Eccles of the Board of Governors of the Federal Reserve System to vary standards, as an instrument of credit control: "Bank examinations should be just what their designation implies, and no attempt should be made to use them for other purposes." As late as 1941, bankers complained to the Senate Banking Committee that their loans and securities were being more severely criticized by examiners than in 1929. Thus the Bank of America had to contend with the classification of their innovative, economically desirable accounts receivable and factoring loans as "slow" or "doubtful."

A joint federal examiners conference, convened at the request of the secretary of the Treasury in September 1934, sought to establish a uniform method of asset appraisal. Loans that would ultimately be repaid, judging by the borrower's net worth, were not to be classified as slow, even though they were illiquid at the time or not secured by saleable collateral. Maturity continued to be emphasized, however.

In July 1938 the three federal banking agencies, in conjunction with the National Association of Supervisors of State Banks, agreed to emphasize intrinsic value rather than liquidity in future examination of loans. Similarly, bonds would be judged on their "inherent soundness" rather than on daily market fluctuations. Marketable securities with a reasonable risk would be valued at cost. The "slow loan" category, used for over two decades for those that did not conform to the concept of self-liquidating loans, was replaced by classification II, where "a substantial and unreasonable degree of risk to the bank" was involved. Loans would not be so classified as long as ultimate repayment was "reasonably assured."

With a major recession as background, the 1938 agreement dealt with the recognized tendency of examiners to be hypercritical during depressions and more easy going in good times, thereby exerting a procyclical influence on bank credit extension. Minor changes in the 1938 approach were made in 1949.[10] The stress on soundness rather than liquidity was also reflected in the uniform examination report form adopted by the federal agencies in 1938 and also used in a majority of states.

The federal agencies expressed the hope in 1938 that these changes would "afford the banks a broader opportunity for service to the community and for profitable outlet for some of their abundant, idle funds." The main impact, however, was felt only after World War II.

Business Loans During World War II

Industrial production more than doubled from the beginning of 1940 to mid-1945, but commercial and industrial loans increased 18 percent. These loans almost paralleled the 45 percent growth in output in the rearmament years 1940-1941. However, in the following 18 months, as the United States military effort assumed gigantic dimensions, bank credit for civilian industry declined by over $4 billion, offset only partially by a $2 billion increase in loans for war production. Though bank loans to commerce and industry expanded moderately after 1943, in the final stage of the war in mid-1945, they were slightly below the 1941 total.

About 55 percent of the manufacturing plant and equipment added during the war years were built at public expense for private operation. Government loans and guarantees were further significant sources of war production financing. The RFC made over $1 billion in loans, mostly at the request of the armed forces. Under the V-loan arrangement, government guaranteed in whole or in part war contractors loans. By the end of 1945, almost 9,000 of these loans had been authorized for over $12 billion, with an average of 85 percent of each loan guaranteed. War procurement agencies also provided working capital through advances and prepayments on government contracts, $2.2 billion at the 1943 peak.

Total bank loans, $21.7 billion at the end of 1941, were again at that level by the end of 1944, after having declined to $18 billion by mid-1943. The $26 billion in bank loans at the end of 1945 represented the highest point since 1931. Reconversion and expansion during 1945 brought a 19.4 percent gain in commercial and industrial loans from a low level of $8 billion at the start of the year.

Agricultural Loans in Wartime

Farm output expanded almost 20 percent from 1940 through 1945, yet short-term loans from all institutional sources (excluding crop price support loans) of $2.5 billion were about the amount that banks alone had made available in 1918. At the end of 1945, bank loans to agriculture were actually $100 million less than the figure 4 years earlier.

Farm mortgage debt increased by 69 percent from 1915 to 1920, creating difficulties in the postwar era. From 1941 to 1946, however, there was a prudent 22 percent reduction. Wartime prosperity enabled farmers to repay $1.7 billion. At the end of 1945, banks had 11 percent of outstanding farm mortgages.

Nonfarm Home Mortgages in Wartime

Nonfarm residential mortgage debt outstanding at the end of 1945 was slightly below the 1941 level and was $3 billion less than at the end of 1930. Bank holdings in 1945 were about the same as in 1941, representing only 2.1 percent of total assets, which was just slightly higher than the 1900 proportion. In 1945, 80 percent of all bank mortgage holdings were for residences, up from the 76 percent in 1941. For the first time ever, total bank holdings of nonfarm residential mortgages at the end of 1945 exceeded those of mutual savings banks. In the next few years, the lead widened significantly.

Consumer Credit Shrinks in Wartime

Consumer credit extension from all sources came under Federal Reserve Regulation W for the first time in September 1941. This anti-inflationary measure, together with wartime prosperity, the unavailability of autos and other consumer durables, and the high rate of personal saving, brought about a 70 percent decline in 2 years from the $1.7 billion consumer instalment loans in commercial banks at the end of 1941. By the end of 1945, there was a slight increase to $.74 billion. Noninstalment consumer bank loans were just under $.70 billion at the end of 1941 and again 4 years later.

Bank loans of all types were a minor factor in the financing of the 50 percent growth in real gross national product, 1940-1945, associated with rearmament and war because of very limited demand from the private sector. With respect to the federal government, the story was very different.

Flood of Federal Government Securities

Commercial banks played a major role in financing World War II by lending to other bond buyers, by handling three-quarters of the war loan campaign sales volume, and above all by adding enormously to their own portfolios. Between July 1940 and the end of 1945 banks bought almost 40 percent of the $187 billion borrowed by the federal government from sources other than the Federal Reserve and government trust funds. Commercial banks held 34.2 percent of the federal debt in 1941 and 33.0 percent 4 years later. At the same time that the Treasury was anxious for the success of each bond drive, it sought a maximum of nonbank purchasers, in the interest of fighting inflation. Almost 60 percent of the $9 billion increase in bank loans from 1940 through 1945 went to finance security acquisitions, mostly United States bonds.

To encourage bond buying by banks, reserve requirements and deposit insurance assessments against war loan accounts were eliminated. A Federal Reserve purchase guarantee made the Treasury bill yielding 3/8 percent risk-free. Bills almost ceased to be a money market instrument as the Federal Reserve Banks came to hold three-fourths of the entire amount outstanding by mid-1945. Commercial banks invested in 7/8 percent certificates in indebtedness, knowing that they could borrow at a preferential discount of 1/2 percent if in need of additional reserves.

New bonds carrying a 2 percent coupon, within 10 years of maturity, were eligible for bank purchase. Higher yielding, longer term issues were reserved for nonbank investors. Almost 45 percent of the government securities acquired by banks from 1941 through 1945 matured within a year. Government obligations maturing in more than 10 years comprised one-third of bank holdings in 1941 but only one-tenth in 1945.

In 1943, bank income from investments exceeded income from loans for the first time. Whereas loans provided 45 percent of current operating earnings from 1934 to 1941, that proportion of banks' earning derived from federal bond interest in 1945.

The commercial banking system used the excess reserves inherited from the gold inflow of the 1930's to expand total deposits created in the course of buying government bonds. As banks absorbed tens of billions of United States government bonds after Pearl Harbor, the enormously swollen excess reserves of the late 1930's disappeared. The $22.5 billion increase in Federal Reserve holdings of government bonds provided commercial banks with reserves needed to acquire whatever securities the Treasury could not sell to other investors. By the end of 1945 excess reserves were less than $1.5 billion, under 10 percent of member banks total reserves. Even this figure was above any seen subsequently.

Between mid-1940 and mid-1945 banks bought a volume of United States bonds equal to their total assets in 1940. With Federal Reserve support of government security prices assured, banks did not fear significant loss or inability to meet any subsequent unforeseen need for liquidity. United States government bonds, 40 percent of total bank loans and investments at the end of 1939, were 73 percent 6 years later. Treasury obligations comprised at least half of total bank assets from 1943 to 1947.

Bank Prosperity

Between 1941 and 1945 total bank assets increased 103.5 percent, while profits doubled despite large tax payments. The rate of return on national bank capital in 1945 was the highest in the 75 years for which official records were available. Since 1870 they had averaged 7 percent on total capital; 1945's record of almost 11 percent was not surpassed until 1969 and 1970.

Bank capital shrank by a third from 1930 to 1933. Despite retention of the bulk of subsequent net earnings, the 1930 total was not reached again until 1946. The ratio of capital to total assets, which had been trending downward since 1875, when the series begins, reached a low of 5.5 percent in 1945. However, the ratio of capital to assets other than cash plus United States government obligations was 25.5 percent in 1945, about the same as in the late 1930's. The FDIC was reassured by the fact that the ratio of assets rated substandard by bank examiners—48.2 percent of adjusted capital as recently as 1939—was down to 7.6 percent in 1945, the lowest level since the beginning of deposit insurance. By the end of World War II, the financial damage inflicted on the banking system by the Great Depression had been repaired. Banks were in a strong position to meet the demands of the postwar economy.

Notes

1. H. Parker Willis, "The Future in Banking," *Yale Review* 23 (Winter 1934), p. 247.

2. Gurden Edwards, "Banking and Public Opinion," *Public Opinion Quarterly* 1 (April 1937), p. 11.

3. Neil H. Jacoby and Raymond J. Saulnier, *Business Finance and Banking* (New York: National Bureau of Economic Research, 1947), p. 139.

4. In the first 20 years, the Export-Import Bank made loans totalling $4.6 billion, mostly during 1945-1953.

5. H. Parker Willis, *The Federal Reserve System* (New York: Columbia University Press, 1923), p. 1523.

6. Legislation passed in 1971 authorizes statewide branching in New York effective in 1976.

7. Conference on Unemployment, *Recent Economic Changes in the United States* (New York: McGraw-Hill, 1929), vol. II, p. 690.

8. Ray B. Westerfield, *Money, Credit, and Banking* (New York: Ronald Press, 1938), p. 297.

9. The original FDIC legislation (not an administration measure) provided for compulsory membership for all insured banks after 1 July 1936. However, banks with deposits under $1 million were exempted in 1935; in June 1939 the membership requirement was eliminated before it was to go into effect.

10. *Federal Reserve Bulletin* 35 (1949), p. 776.

CHAPTER XV

DYNAMIC INDUSTRY SINCE 1945

Sixteen years of depression and war had largely transformed American banks into bond-holding institutions. Treasury securities alone were 57 percent of all assets at the end of 1945. The proportion of loans to earning assets was at an all-time low of just over 20 percent by 1945, compared with 70 percent in 1929 and 50 percent in 1934. As of mid-1945, Comptroller of the Currency Preston Delano described the functions of the national banking system as "the handling of the Nation's current funds—the investment of those funds in Government securities and Government-guaranteed loans, the direct creation of credit for governmental use, and the performance of certain quasi-governmental services."[1]

The bank share of net corporate long- and short-term debt, already down to 14.0 percent at the end of 1939, was 13.7 percent 5 years later. Loans of all types were less than one-sixth of total bank assets in 1945. United States government securities owned by banks were over 3.5 times the amount of their loans. "Commercial" hardly seemed an accurate label to describe bank activities. Not a few observers doubted whether banks would be called upon to resume their commercial lending function in the postwar economy.

Spirited Revival of Lending

Within a decade after the end of World War II, however, loans had surpassed investments; by 1972 they were over twice as large. With the resurgence of lending, by 1953 the share of loans in total assets was double the 16.2 percent of 1945. Even so, the 53.8 percent of 1972 was still below the 57.9 percent of 1929. The ratio of bank loans to the gross national product stood at 35 percent in 1929, 11 percent in 1945, and 29 percent in 1972.

Commercial banks continue as the outstanding source of funds for the broadest range of customers, industries, and purposes. After 1945 banks became more determined and effective competitors of the specialized financial institutions such as the home mortgage oriented savings and loan associations and the finance companies serving consumers and business. Borrowers were now sought after: "The successful bank lending officer is a salesman at heart," one inclined to be favorable to the applicant, stated a widely used text of the 1950's and 1960's.[2]

"Soaring," appropriately described bank loans in the 1960's as they rose at a compounded annual rate of 9.5 percent. Slow growth occurred only in the recession year 1961 (4.6 percent) and the "minirecession" of 1967 (6.7 percent). Again during the 1970 recession total loans increased 4.7 percent, rebounding with a 10 percent gain in 1971 and a further 19 percent in 1972. From 1946 through 1956, commercial banks advanced directly, on average, just over 20 percent of total funds raised in credit markets each year; from 1961 through 1968 they advanced almost 36 percent.

Business Loans

The line-of-credit device was used by over half of all member banks usually in dealing with larger and established borrowers, the Federal Reserve Business Loan Survey of 1955 found. Some banks formalize the arrangement into a revolving credit, normally for a period of more than 1 year, charging a fee for the unused portion.

As of the mid-1950's, bank loans represented almost 80 percent of borrowings, exclusive of trade credit, of established small- and intermediate-sized firms and 70 percent of credit needs of new business. A number of large banks have opened special departments to serve the needs of small business. The post-1951 revival of monetary policy brought several periods of tight money. Their effect on small business was a matter of concern and controversy; the issue is still unresolved. Certainly to the present, most of the nation's banks are small and perforce can lend only small amounts to anyone borrower.

The ability of banks to accomodate borrowers during periods of monetary restraint diminished sharply by the late 1950's; swollen portfolios of readily marketable Treasury securities to liquidate for the purpose were no longer available. Banks financed an average of 19 percent of the credit needs of nonfinancial business during 1955-1959 and 31 percent during 1965-1968. This trend to greater use of bank credit was reversed during the 1969 credit squeeze. Nevertheless, even in 1969 total bank loans grew by 10.9 percent.

Term loans had become the largest single asset category in New York City banks by the mid-1960's, comprising almost 65 percent of their business loans at the end of 1969. They expanded greatly during periods of heavy business investment outlays in the mid-1950's and a decade later. These intermediate-term business loans were 14 percent of the total for all member banks in 1946 and 19 percent in 1957, as business loans maturing in a year or less dropped from 66 to 62 percent of the aggregate. Term loans comprised over 38 percent of commercial and industrial loans made by large banks at the end of 1972.

The prime rate was unchanged at 1½ percent from the time of its introduction in 1934 until December 1947. Considerable flexibility was subsequently displayed, especially after 1965. From early 1966 through 4 November 1971, twenty-eight changes were made. A record high of 10.0 percent was quoted in 1973. In the late 1960's individual banks appeared to be moving away from a uniform rate, particularly when local businesses were involved. A further departure occurred when several major New York banks announced in the fall of 1971 that their minimum loan rate would be governed by open market rates, with weekly changes if necessary, in accordance with a formula. Term loans used to be made on a fixed rate generally. More recently they are increasingly on a floating rate basis, often tied to the prime rate.

Among numerous lending innovations of recent decades one will serve as an example. In the late 1950's a considerable number of banks entered the field of financing business equipment indirectly by lending to lessors. In 1963 national banks were authorized to participate directly by becoming owner-lessors. In the latter case, the bank itself makes the machinery available to the lessee. Fewer than 10 percent of all national banks were in direct lease financing in early 1972.

From 1946 through 1965 nonfinancial corporations borrowed from banks, for short or intermediate term, a net amount equal to one-seventh of their external financing and about two-thirds of the increase in their inventories over the two decades. Short-term bank loans have become "a marginal source of external funds," yet "indispensable" for needs arising out of seasonal and cyclical upswings.[3] Bank loans of all maturities comprised over 18% of all non-financial corporation debt outstanding in the 1969-1972 period.

Agricultural Loans

Banks had almost $4 billion in farm loans, other than on real estate, at the start of 1921. The 1949 total was half as large; not until 1958 was 1921's surpassed. These loans, which do not include CCC-guaranteed crop support operations, reached $14.3 billion by the end of 1972. At 3.6 percent of total bank loans, the share was below 1935's, reflecting in part the declining importance of agriculture in the national income. Production credit associations, now numbering 442, have become the second main source of non-real-estate loans, providing farmers with a steadily rising proportion of total non-real-estate farm debt supplied by institutions, some 31 percent in mid-1972.

Farm departments headed by men trained in agriculture not only lend funds in many banks but also counsel farmers about their operations and finances. Most banks serving agriculture today have more nonfarm deposits to draw on than in the past and better correspondent arrangements for loans too large for them to handle.

Bank farm mortgage holdings in 1945 were at their lowest level since the early 1900's, only 10.4 percent of the total outstanding. Although banks held a record volume, 12.8 percent of the total, in 1972, they have never regained the position lost to life insurance companies in the early 1920's.

Banks finance operating expenses; farm living; and various farm assets such as livestock, machinery, and real estate. One-third of the bank loans in 1966 were originally for a period of 9 to 12 months, and over 70 percent were secured.

The bank share in total agricultural credits was 29.7 percent in 1913 and 28.2 percent in 1960, after having been as low as 15.0 percent in 1940. The thousands of rural banks serve as "farm credit service stations."[4] In 1972 there were 2460 banks whose farm loans were at least half of all their loans, and another 2955 whose farm loans were 25 to 49 percent.

Real Estate Loans

The heavy reliance of the construction industry and home buyers on outside credit made for marked year-to-year countercyclical fluctuations. Banks participated not only as direct sources of mortgages but indirectly through interim financing of intermediaries in the mortgage market.

The bank share of government-underwritten home mortgages (FHA and VA) decreased sharply, from 37 percent of the total outstanding in 1946, to 12.5 percent in 1965 and only 9.0 percent in 1972. Under 20 percent of the amount of nonfarm residential mortgages held by banks at the end of 1972 were guaranteed by the FHA and VA.

At last in 1964 national banks could offer borrowers the same terms as savings and loan associations on conventional mortgages, as the maximum maturity was extended to 25 years and the maximum loan-to-value ratio raised to 80 percent. Nonfarm residential mortgages were 8.3 percent of bank assets at the end of 1964 and 8.0 percent in 1972.

In 1949 banks matched their previous record proportion of total assets in all types of mortgages, 5.5 percent as in 1933; by 1965 it had risen to 8.6 percent and in 1972, 12.2 percent. The bank share of all types of mortgage debt outstanding ranged from 16 to 18 percent in the post-1945 era, well above the 11 to 12 percent in the years just preceding.

Consumer Credit

Once again by the early 1950's aggregate consumer credit attained the ratio of 11 percent of disposable income seen just prior to World War II. The ratio in 1960 was 16 percent and in 1972, 18 percent of disposable income. The bank share of the swelling total was 25 percent in 1945, 34 percent in 1955 (having exceeded credit extended by nonfinancial businesses for the first time in 1953), and 40 percent at the end of 1972.

In automobile credit, the largest single category of installment credit, bank participation was 40-45 percent of the total from 1945 to 1960, rising to 57 percent by 1972. Increasingly after 1950, banks bought automobile paper directly from dealers. Marked liberalizations of credit terms in 1954-1955 led to a sharp rise in auto purchases.

The Board of Governors encountered enforcement difficulties with Regulation W in dealing with thousands of retail outlets between September 1948 and June 1949 and again during the Korean War from September 1950 to May 1952. Though viewed by some as a destabilizing factor, consumer lending was subsequently left unconstrained in part because of board opposition to reinstitution of controls.

By the end of 1955 all but 3 percent of commercial banks were making consumer installment loans. Attracted by the favorable return from this source, most banks overcame their earlier reluctance. Consumer credit, 0.9 percent of total bank assets in 1945, rose to 8.6 percent in 1972.

Bank Credit Cards

Bank-sponsored credit cards began with Franklin National's effort to assist retail merchant in Nassau County, New York, in 1951. Only 27 of the 100 plans initiated from 1951 to 1955 were still active by the end of 1955. Some large banks introduced credit cards in the late 1950's, but entry on a large scale started only in 1966. There were 197 bank plans in September 1967 and

1,631 by the end of 1972. In addition, over 7,000 banks act as local agents of large city correspondents.

The largest bank in the country set up its own Bank Americard on a California-wide basis in October 1959. Later the Bank of America formed the first nationwide system of licensees. In 1969 Interbank Card Association, a nonprofit corporation of banks operating their own plans, took over Master Charge, the other nationwide bank credit card system.

Over 15 million cardholders charged purchases from more than 1 million participating merchants in 1970. Not until August 1968 did the amount outstanding on bank credit cards reach $1 billion; 4 years later, it was $4.6 billion. Despite rapid growth, amounts outstanding on bank credit cards represented less than one-fifth of total bank consumer instalment credit at the end of 1972; although the great majority of all families were not using bank credit cards, they appeared to have a promising future.

The check credit plan, a related development, introduced by the First National Bank of Boston in 1955, provides consumers with a prearranged line of credit. Over 1,600 banks offered check credit plans in 1972, as a substitute for, or supplement to, the credit card. The amount outstanding tripled between February 1968 and October 1972; even then, it came to only $1.7 billion.

Commercial Paper

After languishing for two decades, commercial paper, the oldest short-term money market instrument in the United States (found elsewhere only in Canada) showed renewed vigor. Dealer-placed paper grew at an annual rate of 57 percent from mid-1966 to mid-1970, compared with 15 percent in the preceding decade. Paper of all kinds (including directly- and dealer-placed paper) was under $1 billion in 1950, $4.5 in 1960, $31.8 billion at the end of 1970, and $35.8 billion in mid-1973.

The number of nonbank firms issuing commercial paper increased from 335 in 1965 to 575 in 1970. Tight money episodes in 1966 contributed to its popularity. For a time following the Penn Central default in June 1970, only the strongest firms could look to this source.

Banks, especially those in rural areas and small cities, were traditionally the main buyers of commercial paper. By the end of the 1950's, however, they held less than half; a decade later they held under one-fifth of the greatly expanded total.

Bankers Acceptances

Around 100 banks important in international trade participated in acceptance financing in the 1960's. Less than $400 million bankers acceptances were outstanding in 1950. By 1960, 1929's $1.6 billion had been exceeded; 11 years later the total was almost five times as great.

Accepting banks hold a larger proportion of their own acceptances in periods when they are not under pressure from the Federal Reserve. Thus in 1964 they held 49 percent of outstanding acceptances but in 1969, only 29 percent. Dollar acceptances became increasingly important in international trade financing in the 1960's, with the Japanese being the major users of the instrument.

Federal Government Credit

Federal credit—loans, loan insurance, and guarantees—continued to grow after World War II. The total was 2.2 percent of the 1945 gross national product, 3.8 percent of the 1953 GNP, and 5.8 percent of the 1962 GNP. Still mainly in housing and agriculture, the focus was increasingly directed toward the stimulation of American exports, community development, small business, and higher education. The Federal Land Banks became privately owned in 1947, as did the Federal Intermediate Credit Banks, the Banks for Cooperatives, and the Federal National Mortgage Association in 1968. Certain housing aid programs were taken over by the newly created Government National Mortgage Association in 1968. FGA and the Export-Import Bank continue to be owned by the federal government.

Various sectors of the economy benefitted from seventy-four distinct federal credit programs as of mid-1963. Direct loans of $15.8 billion were made in fiscal 1962, mainly to agriculture and foreign governments; an equal amount was insured, overwhelmingly in housing. The cumulative total outstanding in mid-1962 included $32 billion in direct loans and $71 billion insured. At the end of 1971 the government agency loan total included $8.8 billion in agriculture, the Rural Electrification Administration alone had $6 billion of this; $9.1 billion in housing; and $1.8 billion in industry, of which the Small Business Administration had $1.3 billion. Assets of government sponsored lending agencies grew considerably more rapidly than commercial banks' between 1955 and 1965 and represented 4.1 percent of assets of all main types of financial intermediaries in 1965.

Bank Holdings of Federal Debt

Investments declined from over 60 percent of total bank assets in 1945 to 32 percent by 1960 and under 24 percent in 1969. Slackening of loan demand brought the proportion up again to 26.5 percent in 1971 only to fall again to 23 percent in 1973. The dollar total of investments fell from 1946 through 1948 and in 1950, as banks moved out of Treasury obligations into loans. Total investments declined from 1955 through 1957 and again in 1959, in periods of Federal Reserve credit restraint.

The bulk of the investment portfolio until 1966 consisted of United States government bonds. The 1950 proportion was 83 percent despite a 32 percent ($29 billion) decline in these holdings in the preceding five years. The United States government bond total of $62 billion in 1970 was the same as in 1950 but represented only 42 percent of total investments. Over the two decades, Treasury securities as a share of total assets dropped from 56.5 to 10.7 percent. In between, holdings rose in years of business slowdown marked by slack loan demand and growth of bank reserves: the $5 billion increase in 1961 brought United States bond holdings of banks to a high for the decade of $66.6 billion. When business demand for loans increased sharply, banks would sell off these bonds. Liquidation of $10 billion worth in 1969 brought their holdings to a low for the 1960's of $54.7 billion. Of the total public debt, commercial banks owned about one third in 1945, one fourth in 1950, one fifth in 1960, and only one sixth in 1970.

Following the Treasury-Federal Reserve accord of March 1951, banks lost the assurance that government bonds would not fall below par value. In 1946, when the Fed's policy of supporting the price of these bonds was still in effect, the percentage of United States Treasury bonds owned by banks falling due in 5 years or less was only 45.7; a decade later, 71.7; and in 1972, 86.9. Over the same years, the percentage of banks' United States Treasury portfolio maturing in 5 to 10 years, dropped from 41.0, to 19.6, to 12.1.

Banks moved out of direct Treasury obligations but invested increasingly in the higher yielding issues of federal government sponsored agencies. Most of these securities do not carry a guarantee, though some federal backing is implied. Holdings jumped from $2.3 billion in 1960 to $22 billion in 1972, when banks came to own 44 percent of the total agency issues outstanding.

Municipal Bonds Soar

Municipal bonds represented only 2.5 percent of bank assets in 1945. Not until 1952 was the 5.3 percent of 1939 matched. By 1960, the proportion was 6.8 percent. Unlike the case with Treasury obligations, banks' holdings of state and local government bonds increased year after year, except for a 1.4 percent decline in 1969. Despite this, the 1969 total exceeded Treasury bonds for the first time ever. Municipals conprised 12.9 percent of total bank assets in 1972. Banks held one-fourth of all municipals outstanding in 1945, a slightly higher proportion in 1960, and just under half of the aggregate outstanding by 1972. Slightly more than half of the bank holdings matured in 5 years or longer.

Other Securities

Banks owned around 10 percent of total corporate bonds outstanding in the late 1930's and early 1940's but only 4 percent by 1958 and under 1 percent in 1972. In the postwar period, banks preferred to lend directly to business corporations. The share of assets represented by their bonds dropped from 1.8 percent in 1945 to a fraction of 1 percent in 1972.

Demand Deposits

Total deposits have grown in every year since 1948. The declines of 7.3 percent in 1946 and 7 percent in 1947 were related to the Treasury's use of swollen tax and loan accounts at commercial banks to repay mainly bank-held short-term debt. At the end of 1972, demand deposits were 2.2 times the total of 1945, while time deposits were 9.1 times as great. The percent of total bank liabilities plus capital represented by demand deposits dropped from 74.7 in 1945 to 40.2 in 1972.

Enormous wartime growth brought demand deposits to a ratio equal to 55.6 percent of 1945's GNP. This abnormal situation, reflecting an exceptionally low turnover rate, could not last. By 1955 the ratio was 35.4 percent and in the late 1960's, around 25 percent, about the level of 1929.

Corporations pared cash holdings, converting their idle funds into income yielding money market investments. Nonfinancial corporations reduced their demand deposits, including some currency, from a high of $33.6 billion in 1958 to $28.8 billion in 1968. At the end of 1970, their cash holdings were the same as in 1955, $31.3 billion, despite inflation and a much larger GNP.

All types of nonfinancial businesses held $50.3 billion in cash in 1970, matching 1955's total; the next 2 years, however, saw a $5 billion growth. Nonfinancial business decreased its share of total demand deposits from 57.3 percent in the late 1940's to 50.4 percent in early 1971. This downward trend occurred despite the increased insistence on compensating balances by larger banks. Interbank demand deposits ranged around 12 percent of total demand deposits in 1947 and 1971. Meanwhile, households increased their share of total demand deposits from 27.5 percent in 1947 to 32.0 percent in 1971. In 1946, 34 percent of households had checking accounts; a decade later, 50 percent; by 1970, 75 percent.

Check volume rose from under 4 billion pieces in 1941 and 5.3 billion in 1945 to some 23 billion in 1971. Without new techniques, this flood of paper could not have been handled expeditiously and economically. In 1945 the American Bankers Association developed the check routing symbol (the denominator of the fraction printed in the upper right-hand corner of checks), and later encouraged magnetic ink encoding to enable electronic handling. By the middle 1960's, nearly 90 percent of all checks were electronically sorted and accounted for. After 1 September 1967 the Federal Reserve Banks handled only checks that could be processed on high-speed electronic equipment.

If the number of checks written continues to grow at a 7 percent compounded annual rate, 42 billion would have to be handled by 1980. Some authorities envision a less-check and others a checkless society in the not too distant future. Meanwhile, despite rapidly growing check usage, the currency and coin component of the money supply increased from 20.3 percent in 1960 to 23.0 percent a dozen years later.

Surge of Time Deposits

Commercial banks dominated the liquid savings field in 1920, with 61.1 percent of the total, which also included accounts in mutual savings banks, savings and loan associations, postal savings, and credit unions, but by the end of 1940 they had declined to 48.3 percent. The commercial bank share of time deposits owned by individuals and business firms in 1945 was the same as in 1930, 53.5 percent. By 1960, however, it was less than 40 percent.

The postwar loss of position was a source of great concern, as simultaneously demand deposit growth slackened. Bankers complained about the unequal competition for savings: mutual thrift institutions (savings banks, savings and loan associations and credit unions) paid much lower taxes and enjoyed regulatory advantages, including the absence of a legal reserve requirement on their deposit type obligations.

Interest rate ceilings on time deposits were of no consequence to commercial banks in the first two decades of their application. Some banks began to feel constrained by Regulation Q in the early 1950's, though the 2.5 percent limit was above the prevailing average. The first increase in ceiling rates took effect at the beginning of 1957. Time deposits rose 11 percent that year and even more in 1958, a recession period. As the ceiling's impact became increasingly restrictive, the Board of Governors raised it again as of 1962. In the next years the differential between the rate offered by commercial banks and the mutual thrift institutions on passbook savings narrowed. It might have vanished altogether if Regulation Q had not been amended in 1966 under special legislation aimed at preventing this.

Time deposits owned by nonfinancial corporations were less than $1 billion until 1954, $2 billion in 1959, and $26.4 billion at the end of 1972. These deposits came to take the form mainly of negotiable certificates of deposit (CDs) in denominations of $100,000 and over. They were first issued by the First National City Bank of New York in February 1961; other large banks quickly followed. Investors needing funds before maturity could sell the CDs in the open market, where these obligations of leading banks soon became a major instrument.

Important Wall Street banks did not pay interest on business time deposits until 1961. They were forced to change their attitude as total deposits in New York's leading banks grew insignificantly in the post-1945 era. Large denomination CDs soared to $18.6 billion by August 1966 only to decline by $3 billion in the next 3 months because the Board of Governors refused to raise the ceiling rates at a time when investors could get a higher interest return in the open market. Again from November 1968 to December 1969 these CDs shrank, this time by 60 percent—over $14 billion—because of the unfavorable differential between what banks were permitted to offer and the open market rates.

Nonnegotiable CDs were not a new instrument, but in the 1960's they were promoted vigorously. As a result, noncertificate savings deposits, over 75 percent of total time deposits as recently as the end of 1961, were just over 45 percent a decade later.

Time deposits were 20.3 percent of total deposits in 1945 and 26.2 percent in 1955. After 1945, the time deposit total declined only in 1969; the $9 billion drop was the consequence of the low ceiling under Regulation Q. At the end of 1972, time deposits were a record 51.1 percent of total deposits, compared with 40.2 percent in 1929 and 33.4 percent in 1961.

Federal Funds

Banks actively seeking loanable funds did not confine themselves to attracting time deposits. Near the end of 1964 Morgan Guaranty Bank of New York announced it would use federal funds as a long-range resource instead of merely as a temporary device for reserve adjustments. Since then, the rate on federal funds has been almost continuously above the Federal Reserve discount rate, the premium reaching 1½ percent at times. Average daily volume was less than $2 billion in 1955 but was seven to nine times as great in the late 1960's. In August 1973 volume averaged $14 billion a day, as the rate reached a record high of 10.79 percent.

Increasing numbers of small banks became sellers of federal funds as the rate offered became more attractive. Large correspondent banks agreed to place small amounts for them. Today's market is much broader than in the 1920's. Many banks have come to view the sale of federal funds as an alternative to acquisition of other secondary reserves.

Eurodollar Borrowings

Major banks suffering sharp runoffs in their CDs in 1966 and 1969 resorted to the Eurodollar market to avoid a decline in lending capacity at a time when customers were clamoring for funds. Eurodollars are deposits expressed in American dollars owed by banks located outside the United States, though not necessarily in Europe. Only a few dozen banks borrow in this market.

Such borrowing came to less than $1 billion before the summer of 1964. American banks doubled their borrowings from their own foreign branches in the second half of 1966, going beyond $4 billion. From January through September 1969 borrowings doubled to a level of over $14 billion. The Board of Governors, concerned that its efforts at keeping money tight were being circumvented, imposed a reserve requirement on Eurodollar borrowings for the first time in October 1969. As loan demand weakened in 1970 and reserves became more ample, these borrowings were paid off rapidly.

Other Nondeposit Sources of Funds

Eurodollars constituted the largest nondeposit source of bank funds in 1969. At the time, banks also sold outright to the nonbank public some of the loans in their portfolio and participations in loan pools—$1.8 billion at the peak in April 1970. Loan sales to bank affiliates reached almost $8 billion by the middle of 1970. Additional loans were sold under repurchase agreements, whereby the bank committed itself to buy back the paper at a predetermined price. Such sales attained a peak in July 1969—$1.3 billion going to the nonbank public and another $.6 billion to bank affiliates. Loan repurchase arrangements dropped greatly after 25 July 1969, when such transactions were made subject to reserve requirements and Regulation Q.

Affiliates of bank holding companies acquired funds for buying loans through the sale of commercial paper. Only $800 million of bank-related commercial paper was outstanding in May 1969; July 1970 volume was almost ten times as great, with some sixty banks in the market. In August 1970, the Board of Governors subjected bank-related paper to regulation; the amount outstanding fell off sharply by year-end.

Yet another nondeposit liability, negotiable, unsecured short-term promissory notes, had a brief vogue following their introduction by First National Bank of Boston in September 1964. About $500 million were outstanding in late 1965. In mid-1966 the Federal Reserve subjected notes maturing in less than 2 years (subsequently made 5 years) to reserve requirements and interest ceilings.

Techniques of liability management banking—negotiable CDs, federal funds, Eurodollars, bank-affiliated commercial paper—were devised by aggressive lending banks faced with slowly growing demand deposits and, at times, with Regulation Q ceilings which precluded retention of previously attained time deposit volume. The Board of Governors moved to discourage the use of most of these devices in periods when it aimed to restrain credit.

Computerization

The very first commercial computer in the United States was put into operation at the Bureau of the Census in 1953. Within 2 years, the Bank of America and the First National City Bank of New York began to experiment with computer processing. Most banks with deposits of over $100 million turned to electronic data processing (EDP) over the next decade. By the end of 1967, banks holding three-fourths of all deposits were using computers, as were increasing numbers of smaller banks.

EDP was first applied to demand deposit operations. Pressure to reduce clerical costs subsequently brought computerization to various other operations, such as savings deposits, instalment loans, and mortgage loans. In 1968, banks were the largest users of commercial EDP on-line computer services, and they employed 20 percent of all programmers and systems analysts in the United States. Banks with their own computer installations offered computer time for sale, payroll handling, account reconciliation, and on-line teller arrangements, among other services, usually on a fee basis. The computer has made it possible for banks to perform efficiently a wider range of services over a broader geographic area.

Expanding Functions

The range of bank activities expanded notably after 1945, particularly during James Saxon's term as Comptroller of the Currency (1961-1966). Factoring is a case in point. The buying of accounts receivable on a notification basis by national banks was authorized in 1963. By the end of 1967, banks had 38 percent of total factoring volume.

Saxon, who welcomed innovation, allowed entry into a number of areas. National banks could now engage in direct lease financing, service mortgages, operate credit bureaus, extend credit through use of credit cards, process data for bank customers on computers, commingle investments in a common trust fund, offer travel services, act as insurance agent (writing insurance "incidental to banking transactions"), and underwrite revenue bonds of state and local governments. Nonbank competitors challenged the latter five areas in the courts, often successfully, as improper extensions of "the business of banking." The one-bank holding company device was adopted in 1968-1969 by banks hoping to escape from this harassment.

A wide and increasing variety of noncredit services were being offered by the late 1960's, the extent depending on the size of the bank and its location. For nonfinancial businesses, nonprofit organizations, and local governments there were such services as credit information, lock boxes, bank statement reconciliation, payroll accounting, business income-expense record keeping, billing and collection of accounts receivable, purchase and sale of securities, portfolio management, property management, securities registration, equipment leasing, freight payments, and foreign banking. Noncredit services available to correspondents included demand deposit accounting and investment and portfolio advice. Consumers might find special checking accounts, automatic transfer of funds to savings accounts, automatic customer bill payments, purchase and sale of securities, safe deposit boxes, a range of trust services, and family budget planning. Explicit fees were charged for some of these services, others called for keeping compensating balances; some required a combination of both fees and balances.

In the field of investment banking, commercial banks were the leading underwriters of United States Treasury issues. Between 1953 and 1960 commercial banks were allotted almost 90 percent of all securities on cash offerings, 53 percent of those issued in exchange for existing securities, and over 65 percent of the $250 billion aggregate. In municipal bonds, bank-managed syndicates increased their proportion of general obligation underwritings from 23.3 percent in 1957 to 38.5 percent in 1965.

Comptroller Saxon took the position that banks should not be excluded from any financial market. Both he and his successor William Camp argued that solvency and liquidity were the only considerations that might restrain the manner in which banks performed a financial function. The 1970 amendments to the Bank Holding Act, the result of a hard battle in Congress over the issue, gave the Board of Governors the task of defining bank-related functions, insofar as banks were part of a holding company.

Branch Banking Comes of Age

Branching is clearly the outstanding structural development of the twentieth century. Banks without any branch offices (unit banks) comprised 99 percent of the total in 1900, 98 percent in 1921, and 92 percent at the end of World War II. Today they comprise 70 percent.

Unit banks, with 72 percent of all offices in 1945, operated half or more until 1959. In 1964, branches exceeded the number of commercial bank head offices for the first time. Banks with at least one branch operated 73.7 percent of the 36, 672 offices at the beginning of 1973, compared with 28.2 percent of 17,958 at the end of 1945. Upwards of 1,000 new branches have opened annually since the start of 1963. The increase in the next 10 years (net of closings) was 2,462 more than from 1935 through 1962. At the start of 1973, there were over twice as many branches as a decade earlier.

Newly opened (*de novo*) branches comprised over 85 percent of the gross additions from 1956 through 1972. This is a marked increase over the 70 percent de novo from the bank holiday of 1933 to 1951 and the 80 percent for the period 1951-1961. Despite the extensive merger movement, converted head offices of acquired banks represent fewer than one sixth of the almost 18,000 branches added (net) from 1952 through 1972. Discontinued branches averaged 90 from 1967 through 1972, compared with an annual average of 49 from 1960 through 1966.

The tidal wave of branching is as striking when measured by deposit volume as when the number of offices is aggregated. Unit banks had over half of the dollars on deposit until around 1934-35. Their share was down to 46.6 percent by 1939 but a decade later had increased to 47.8 percent. By mid-1972, however, less than one-fourth of commercial banks deposits were in unit banks.

Single-office banks tend to disappear in those states that permit branching. As recently as 1962, even the seventeen jurisdictions where statewide branching prevailed had more unit than branch banks; today, fewer than 35 percent of their banks are branchless. Nationally, unit banks declined by over 25 percent from the end of 1945 to the end of 1972, though they continue to increase in states that forbid branching.

The total number of offices diminished without interruption from late 1922 until 1945 (except for the 1933-1934 reopening of many suspended banks). Around mid-1922 there had been almost 32,000 offices. Not until

1968 was this aggregate again reached. Even the shrunken 1935 total, 42 percent below that of 1922, was not exceeded until 1949.

By the mid-1930's the population per office was double 1920's ratio of 1 per 3,400. A peak for the twentieth century of 8,000 was reached in the early 1950's. At the end of 1960, there was one office for 7,500 people, about 200 more than at the end of 1945. By mid-1972, however, the population per office was 5,800 in unit banking states, 5,300 in limited branching states, and 4,700 in statewide branching states. Nationwide, the striking upsurge of branching has been mainly responsible for bringing down the average population served per office from 7,300 in 1945 to 5,500 in 1972, around where it stood in 1900, despite the great improvement in transportation since the horse and buggy era.

Three-fourths of the increase in branches from the 1933 bank holiday until the end of 1951 was *outside* the head-office city, as was two-thirds of the net growth in the next two decades. Head-office city branches comprised 43 percent of the total in 1945; their share today is 35.2 percent. Meanwhile, since 1945, branches in the head-office county outside the head-office city went from 23 to almost 31 percent, and contiguous county branches went from 12.4 to 17.1 percent. Noncontiguous county branches have ranged narrowly around one-sixth of all branches throughout the post-1945 period.

Despite a tripling from 1956 through 1972, branching shows no signs of leveling off. Rivalry in the form of offering convenient banking locations is likely to continue, at least until such time as computer technology makes such offices obsolete.

Holding Company Expansion

Bank holding company legitimacy was validated on the federal level in 1956. Since that time organizations with 25 percent control of at least 2 banks have had to register with the Board of Governors of the Federal Reserve System. From 1956 to 1965, banks belonging to these groups comprised just over 3 percent of all commercial banks and held some 8 percent of deposits. A sharp rise began in 1966 after the law was amended. At the end of 1972, 210 registered multiple-bank holding companies (157 more than 7 years earlier) included 10.5 percent of all banks, 20.0 percent of all bank offices, and 31.4 percent of all deposits.

No longer mainly a unit banking state phenomenon, multiple-bank holding companies in 1970 had about the same deposit share in statewide and limited-branching states as in unit states. It is unlikely that this situation would exist, however, if unconditional statewide branching were allowed.

The one-bank holding company movement of the late 1960's became a source of concern, culminating in the 1970 amendments bringing them under the Bank Holding Company Act. In 1955, there were 117 known cases where a corporation owned a single bank; although the number had grown to 550 by 1965, their share of all commercial bank deposits dropped from 6.3 percent to 4.5 percent. As of the end of 1970, when legislation took effect, over 1,350 banks, holding 38 percent of all deposits, were affiliated with one-bank holding companies.

Many of the larger banks took on this form in 1968-1969, hoping to expand their nonbank operations more freely than before. Since 1971 their activities have been subject to the same restrictions as multiple-bank holding companies. A number of one-bank holding companies subsequently acquired additional banks, among them several New York City giants.

New Bank Entry Developments

The total number of commercial banks increased by 357 (net) from the beginning of 1963, when there were fewer banks than in any year since 1901, to the end of 1972. Nevertheless, there were 84 more banks in 1945 than in 1972. An average of 217 new banks opened in 1970-1972 compared with 108 in 1966-1969 and 102 in 1956-1959. In 1963 300 new banks began operations and in 1964 335 new ones opened, numbers not seen since 1926. However, mergers more than offset these newcomers in the 1960's.

From 1945 through 1972, some 300 banks were permitted to open without FDIC insurance. Thus, although ultimate federal control with respect to new charters is not complete, over 90 percent of all new commercial banks since 1944 have been insured from the start. At the end of 1945, 93.8 percent of all commercial banks were insured; today 98.7 percent are.

Financial difficulties forced the closing of 501 insured commercial banks from the FDIC's beginning in 1934 through 1972. The combined total over the 39-year span, even including the 134 closed noninsured institutions, is no more than the number of failures in a single year in the late 1920's. Losses to the FDIC have averaged $2 million a year. From 1945 through 1972 failures averaged about four a year.

Few mergers since 1945 (with 50 involving insured banks) have been failure-related, the most important being the 1966 acquisition of the $120 million Public Bank in Detroit by Bank of the Commonwealth and the 1973 purchase of assets of the $1 billion United States National Bank of San Diego by Crocker Bank in California. From 1960 through 1971, bank mergers averaged 144 each year, 5 more than in the preceding dozen years. Passage of the law in 1960 did not reduce the total number of mergers, but it has prevented anticompetitive combinations.

Concentration Patterns

Nationally, the 100 largest banks had 58 percent of all commercial bank deposits in 1940 and 48.3 percent by 1945. In no subsequent year has it been that high. At the end of 1959, shortly before the passage of the Bank Merger Act, the share of the top 100 banks was 46.6 percent and a decade later, 44.4 percent.

While twenty-one of the thirty largest industrial firms are headquartered in America, the United States has only nine of the thirty largest banking giants in the noncommunist world. Given the national penchant for size, restrictive state branching laws would appear to account for much of this difference. New York City, in first place since the demise of the former Second Bank of the United States in 1841, yielded to California's Bank of America in October 1945. Nevertheless, the next six largest American banks made their head office in New York in 1973.

The median-sized commercial bank in 1970 had $8.4 million in deposits, compared with $3 million in 1957. As recently as 1935, over half the nation's banks had under $500,000 in deposits.

By the early 1930's, two or three banking organizations controlled 60-80 percent of resources in every large city. Concentration in American cities may have been even higher than in Western Europe or Canada, where the great banks had representation in every major city: three in Germany, four in France and Canada, five in Britain, often supplemented by one or two significant regional banks. Between 1939 and 1959, asset concentration on the Census Bureau's Standard Metropolitan Statistical Area (SMSA) level tended to decline in forty-five reserve city locations. The share of the top five fell in 35 locations but rose in the remaining ten from 3 to 12 percentage points. Mid-1972 concentration was lower in thirty-eight of these forty-five centers than in 1939.

Some deconcentration thus appears to be taking place in most metropolitan areas. Deposits are also being dispersed geographically. Whereas in 1945 all reserve city member banks combined had twice as much in deposits as all "country" member banks, by 1972 the multiple was down to 1.5.

Branch Law Policy and Evolving Structure

"Commercial banking in this country is primarily unit banking," the Supreme

Court remarked in June 1963. This is still the case only as regards the total number of banks, 9,652 out of 13,784 at the end of 1972. With respect to deposit volume, the statement had ceased to be true around 1935; as regards offices it became obsolete in 1964, soon after the *Philadelphia National Bank* merger decision was written.

The dominant tendency has been toward easing restrictions, but over six decades after the passage of California's 1909 law, a majority of the fifty-one jurisdictions continued to forbid statewide branching. Of the twenty-three states that had legislated prohibitions against branching by 1930, twelve were still unit banking states 42 years later. Only Oklahoma enacted a ban after 1930, waiting until 1957 to do so. Of the twenty jurisdictions with statewide branching today, seventeen had joined this category by 1935.

Foreign Branches

At the end of World War II, seven American banks operated 72 foreign branches, less than half the 1920 total and 38 fewer than in 1939. Not until 1965 was the 181 of 1921 surpassed. Seven years later, one hundred and seven member banks operated 627 branches in seventy-three foreign countries. Between 1967, when only fifteen banks had foreign branches, and 1972, the number of branches more than doubled. Bankers followed their corporate customers, whose interests had become increasingly global.

The drive for these branches was strengthened when large banks came to use Eurodollars as a source of loanable funds. Branches of American banks in London, the center of the Eurodollar market, grew from thirteen in 1968 to forty-nine by 1970. The British-owned Bahamas has only two American branches in 1965, but there were ninety-four by 1972. Assets in the foreign branches were $9 billion as recently as 1965. Seven years later they soared to over $77 billion, of which 52 percent was in the United Kingdom and 15 percent in the Bahamas.

American banks have been empowered to organize corporations to engage in foreign banking and other financial operations ever since 1919. After 40 years, there were only six of these "Edge Act Corporations," all but one of which had been formed after 1948. By 1972, however, there were eighty in active operation, reflecting the recent growth of interest in international banking transactions. Among those corporations are twenty subsidiaries established by out-of-state banks in New York City in the 1960's. More recently fourteen more have been opened elsewhere, especially in Miami, for Latin American trade, and Los Angeles, for the Far East. A few out-of-state banks have also located Edge Act subsidiaries in San Francisco, Chicago,

Houston, and New Orleans. Although legally restricted to international trade activities, some view these offices as a step toward interstate branching.

The tradition of locally oriented banks was respected by the federal government from the beginning of the national banking system. Today, only five states are without multi-bank holding companies or full service branches: Illinois, Kansas, Nebraska, Oklahoma and West Virginia. Business and economic forces long ago rendered state boundaries irrelevant with respect to larger depositors and borrowers. In time to come, branching laws may recognize this fact formally. Meanwhile bank holding companies represent an even more powerful factor diminishing the significance of state lines. All of their nonbank subsidiaries, not only Edge Act subsidiaries, may operate anywhere, with the authorization of the Board of Governors.

Structural change and functional innovation characterized commercial banking after World War II. *Fortune*'s reference in May 1948 to "the quasi-civil service nature of a banking career" may have been appropriate for an era that was ending. In the decades which followed, resourceful bankers instilled a new dynamism in an old industry.

Notes

1. Comptroller of the Currency, *Annual Report 1944* p. 4.

2. Roland I. Robinson, *The Management of Bank Funds* 2nd ed. (New York: McGraw-Hill 1962), p. 146. In the 1951 edition this appears on p. 94.

3. Raymond W. Goldsmith, *Financial Institutions* (New York: Random House 1968), p. 135.

4. Aaron Nelson and William Murray, *Agricultural Finance*, 5th ed. (Iowa City, University of Iowa Press, 1967), p. 320.

CHAPTER XVI

SOME PERSPECTIVES ON AMERICAN BANKING

Commercial Banks and Other Financial Intermediaries

Among American financial intermediaries, commercial banks have always occupied a commanding position. Their 64.1 percent share as late as 1912 was not much below the 66.7 percent of 1860. After 1913, Federal Reserve Banks as well as various federal lending and investing agencies, appeared on the scene. Excluding these government instrumentalities, the bank share of all private intermediaries' assets dropped to 53.6 percent by 1929 and 48.5 percent in 1933, recovering sharply to 63.0 percent by 1945. Twenty years later, however, banks were down to 38.3 percent. If all financial intermediaries, including governmental, are considered, the drop from 1945 to 1965 is not quite as great, from 46.1 percent to 31.7 percent. The percentage of commercial bank assets to GNP was 52.3 in 1965 (just slightly below that of 1900), though much less than 1945's exceptional 75.1. By 1972 this crude measure of banking's importance had risen to 61.2 percent, about the same as in 1908.

From the beginning, commercial banks have been the leading financial intermediary in the United States. Insurance companies, mutual savings banks, savings and loan associations, and other institutions appeared over the decades; though as recently as 1900, investment companies, finance companies, and small loan companies were unknown or insignificant. As these succeeded in establishing themselves, banks were destined to diminish in relative importance. The notable adaptability of banks in increasing the variety of their loans, debt obligations, and financial services made it possible for them to retain their position of primacy.

Changing Role of Banks

At first very exclusive organizations for well-connected seaport merchants, banks became more accessible as competition arose to serve a widening range of aspiring businessmen in rural as well as urban areas, even before the era of free banking. The national banking system, at least before 1913, was not well-suited to meet the requirements of agriculture directly. State chartered institutions could better fill rural needs, but their inability to issue bank notes after 1866 was a handicap until the farm sector became habituated to doing business by writing checks.

Retail banking came to be increasingly prominent in the 1920's. Households were encouraged to become depositors and borrowers, even when the sums involved were small; consumer debt gradually lost its connotation of moral turpitude. Diversification efforts, notable in the 1920's, persisted in the 1930's. New opportunities for the employment of bank funds were sought. Only in the field of investment banking was there retrenchment, first as a result of declining security flotations, and then because of government enforced separation under the Banking Act of 1933.

Swelling excess reserves and persistent low earnings after 1933 pressured banks into modifying their lending practices and extending new types of accommodations—most notably the term loan. Lending directly to consumers, as well as indirectly through advances to consumer and commercial finance companies, became significant by the 1930's. As they extended the scope and nature of their lending activities, banks found themselves increasingly in competition with other financial institutions.

The full flowering of retail banking arrived only after 1945. The combined total of loans to individuals and real estate loans, mostly on residences, has exceeded commercial and industrial loans year after year since 1953 and by a widening margin. Banks, by tradition lenders to business, were now increasingly financing the household sector of the economy. By 1960 there remained few exclusively wholesale banks dealing only with large business customers.

The dynamic transformation of banking which took place in the post-World War II era became especially notable after 1960. Banking's share of credit markets about doubled to around a 40 percent level between the late 1950's and the late 1960's. This vigorous activity notwithstanding, the commercial bank percentage share of financial assets of all financial institutions was 34.6 in 1970, just slightly above the 34.2 of 1960 but well below the 42.7 of 1950.

The relative share of demand deposits per dollar of time deposits slumped from $2.40 in 1947 to $.80 in 1972. Early in 1961, demand deposits were five-eighths of total commercial bank deposits; in 1971 they fell below one-half. Time deposits exceeded half of the total excluding interbank and U.S. government deposits by 1965; 7 years later they were some 55 percent of the aggregate. To the present, checking accounts remain in the category of financial services the Supreme Court described as "so distinctive that they are entirely free of effective competition from . . . other financial institutions," but they represent a declining proportion of a bank's sources of funds.

Check volume, 5.4 billion in 1947, swelled to 25 billion in the next quarter of a century. The major revolution in the payments mechanism presently under way may alter significantly the role of commercial banks in this mechanism, as well as the structure of the banking industry.

Banks have increasingly acted as money brokers. Time deposits were being actively sought by 1900, especially after 1913 until the early 1930's, and again after 1960. More recently, banks have also been eager for non-deposit funds. Earlier generations of bankers looked askance at the practice of paying interest for loanable funds. However, in each year since 1964 interest expenses of commercial banks have exceeded wage and salary payments plus fringe benefits. Despite this growing cost of funds, net profits in 1967-1972 were well above the 1945-1970 average of 9 percent on total capita.

Banks rather than the federal government have supplied the greater part of the circulating medium ever since the early 1800's. At first mainly bank notes, deposits subject to check predominated after the mid-nineteenth century. All bank notes became safe only after a punitive federal tax swept away the various state bank issues, and United States government bond-secured uniform national bank notes took their place in 1866. Another 70 years elapsed, with considerable losses, especially in 1930-1933, before the organization of the FDIC gave most bank depositors federal protection. Deposit insurance not only restored confidence in the battered banking system but also assured the survival of small unit banks.

Structural Developments

The unit banking heritage has left the United States with almost 14,000 bank entities, unlike the situation in any other country. With further liberalization of banking laws probable in the years ahead, many of these are likely to be merged into other institutions.

Branch banking is an irreversible trend. Over time, ambitious, growth oriented bankers in unit banking states are likely to spearhead a movement to eliminate long-standing branching restraints and catch up with the rest of the nation. At the end of 1972, over 62 percent of all banking facilities in the United States were branch offices, compared with less than 27 percent as recently as 20 years earlier. Should Congress broaden national bank branching powers, the trend would accelerate further.

Meanwhile, as a consequence of the one-bank holding company movement and the 1970 Congressional response, bank holding companies registered with the Board of Governors (most having a single bank) owned under one-fifth of all banks in 1972; these had three-fifths of all deposits. Registered bank holding companies could acquire finance-related nonbank subsidiaries anywhere in the United States, and many are actively expanding their role.

Americans have traditionally feared bigness in banking, even more so than in other industries. This aversion has not prevented multibillion dollar banks from developing, however. The National City Bank in New York was first to attain an asset size of $100 million in 1897. It was ten times as big in 1925. By the end of 1972, there were ninety-two banks with total assets of $1 billion or more.

Between 1900 and 1949 the deposit share of the 10 largest banks almost doubled to 19.7 percent of the United States total, while the 100 largest grew from 35.3 percent to 45.5 percent. Concern over concentration is reflected in the long-standing, deep-seated suspicion of Wall Street; in unit banking legislation; in prohibition of interstate banking; and in limits placed, in 1956 on multiple-bank holding company expansion, in 1960 on growth by merger, and in 1970 on one-bank holding company movement into other industries.

New York City, the financial center of the United States by the 1830's, retains a special position despite significant slippage in its share of the nation's deposits: 25.4 percent in 1939, down to 18.4 percent by 1949. Assets of New York City member banks fell from 20.5 percent of the national commercial bank total in 1945 to 14.3 percent in 1972. Although important regional financial centers have developed elsewhere, corporations of national and international scope have not been able to dispense with the services perfected by Wall Street banks over the generations.

Regulation

The present dispersal of federal banking regulation among three separate agencies is a consequence of a series of historical accretions rather than design. The Comptroller of the Currency was alone in the field from 1863 until the Federal Reserve appeared on the scene 51 years later. Neither welcomed the organization of the FDIC in 1934. The corporation has enjoyed vigorous support, particularly from the insured state nonmember banks, numerically the majority of all United States banks. The pattern of divided and overlapping federal jurisdiction is likely to continue; proposals for unification which have been made from time to time have met with strong banker opposition.

Most state banks never joined the Federal Reserve System; many that did, left it over the years. Only about 7 percent of the 1600 new state banks chartered 1960-1972 became members. Numerous national banks have also taken out a state charter for the purpose of becoming nonmembers. Member banks hold under 78 percent of total deposits, down from 86 percent in 1945.

From 1963 through 1966, 104 state banks converted to national bank status, attracted by Comptroller Saxon's liberal policies. Advocates of a dual banking system were especially fearful when New York's Chase Manhattan Bank, the largest state bank in the nation, switched in 1965. Further tremors were felt in 1968 when the largest bank in the Southeast, Wachovia, and the largest outside New York City, Wells-Fargo, joined the national fold. Despite the conversions, state banks had over 41 percent of total deposits at the end of 1972, a loss of but 2 percentage points since 1945.

Notwithstanding the mass of statutory restrictions from an early period, there was actually little government interference with banking practices until the collapse of the early 1930's. Outside the national banking system, examination was generally perfunctory. Even the Comptroller of the Currency refrained from undue meddling, lest national banks switch allegiance.

From the 1930's through the 1950's the negativism of the regulatory authorities, anxious to assure bank solvency, dampened banking enterprise. The attitude of the supervisory authorities was colored by the view that before the collapse "there were too many banks engaged in unregulated and unrestricted competition," as the chairman of the FDIC told a congressional committee in 1957. Comptroller Saxon's policies encouraged reinvigoration in 1961-1966. His farewell address before the American Bankers Association rightly hailed "a new spirit . . . confident in its outlook, aggressive in its conduct, and optimistic of the future." The regulatory climate in all jurisdictions did change significantly in the 1960's. Yet President Nixon's Commission on Financial Structure and Regulation (the Hunt Commission) had good reason to complain in 1971 that "the existing regulatory system is, on balance, too restrictive."

Increased reliance on competition and less on regulation to obtain good performance was a pronounced trend under way in the 1960's. The Supreme Court upheld the Justice Department's position in opposition to certain acquisitions, previously approved by the banking agencies, where anticompetitive consequences were foreseen. Larger banks, prohibited from growing by combining with other local institutions, opened new offices and sought out distant partners where permitted. More significant was the channeling of management's energies into divising new ways of better serving customers.

Commercial banking in the early 1970's was well prepared to continue the process of renewal which, as on several earlier occasions, has given the industry increased strength and importance. The slogan "a full service bank" reveals an ambition on the part of commercial banks to perform an ever-widening range of activities, constrained only by executive capabilities and the limits set by regulatory constraints.

Enactment of the Hunt Commission's recommendations would increase further the competition from other financial institutions, especially in the consumer financial services category. However the commission did not propose any change that would diminish the importance of commercial banks in their venerable, specialized role as a source of credit and third party services to the business sector of the American economy.

American Bankers Association. *The Commercial Banking Industry. A Monograph Prepared for the Commission on Money and Credit.* Englewood Cliffs: Prentice Hall, 1962.

Andersen, Theodore A. *Century of Banking in Wisconsin.* Madison: State Historical Society of Wisconsin, 1954.

Barnett, George E. *State Banks and Trust Companies since the Passage of the National-Bank Act.* Washington: Government Printing Office, 1911.

Board of Governors of the Federal Reserve System *Banking Studies.* Baltimore: Waverly Press, 1941.

Beckhart, Benjamin H. *The Federal Reserve System.* New York: Columbia University Press, 1972.

Burr, Anna R. *Portrait of a Banker: James Stillman, 1850-1918.* New York: Duffield, 1927.

Cable, John R. *Bank of the State of Missouri.* New York: Columbia University Press, 1923.

Caldwell, Stephen. *Banking History of Louisiana.* Baton Rouge: Louisiana State University Press, 1935.

Colwell, Stephen. *Ways and Means of Payment.* Philadelphia: J. B. Lippicott, 1859.

Dewey, Davis R. *State Banking before the Civil War.* Washington: Government Printing Office, 1910.

Dowrie, George W. *Development of Banking in Illinois.* Urbana: University of Illinois Press, 1913.

Fischer, Gerald C. *American Banking Structure: Its Evolution and Regulation.* New York: Columbia University Press, 1967.

Forgan, James B. *Recollections of A Busy Life.* New York: The Bankers Publishing Company, 1924.

Friedman, Milton, and Schwartz, Anna J. *A Monetary History of the United States, 1867-1960.* Princeton: Princeton University Press, 1963.

Goldsmith, Raymond W. *Financial Institutions.* New York: Random House, 1968.

———*Financial Intermediaries in the American Economy since 1900.* Princeton: Princeton University Press, 1958.

Gouge, William M. ed. *The Journal of Banking from July 1841 to July 1842.*

Gras, N. S. B. *Massachusetts First National Bank of Boston.* Cambridge: Harvard University Press, 1937.

Green George D. *Finance and Economic Development in the Old South.* Stanford: Stanford University Press, 1972.

Gruchy, Allan G. *Supervision and Control of Virginia State Banks.* New York: D. Appleton-Century, 1937.

Hales, Charles A. *The Baltimore Clearing House.* Baltimore: Johns Hopkins Press, 1940.

Hammond, Bray. *Banks and Politics in America from the Revolution to the Civil War.* Princeton, N.J.: Princeton University Press, 1957.

Hedges, Joseph. *Commercial Banking and Stock Market before 1863.* Baltimore: Johns Hopkins Press, 1938.

Helderman, Leonard. *National and State Banks: A Study of Their Origins.* Boston: Houghton Mifflin, 1931.

Gallatin, A. *Considerations on the Currency and Banking System of the United States.* Philadelphia: Carey and Lea, 1831.

Jacoby, Neil H., and Saulnier, Raymond J. *Business Finance and Banking.* N.Y.: National Bureau of Economic Research, 1947.

James, F. Cyril. *The Growth of Chicago Banks.* New York: Harper, 1938.

James, Marquis. *Biography of a Bank: The Story of Bank of America.* New York: Harper, 1954.

Kane, Thomas P. *The Romance and Tragedy of Banking.* New York: Bankers Publishing Co., 1922.

Knox, John Jay. *History of Banking in the United States.* New York: Bradford Rhodes, 1900.

Krooss, Herman, and Blyn, Martin. *History of Financial Intermediaries.* New York: Random House, 1971.

Miller, Harry E. *Banking Theories in the United States before 1860.* Cambridge: Harvard University Press, 1927.

Mints, Lloyd W. *History of Banking Theory in Great Britain and the United States.* Chicago: University of Chicago Press, 1945.

Myers, Margaret. *New York Money Market: Origins and Development.* Vol. 1, New York: Columbia University Press, 1931.

Popple, Charles S. *Development of Two Bank Groups in the Central Northwest.* Cambridge: Harvard University Press, 1944.

Preston, Howard H. *History of Banking in Iowa.* Iowa City: The State Historical Society of Iowa, 1922.

Raguet, Condy. *Treatise on Currency and Banking.* Philadelphia: Grigg & Elliot, 1840.

Redlich, Fritz. *Molding of American Banking: Men and Ideas.* New York: Hafner, 1968. This reprint contains a new introduction updating part I, published in 1947, and part II, published 1951.

Robertson, Ross M. *The Comptroller and Bank Supervision.* Washington: Office of the Comptroller of the Currency, 1968.

Rodkey, Robert G. *Legal Reserves in American Banking.* Ann Arbor, Mich.: University of Michigan Press, 1934.

Scroggs, William O. *A Century of Banking Progress.* New York: Doubleday, 1924.

Shultz, William J. and M. R. Caine, *Financial Development of the United States.* New York: Prentice-Hall, 1937.

Smith, Norman Walter. *"History of Commercial Banking, New Hampshire 1792-1843."* Ph.D. diss., University of Wisconsin, 1967.

Smith, Walter Buckingham, *Economic Aspects of the Second Bank of the United States.* Cambridge: Harvard University Press, 1953.

Sparks, Earl S., and Carver, Thomas N. *History and Theory of Agricultural Credit in the United States.* New York: Crowell, 1932.

Studenski, Paul and Herman E. Krooss, *Financial History of the United States.* New York, McGraw-Hill, 1963.

Sumner, William G. *A History of Banking in the United States.* New York: Journal of Commerce and Commercial Bulletin, 1896.

Sylla, Richard. *"American Capital Market 1846-1914."* Ph.D. diss., Harvard University, 1969.

Taus, Esther R., *Central Banking Functions of the United States Treasury, 1789-1941.* New York: Columbia University Press, 1943.

Trescott, Paul B. *Financing American Enterprise.* New York: Harper & Row, 1963.

Tucker, George. *Theory of Money and Banks.* Boston: Little & Brown, 1839.

U.S. Senate Committee on Banking and Currency, Federal Banking Laws and Reports. A compilation of major federal banking documents. Washington: Government Printing Office, 1963.

Wainwright, Nicholas. *History of Philadelphia National Bank.* Philadelphia: Historical Society of Pennsylvania, 1953.

Watkins, Leonard L., *Commercial Banking Reform in the United States.* Ann Arbor: 1938. Michigan Business Studies, Vol. 8, No. 5.

White, Horace. *Money and Banking.* Boston: Ginn, 1914.

Willis, H. Parker, and Chapman, John M. *The Banking Situation.* New York: Columbia University Press, 1934.

Accommodation paper, 35
Accounts receivable financing, 147
Affiliates, Bank, 65-66, 82, 140, 178
Agricultural Credits Act, 114
Agricultural loans, 30, 37, 78-79, 110, 114, 149, 169-170
Aldrich Bill, 107-108
Aldrich Vreeland, Act, 92, 109
American Bankers Association, 77, 89, 96, 108, 121, 124, 126, 156, 157, 158, 160, 176
American Institute of Banking, 89

Bank Capital, 10-11, 57, 58, 135, 136, 145-146, 164
Bank Credit Cards, 171-172
Bank directors favored, 36

Bank Examinations, before 1863, 41, 42, 95, 160-161
1863-1914, 95, 96-97
1920's, 128-129
1930's, 160-161
Bank Failures 23-24, 37, 48, 58, 87-88, 125, 129, 131-132, 134, 137-138, 183
Bank Holding Company Act, 183
Bank holding companies, 60, 127-128, 159, 178, 182-183 186, 190
Bank holiday, 133-135
Bank Merger Act, 184
Bank Mergers, 125, 158, 181, 183, 184
Bank notes, ban on issue, 11, 12, 13, 42
Bank notes, counterfeits, 17-18, 20

Bank notes, par redemption, 24-25, 54, 55, 64

Bank notes, protection for holders, 23-24, 42

Bank notes, redemption, 20-23

Bank notes, small denominations, 18-19

Bank notes, state, 2, 10, 11, 12, 13, 17-28, 32, 42, 44, 47, 48, 49, 50, 54, 55, 57, 63

Bank of America, NT & SA, 151, 184

Bank of Maryland, 2-3

Bank of New York, 3

Bank of North America, 2, 3, 34, 37

Bank reports of condition, 41

Bank underwriting of securities, *see* Investment banking.

Bankers, caliber of, 100, 138, 141, 143 fn. 13

Bankers, public opinion of, 98-99, 145

Bankers Acceptances, 116, 173

Bankers balances, *see* Interbank balances.

Banking Act of 1935, 137, 148, 153, 154, 157

Banking powers, 40-41, 99-100, 179-181

Banking privilege, 32-33

Banks, oldest, 3, 4-6

Banks usefulness of, 2, 49-51

Banks and business fluctuations, 47-48

Banks, rural, 78

Banks, state-owned, 39-40

Bartar transactions, 9

Biddle, Nicholas, 44

Bills of credit, 1

Board of Governors of the Federal Reserve System *see* Federal Reserve Board.

Branches, bank, 13-14 59-61, 71, 126-127, 158-159, 181-182, 184-188, 190

Branches, foreign, 127, 185-186

Branches, national bank, 59, 126, 158-159

Brokers' loans, 117, 118, 152

Business loans, 111-113, 146, 161-162, 168-169. *see* also Commercial loans.

Clearing houses, earliest, 26-27, 88-89
    functions, 89
    par collection, 66

Call loans, 33, 79-80, 89, 117, 152

Certificates of deposit (CDs), 177, 178, 179

Chain banking, 60, 127-128, 159

Charter policy, need test, 56, 58, 124-125, 157-158, *see* also Free banking

Chase, Salmon P., 55, 63, 80-81

Check credit plan, 172

Check usage, 25-26, 27, 66, 67, 68, 176, 189

Checking Accounts, service charges, 121

Checks, par collection, 67-120-121

Chemical Bank, New York City, 32

Clearinghouse agreements, 123

Clearinghouse certificates, 88, 90, 91-92

after 1863, 60, 90-92, 103,
    138-139, 156-157
Collateral, loan, 31, 33, 113, 147
Commercial loans, 75, 76, 112,
    146.
    see also Business loans.
Commercial paper, 80, 104, 107,
    116, 172, 178-179
Commodity credit corporation
    loans, 149
Compensating balances, 27, 76, 112
Comptroller of the Currency, 53,
    59, 66, 77, 79, 82, 88, 89,
    91, 92, 95, 96, 97, 106, 110,
    124, 128, 129, 138, 153,
    157, 158, 191
Computerization, 179
Concentration, banking, 71, 125,
    184, 190
Consumer loans, 115, 151-152,
    163-163, 171
Corporate bonds, bank holdings of,
    81, 119, 175
Correspondent balances,
    see Interbank deposits
Correspondent banking, 69, 71, 72,
    99, 105
Credit departments, bank, 77, 113
Currency Act of 1863
    see National Currency Act

Demand deposits, 25-26, 27, 67-69,
    122, 155, 175-176 179, 189
Department store banking, 100,
    120
Deposit insurance, state, 128,
    136-137, 139

Deposit rate ceilings, 138-139,
    see also Regulation Q
Deposit Liquidiation Board, 136
Discount Facilities of Federal
    Reserve Banks, 105, 109,
    119, 132-133, 148
Domestic exchange, 24, 64
Double liability, 11, 136
Dual banking system, 57, 128,
    159-160, 191

Edge Act subsidiaries, 185-186
Elastic currency, 67-68, 101,
    103-104, 134
Emergency Banking Act of 1933,
    135
Equipment leasing, 169
Eurodollar market, 178, 185
Excess reserves, 154, 164
Export-Import Bank, 150

Federal banking regulation,
    190-191
Federal Deposit Insurance
    Corporation (FDIC), 132,
    135, 136, 137-138, 139, 141,
    142, 155, 157, 158, 159,
    160, 164, 165 fn. 9, 183,
    189, 191
Federal funds, 118, 177-178, 179
Federal home loan banks, 150
Federal Housing Administration
    (FHA), 150, 151, 170, 173
Federal Intermediate Credit Banks,
    114
Federal Land Banks, 114, 149, 173

Federal National Mortgage
    Association, 150, 173
Federal Reserve Act, 53, 57, 69,
    72, 75, 84, 92, 97, 98, 104,
    106-108, 109, 112, 116, 117,
    122, 124, 132, 134, 142,
    148, 154
Federal Reserve Banks, 106, 107,
    116, 117-118, 121, 122, 132,
    133, 134, 135, 142, 153,
    154, 155, 163, 176, 187
Federal Reserve Board, 107, 108,
    117-118, 119, 120, 121, 123,
    126, 128, 132, 133, 138,
    139, 141, 152, 154, 155,
    159, 160, 173, 177, 178,
    179, 181, 182, 186, 190, 191
Federal Reserve Notes, 132, 155
First Bank of the United States, 3,
    7, 18, 19, 25, 34, 44
Foreign exchange, 12, 18, 65
Forstall, Edmond, 35
Free banking, 9-10, 41, 43, 55-56,
    57, 59, 97, 124, 157
Friedman, Milton and Anna I.
    Schwartz, 68, 91, 100, 141

Gallatin, Albert, 7-8, 18, 20, 25,
    26, 29, 42
Giannini, Amadeo P., 125, 127
Girard's Bank, 11, 31, 34
Glass, Carter, 101, 107, 141
Glass-Steagall Act, 132
Gold holdings, 133, 135, 155, 164
Gold Standard Act, 64
Gouge, William, 44
Greenback party, 56
Group banking,
    see Bank holding companies

Hamilton, Alexander, 2, 7, 36
Hammond, Bray, 9, 26
Hepburn, Alonzo Barton, 60, 67,
    75, 100
Home Owners Loan Corporation,
    150
Hunt Commission, 191, 192

Independent Treasury, 44-45, 98,
    122
Interbank deposits, 27, 33, 55, 71,
    105, 121-122, 138-139, 157
Investment banking, 33, 82,
    139-141, 180

Joint-stock land banks, 114

Knox, John J. 49, 56, 65, 68, 75,
    100

Land banks, colonial, 1, 30-31
Liability management, 179
Line of credit, 168
Loan availability, 145, 146
Loan limits, legal, 76-77
Loan maturities, 34-35, 148.
    see also long-term loans
Loans, bank, to states, 33
Loans, federal government to the
    private sector, 149-150, 173
Long-term loans, 13, 35, 36, 76,
    148

Machines, bank office, 99
Manufactures, loans for, 31
Margin requirements, 117, 152
Massachusetts Bank, 3, 27

McCulloch, Hugh, 23, 54, 55, 56, 100

McFadden Act of 1927, 126, 128

Member banks, 106, 108, 128

Money orders, 65

Money Trust, 71

Morgan, J. P. & Co., 82, 90, 140

Morris, Robert, 2

Municipal bonds, bank holdings of, 81, 120, 174-175, 180

Murray, Lawrence, 96

Mutual Savings Banks, 65

National Bank Act, 10, 11, 17, 53, 55, 57, 59, 69, 72, 76, 97, 99
see also National Currency Act

National Bank notes, 25, 54, 55, 63-64, 97, 101, 120, 154-155, 189

National banking system defects, 104

National banks, 54, 57, 71, 75, 76, 78, 87, 88, 95, 96, 97, 98, 101, 103, 108, 116, 117, 120, 122, 123, 128, 129, 136, 152, 158, 170-171, 191

National Credit Corporation, 132

National Currency Act, 41, 53

National Currency Association, 92

National Housing Act of 1934, 151

National Monetary Commission, 65, 68-69, 79, 92-93, 96, 107, 108

National Recovery Act (NRA), 156, 157

New York City, as financial center, 27, 69, 71, 123-124, 157, 184

New York Clearing House Association, 26, 54, 84, 88, 138-139

Nonbank Lenders, 117

Nondeposit sources of funds, 178-179

Nonpar banks, 108, 121, 156

One-bank holding company, 183

Overbanking, 8, 59, 124, 141-142, 158

Panics, Banks and, 47, 89, 104

Panic of 1907, 90-93, 125

Pet banks, 44

Post notes, 17

Prime rate, 147, 169

Private Banks, 11-13, 20, 27, 33, 41, 58, 124

Production Credit Associations (PCAs), 148-149, 170

Property banks, 31, 40

Protected circulation, bank notes, 21

Raguet, Condy, 22, 26

Railroads, loans to, 31, 81

Real bills, 35, 105

Real Estate loans, 30-31, 78, 79, 112, 113-114, 115, 150-151, 162, 170-171

Reconstruction Finance Corporation (RFC), 132, 133, 134, 135-136, 137, 149, 150, 162

Rediscounting,
see Discount facilities of Federal Reserve Banks

Redlich, Fritz, 26, 49, 100

Regulation Q, 139, 176-177, 179

Reserve cities, 69, 70
Reserve requirements, 43-44,
        69-72, 84, 89, 91, 97, 98,
        105, 106, 122
Retail banking, 188
Ricardo, David, 22
Safety fund, 23, 41
Second Bank of the United States,
        7, 8, 13, 19-20, 24, 34, 44
Securities Exchange Act, 152
Service charges, demand deposits,
        121, 156
Short-term commercial loans, 29,
        35, 75, 76, 112
Small Business Administration,
        149, 173
Smith, George, 12
Specie, 1, 50
Specie payments, suspension, of 23,
        47
State Bank of Indiana, 13
State banking departments, 95, 129
State banks, 54, 55, 57, 77, 81, 87,
        124, 159, 191
State shareholdings in banks, 40
Suffolk System, 24

Term loans, 147-148, 169
Time deposits, 65-66, 113,
        122-123, 139, 155, 176-177,
        189
Treasury bills, 153, 154, 163
Treasury notes, 153
Trust Companies, 27, 82-84, 100
Trust departments, bank, 84, 100,
        120
Tucker, George, 41

United States government bonds,
        bank holdings, 81, 109, 119,
        131, 142, 153, 154, 155,
        163, 164, 167, 174
United States government deposits,
        44, 97, 103, 122,
    see also Independent Treasury
United States Mint, 18

Walker, Franics A., 50, 68
Warburg, Paul, 103, 107
Wildcat banking, 50